Inconsistency in Roman Epic

How should we react as readers and as critics when two passages in a literary work contradict one another? Classicists once assumed that all inconsistencies in ancient texts needed to be emended, explained away, or lamented. Building on recent work on both Greek and Roman authors, this book explores the possibility of interpreting inconsistencies in Roman epic. After a chapter surveying Greek background material including Homer, tragedy, Plato and the Alexandrians, five chapters argue that comparative study of the literary use of inconsistencies can shed light on major problems in Catullus' *Peleus and Thetis*, Lucretius' *De Rerum Natura*, Vergil's *Aeneid*, Ovid's *Metamorphoses*, and Lucan's *Bellum Civile*. Not all inconsistencies can or should be interpreted thematically, but numerous details in these poems, and some ancient and modern theorists, suggest that we can be better readers if we consider how inconsistencies may be functioning in Greek and Roman texts.

JAMES J. O'HARA is George L. Paddison Professor of Latin at the University of North Carolina, Chapel Hill. He is the author of *Death and the Optimistic Prophecy in Vergil's Aeneid* (1990) and *True Names: Vergil and the Alexandrian Tradition of Etymological Wordplay* (1996), as well as numerous articles and reviews on Latin literature.

ROMAN LITERATURE
AND ITS CONTEXTS

Inconsistency in Roman Epic

ROMAN LITERATURE
AND ITS CONTEXTS

Series editors:
Denis Feeney and Stephen Hinds

This series promotes approaches to Roman literature which are open to dialogue with current work in other areas of the classics, and in the humanities at large. The pursuit of contacts with cognate fields such as social history, anthropology, history of thought, linguistics and literary theory is in the best traditions of classical scholarship: the study of Roman literature, no less than Greek, has much to gain from engaging with these other contexts and intellectual traditions. The series offers a forum in which readers of Latin texts can sharpen their readings by placing them in broader and better-defined contexts, and in which other classicists and humanists can explore the general or particular implications of their work for readers of Latin texts. The books all constitute original and innovative research and are envisaged as suggestive essays whose aim is to stimulate debate.

Other books in the series

Joseph Farrell, *Latin language and Latin culture: from ancient to modern times*

A. M. Keith, *Engendering Rome: women in Latin epic*

William Fitzgerald, *Slavery and the Roman literary imagination*

Stephen Hinds, *Allusion and intertext: dynamics of appropriation in Roman poetry*

Denis Feeney, *Literature and religion at Rome: cultures, contexts, and beliefs*

Catharine Edwards, *Writing Rome: textual approaches to the city*

Duncan F. Kennedy, *The arts of love: five studies in the discourse of Roman love elegy*

Charles Martindale, *Redeeming the text: Latin poetry and the hermeneutics of reception*

Philip Hardie, *The epic successors of Virgil: a study in the dynamics of a tradition*

Alain Gowing, *Empire and memory: the representation of the Roman Republic in imperial culture*

Richard Hunter, *The shadow of Callimachus: studies in the reception of Hellenistic poetry at Rome*

Inconsistency in Roman Epic

Studies in Catullus, Lucretius, Vergil, Ovid and Lucan

James J. O'Hara

Paddison Professor of Latin
The University of North Carolina at Chapel Hill

CAMBRIDGE UNIVERSITY PRESS

CAMBRIDGE UNIVERSITY PRESS
Cambridge, New York, Melbourne, Madrid, Cape Town, Singapore, São Paulo

Cambridge University Press
The Edinburgh Building, Cambridge CB2 8RU, UK

Published in the United States of America by Cambridge University Press, New York

www.cambridge.org
Information on this title: www.cambridge.org/9780521646420

© Cambridge University Press 2007

First published 2007

Printed in the United Kingdom at the University Press, Cambridge

A catalogue record for this publication is available from the British Library

ISBN 978-0-521-64139-5 hardback

ISBN 978-0-521-64642-0 paperback

For Marika

Contents

Acknowledgments	*page* xiii
Introduction	1
1 Greek versions	8
2 Catullus 64: Variants and the virtues of heroes	33
3 Death, inconsistency, and the Epicurean poet	55
4 Voices, variants, and inconsistency in the *Aeneid*	77
5 Inconsistency and authority in Ovid's *Metamorphoses*	104
6 Postscript: Lucan's *Bellum Civile* and the inconsistent Roman epic	131
Bibliography	143
Index of passages discussed	159
General index	163

Acknowledgments

Like many short books this one has had a long gestation period. I need to thank all of my colleagues at Wesleyan University, where the most important work on the book was done, and at the University of North Carolina at Chapel Hill, where it was finished.

Many portions of the book were presented before audiences that asked tough and useful questions: I thank scholars at the University of Virginia (in both 1992 and 2003), Rutgers University (in both 1993 and 2003), Harvard, the College of the Holy Cross (my alma mater), Boston University, Smith College, the University of Michigan (where I did my graduate work), the University of Chicago, Agnes Scott College, the University of Georgia, Yale, the University of North Carolina at Chapel Hill, the University of Tennessee at Knoxville, Loyola College in Maryland, the North Carolina Classical Association, the Classical Association of Connecticut, and the Classical Association of the Middle West and South. Both after those talks and at other times I learned much from Wesleyan colleagues Michael Roberts, Marilyn Katz and Sean McCann, and from Peter Smith, Bruce Frier, Ruth Scodel, Alden Smith, and Lowell Edmunds.

Thanks go to those who have responded to my questions about forthcoming work: Rene Nünlist, Shadi Bartsch, Fred Williams, Katie Gilchrist, Richard Thomas, and Nicholas Horsfall.

What I have learned from David Ross in graduate school and beyond still informs every page I write.

My student research assistants Katherine Kelp-Stebbins (at Wesleyan), and Dennis McKay and John Henkel (in Chapel Hill) were of great help with my research, and each read the whole manuscript and made useful suggestions on both presentation and argument. Sydnor Roy also offered helpful and challenging marginal comments. My colleagues Sarah Mack (Vergil and Ovid chapters) and Sharon James made helpful criticisms of both style and content, with particular attention to all of my favorite stylistic weaknesses. Richard Thomas and Nicholas Horsfall offered predictably learned and precise criticism of a draft of the whole book.

Over a period of years, series editors Stephen Hinds and Denis Feeney read a number of drafts, some of them amazingly lacunose and rough, and made many invaluable suggestions; only the other authors in the series will know how much they have done to improve this book. Pauline Hire, Michael Sharp and Jayne Aldhouse of Cambridge University Press were a pleasure to work with, and Linda Woodward was a tactful but effective copy editor.

The readers that I have thanked have improved my work a great deal, and saved me from numerous errors. Given my subject matter, all errors that remain are of course deliberate.

My dedication is to my daughter, a very good reader.

Introduction

This short book about long poems explores the possibility of interpreting, rather than removing or explaining away, inconsistencies in ancient texts. My main argument is that comparative study of the literary use of inconsistencies can shed light on major problems in epics written by five Roman authors: Catullus, Lucretius, Vergil, Ovid, and Lucan – though Lucan gets only a short concluding chapter. I hope that the book offers a valuable vantage point from which to consider major recent trends in the study of Greek and especially Latin poetry, and that those who read it will find that it helps them become better readers of the poems treated, and perhaps other works as well.

This book flows from earlier work I have done on Vergil, with my perspective broadened to include the four other Roman poets, a number of Greek authors, and I hope a greater range of interpretive reflection. Too much work in Classics focuses on individual authors, without seeing them in the context of what other more or less similar authors are doing. I believe this is strikingly true for the phenomenon at the heart of this study. I attempt to trace and analyze, in several authors, something a number of scholars have been noticing in isolation in individual authors, often without mentioning work being done by anyone else. Part of the originality of this study lies in bringing these texts and problems together, and part lies in the analysis I do of these texts; the book aims both to synthesize some recent work on Greek and Latin poets and to confront more explicitly and tenaciously certain intriguing questions this work has raised.

A central argument of my book on prophecy in the *Aeneid* (O'Hara 1990) is that some discrepancies between what is said in prophecies in the poem and what either happens, or is predicted to happen, elsewhere in the poem are

I

not signs of Vergil's inability to revise the *Aeneid* before his death. Rather these inconsistencies are indications that characters within the *Aeneid* are being deceived, and that readers may be deceived as well, or at least offered conflicting paths of interpretation. These inconsistencies are products not of the poet's inattention, but of his artistry. They are at least potentially "portals of discovery," to quote a phrase used by Joyce's Stephen Daedalus, who says that with a great poet like Shakespeare, "his errors are volitional and are the portals of discovery." As I was finishing the prophecy book, I realized that it was part of a quiet and for the most part under-analyzed movement throughout classical studies, in which poetic inconsistencies were being seen in a new light. Much of this work has appeared in the form of studies of single authors. This book offers an extensive (though necessarily somewhat cursory) first chapter on recent work on inconsistencies in Greek authors, and then a comparative study of inconsistency in poems by the five Roman authors of my title, who wrote within about a century of one another.

The first chapter's survey of Greek material depends heavily on the work of others. I discuss examples of inconsistency in Homer, Hesiod, lyric and tragedy, and then certain passages in Plato and Aristotle that discuss unity or inconsistency, before finishing with the Alexandrian poets. The Alexandrians are treated in somewhat greater detail because of their importance to the Roman poets both in general and in terms of their interest in inconsistencies and mythological variants. Roman practice owes much to Callimachus and the Alexandrians, but it is also important to note that certain practices commonly labeled Alexandrian have precedent in archaic and classical Greek poetry.

That first chapter has a broader scope than the others, for it discusses poems in a number of genres, while the remaining chapters are each limited to a single "epic" poem. In part this reflects the wide range of influences that produced Roman epic, but there is also a degree to which this first chapter could have been the beginning of a much broader study of Roman poetry – not limited to epic – the outlines of which this book can only suggest. I do believe, however, that the epic texts studied in Chapters Two through Six bear a special relationship to one another with respect to their use of inconsistencies, and that the Roman epic tradition comes to create in the reader certain expectations about how inconsistencies will be treated.

Many of the Greek texts discussed in Chapter One have a particular relevance for the Roman poems that come later, but more generally, the chapter is meant to familiarize the reader with material helpful for contextualizing my argument about Latin poets. Most often, I hope, knowledge of this material will help the reader accept my arguments, but I also realize that it may allow a reader to go beyond what I have argued in this short book, or even refute my arguments. This is fine with me: books in this series are meant to be "suggestive essays whose aim is to stimulate debate."

Chapters Two through Five treat Catullus 64, Lucretius' *De Rerum Natura*, Vergil's *Aeneid*, and Ovid's *Metamorphoses*, and then Chapter Six briefly discusses Lucan's *Bellum Civile*. Each of these chapters begins with a close reading of a passage near the start of the poem, where striking inconsistencies have long been problematic; then I show that central interpretive questions for each author involve how we respond to inconsistencies. Some of these questions involve factual inconsistencies, others inconsistencies of theme, philosophy, and political attitudes, and there may be room to criticize my lack of interest in distinguishing these different types of phenomena. But I believe they all profit from being looked at together, and are all united by the way in which traditional scholarship has mishandled them. I hope that my method will be seen to involve an imaginative search for solutions to problems, open to the best that ancient and modern theory has to offer, but with rigorous testing of any hypothesis against the details of the text. I do not claim that all inconsistencies in ancient texts are of the same type, although I do posit a common willingness on the part of ancient authors to make use of inconsistency. I also try to acknowledge that some inconsistencies can be produced by aspects of the production of ancient texts that make them less interesting or valuable for the purposes of interpretation. Here too I note that a few pages after Joyce's Stephen Daedalus pronounces that a great poet's "errors . . . are the portals of discovery," he is asked, "Do you believe your own theory?" and "promptly" answers, "No." (The question does not refer directly to the statement I cite above, but it might as well have.)

For Catullus 64, the *Peleus and Thetis*, I look at the problem of the first ship, the Argo, and the ship that sailed earlier than the first ship, that of Theseus. I discuss the introduction to the Theseus and Ariadne panel, which says it will be about "heroic manly deeds," as well as its content, which involves dumping Ariadne on an island and sneaking away at night. And I look at the conflict between the happiness predicted for Peleus and Thetis at their wedding, and the notorious unhappiness of their marriage in the whole literary tradition. How we as readers should respond to borrowings from or allusions to mythological variants is a major concern here, as often in the book.

In Lucretius' *De Rerum Natura*, I examine how the initial "Hymn to Venus" is quickly contradicted by the Epicurean claim that gods do not worry about humans, in lines that many have wanted to cut from the text. I then discuss recent scholarship's attention to Lucretius' habit of briefly inhabiting his opponents' positions, for rhetorical purposes, and how this work has provided an alternative to the old theory of the "Anti-Lucretius in Lucretius." And I look at the frequent practice of scholars who brandish inconsistencies as evidence for how Lucretius should have revised or was planning to revise his text – almost as though Roman poets were working with the help of dissertation supervisors. How proems relate to the rest of a work, or even to the rest of a single book, and how a poem's apparent goals might differ from its actual impact are other issues discussed.

My Vergil chapter is the longest. It discusses inconsistencies in prophecies, the extent to which the fully polished *Georgics* also contain a number of inconsistencies, allusions to incompatible mythological variants, the complicated picture of the underworld of *Aeneid* 6, and the war in Italy of *Aeneid* 7–12, for which I focus on contradictory allusions to the myth of gigantomachy. In this chapter, and in the following chapter on Ovid, I look at ways in which inconsistencies in a poem can introduce competing perspectives, a plurality of voices, and conflicting or ambiguous attitudes, and thus can raise questions about authority and power (especially with regard to Jupiter), and create a sense of indeterminacy or uncertainty.

For Ovid's *Metamorphoses* I begin with the philosophical creation, by a rational creator god, which then yields to a world run by a particularly disorderly, un-philosophical, emotional, lustful version of the mythological Olympian gods. I also talk about chronological problems as in Catullus 64, and about Ovid's multiple origin stories for the same animal or flower, which often feature unmistakable cross references that call readers' attention to problems. I discuss Ovid's mixing of genres, and use of mythological variants, and how inconsistent passages raise questions about authority and power in Ovid as in Vergil (again Jupiter will be problematic).

I end with a short discussion of Lucan, which also serves as the book's conclusion, in which I briefly discuss the praise of Nero in the proem to the *Bellum Civile*, the poem's shifting attitudes towards the republic and principate, and the way in which "the poem is at war with itself," to cite a formulation prominent in recent scholarship. My contribution to the study of Lucan is fairly minor, and consists largely in insisting that Lucan be seen in the tradition described earlier in the book, and so this short chapter will look back at earlier chapters as much as it looks at Lucan.

The book's goals are both text-specific and theoretical: a comparative approach can provide better understanding of the passages in question, and the tracing of similar phenomena in several authors may help to establish a framework for understanding the poetic or rhetorical use of inconsistencies in any ancient author, and perhaps in authors of other periods as well. The question at the heart of my book is perhaps this: How should we react as readers and as critics when two passages in a literary work contradict one another? Should we try to emend the text? Should we blame the inconsistency on someone other than the author, who has ruined a consistent original unity by inserting inappropriate material? If we cannot change the text, should we blame the author, and consider him a failure? We cannot overlook this option, but it is not one of my favorites. Should we excuse the author, by reason of biography, citing his untimely death (in the case of Lucretius, Vergil, and Lucan), or even his exile (in Ovid's own words)? Lucretius, the Epicurean poet, naturally says that "Death is nothing to us" (*DRN* 3.830) but is that really true if you die with your poem unfinished? And should we imagine Vergil, as he was dying, thinking with sorrow of his "List of Things to Fix After Trip to Greece"? Ovid introduces the idea in *Tristia* 1.7 that he should be cut some slack because he was exiled and did not get to polish his epic. Is he serious? Kidding? Imitating Vergil? All of the above? Or is Ovid perhaps signaling to readers that his epic contains the inconsistencies they have learned to expect in the genre? For Lucan, we know exactly when he died, and why. Before he died, had his views of Nero changed, and does this account for some of the varied views present in his poem?

My preferred way to respond to inconsistencies is to ask whether we can interpret them, and whether they are being used with some skill to make certain suggestions – whether they have been "thematized," to cite a term of Ruth Scodel's, discussed in my first chapter. These questions will not always yield a positive answer, and should not be forced, but they should always be considered. A text may be inconsistent, for example, because a character is lying, or speaking deceptively for rhetorical purposes. This solution, for which there is precedent in ancient comments on these poems, "saves" the consistency of the world being presented by the text. At times, especially in the start of a work, a poet may be temporarily adopting one attitude, before attempting to move readers to another. More challengingly, a poet may present

5

relentlessly inconsistent material, and different views, with no clear guide as to which view is "right." This inconsistency may come about as a natural result of working with certain ideas in certain genres, or as a deliberate effect sought because it fits certain poetic goals, or from some combination of both factors. Plato complains in *Republic* 2 and 3 about poetry's tendency to present a fragmented voice. In the latter half of the twentieth century many critics said it was only the Vietnam War or some bizarre American fondness for ambiguity that made us see multiple voices in Vergil and other poets. But the problem is right there in the *Republic*. Bakhtin's famous and now famously inadequate claim, that the novel is polyphonic and epic is monologic, certainly does not fit the poems under view here.

Some scholars may argue that all readers or that all readers before the twentieth century would tend to construct a view of the world of a poem or novel that harmonizes or explains away inconsistencies, that concretizes or makes determinate any gaps left in the text, on the theory that the human consciousness naturally seeks unity, wholeness, and coherence. I see little reliable evidence for this either as a fact of human nature or as a claim about the history of reading. Many modern critics, on the other hand, have argued that texts tend to fly apart despite the presumed desires of their authors for them to hold together. I think we are dealing in this book with writers who know that texts tend to fly apart, and that they therefore work with inconsistencies, instead of vainly trying to produce the kind of single-voiced, unified work demanded by many twentieth-century critics.

It may well be that these polytheistic, non-Christian writers saw poems with multiple voices and inconsistent attitudes and even variant versions in one text as the best way to represent their view of the complexity of the world as they saw it. This idea has been suggested for Homer by some, for the Alexandrian poets especially, and for Lucan (and his contemporary Petronius) at the end of our period; it is implicit in much recent work on Catullus, Vergil, and Ovid. Or it may be that they thought that the function of poetry or of epic was the challengingly ambivalent depiction of conflict. A number of our texts deal with issues that can be looked at in two diametrically opposed ways, such as the role of the gods in human endeavors, the nature of heroism, or a poem's attitude toward an emperor, or they depict two-sided conflicts between complicated and flawed foes. It seems implausible to me that it is an accident, or a result of perverse late twentieth-century reading practices, that Catullus 64, the *Aeneid*, the *Metamorphoses*, the *Bellum Civile*, and possibly even Lucretius, as well as a number of poems in other genres written during this period, can be read in two starkly opposing ways. The following chapters explore some of the choices that readers can make in dealing with contradictory poems and passages. Their goal will be to make us better readers, able to respond to more aspects of the poem than we can when we are willing to change or distort texts in the service of anachronistic or at least overly simple notions of unity.

CHAPTER

I

Greek versions

This chapter will offer a selective survey of work on Greek authors who wrote before the five Roman poets to be considered in later chapters. It first sweeps from Homer through tragedy, then stops to consider Plato, Aristotle, and (briefly) the history of the concept of "unity," before finishing with the Alexandrian poets. We shall look both at the poets on whom the Roman poets schooled themselves, and also at the modern aversion to inconsistencies that led scholars to march through the corpus of Greek and Latin authors removing, lamenting, or explaining away inconsistencies. Thus this chapter will demonstrate both the extent to which inconsistency appears in authors to whom Roman poets are indebted, and the scholarly behavior pattern under indictment in this book, in which a work is found wanting because it lacks the simple and organic unity or univocality that came to be identified with value and quality in poetry. Throughout, the stress will be on questions, and in some cases even characters and myths, that recur in later chapters. Discussions throughout the chapter must be brief. Often recent work will be described and put to some critique, but this chapter will present arguments for consideration more than it will analyze them in depth, although there will be a little more detail when we reach the Alexandrians. I leave more extended examination for later chapters.

From Homer to tragedy

Homer is the apparent founder of the genre at the heart of this study, and Homeric scholars are largely the originators of the type of criticism of inconsistencies that became so instinctive and natural to classicists. Modern classical scholarship began with Wolf's study of the "Homeric question" and the work that followed it, which offered a model for the analysis of texts that maintains a powerful hold on the imagination of classicists. Inconsistencies were seen by "Analysts" as reliable clues for identifying layers of redaction in the Homeric poems and other texts, always with the assumption that those texts were originally tightly unified, non-contradictory, and as well organized as a properly supervised dissertation. "Unitarians" often sought to explain away perceived inconsistencies, and later, "Neo-analysts" offered a unitarian view of the poems as a whole, but explained many of their odd features by reference to their origin rather than their function in the poems we have: for them, inconsistencies "point to sources the Homeric poet has adapted in a new composition."[1] More recently, many scholars have offered a number of interesting – if not always fully convincing – suggestions about different ways to deal with inconsistencies in Homeric epic. One tactic has been to argue that strict standards for consistency are inappropriate. Todorov's classic piece on "primitive narrative" describes "laws" that have been wrongly applied to the *Odyssey* concerning verisimilitude, stylistic unity, the "priority of the serious," noncontradiction ("cornerstone of all scholarly criticism"), non-repetition, and digression.[2] Classical scholars have not always accepted the notion that Homer is "primitive," but oral theorists have often argued, fairly plausibly, that texts produced or encountered orally are more likely to contain certain kinds of consistency problems.[3] Throughout this book, we shall have to consider whether apparent inconsistencies in a text can be traced back to the method of composition, incomplete revisions, or textual problems in the manuscript tradition.

Ruth Scodel's monograph on verisimilitude in Homer and tragedy (Scodel 1999) has offered a number of useful ideas. At times her method is like that of Unitarians defending Homer by explaining away inconsistencies, but she is open-minded about whether problems can or should be explained away. Readers or an audience, she argues, can minimize the effect of inconsistencies; to maximize their own pleasure, they can cooperate with the poet to downplay an inconsistency or implausibility through a "principle of inattention," a similar principle of "generosity," or through "naturalization." With "naturalization,"

---

[1] Scodel (1999) 22; cf. Katz (1991) 13–16, with further references.
[2] Todorov (1977) 53–6. For a recent attempt to use "inconsistencies and incoherencies in the texts of the *Iliad* and the *Odyssey*" as evidence for how the texts were composed see Wilson (2000).
[3] Cf. Lord (1960) 28, Tsagarakis (1979), Janko (1998).

problems of verisimilitude can be viewed "not as problems as long as the narrative audience can believe that there is a plausible reason within the fictional world." This suggestion that readers are meant sometimes to minimize problems of consistency and unity in some ways resembles the thesis of Malcolm Heath, that ancient authors paid little attention to thematic unity, or indeed to thematic (as opposed to aesthetic) concerns at all.[4] But Scodel also describes a large number of ways in which an inconsistent detail can be "thematized," or "can be made by the poet (or in some cases merely the reader) into something with important thematic consequences." My study, while aiming to keep in mind various ways to minimize the impact of inconsistencies, will often discuss ways in which inconsistencies are "thematized."[5]

The next few paragraphs will dance through some examples of Homeric inconsistencies and possible responses to them. Homer may, for example, misdirect the audience to some degree, in order to create tension or uncertainty about how the narrative will proceed, as when Zeus predicts how far Hector will get before Achilles returns. Such passages have long been seen by Analysts as signs of multiple authorship, on the false assumption that a poet must provide accurate and dependable foreshadowing of what comes later in his work.[6] Alternatively one might see Zeus as deceiving the other gods – a way of reading discussed in the treatment of Jupiter below in my chapters on Vergil's *Aeneid* and Ovid's *Metamorphoses*. Indeed many inconsistencies are introduced by speakers other than the narrator. Scenes in which characters summarize earlier events are often slightly inaccurate, because of a character's ignorance (e.g. a dead suitor in *Odyssey* 24) or someone's wish to "spin" a story to emphasize or minimize certain elements (e.g. Odysseus to Penelope on his travels, and Thetis to Hephaestus on Achilles' troubles).[7] Ahl and Roisman's study of the *Odyssey* focuses "particularly on instances in which the narrator or an internal speaker seems to be contradicting something stated authoritatively as fact elsewhere in the epic;" their "central concern is with what we would describe as Homeric rhetoric" or the way in which what speakers say is fitted to their rhetorical needs (1996: ix–x). Not all of their examples convince, but such explanations are not without ancient precedent.

---

[4] Heath (1989), discussed below at n. 35.   [5] Scodel (1999) 15–21.

[6] See esp. Morrison (1992); this issue will be important in my Lucretius chapter. On creating tension see also Scodel (1998) on an apparent inconsistency concerning the removal of arms from the hall in *Od.* 16 and 19.

[7] Scodel (1999) 62–3, whose examples I cite.

As I noted in my study of prophecy in the *Aeneid* (O'Hara 1990), ancient commentators on Homer suggest that the *prosopon*, the character who is speaking or the *persona*, is the source of many inconsistencies in Homer or, to look at it in their terms, can be the solution to many problems in the text, so that one critic even calls this the "solution from the character speaking," which de Jong says is the ancient term for "focalisation."[8] When different Homeric passages disagree on whether wine gives strength to a warrior or weakens him, or whether the Cyclopes "trust in the immortal gods" or "do not care about aegis-bearing Zeus," scholiasts note that "the characters (*prosopa*) who speak are different" or that readers should "consider the character speaking." The general principle is that

> It is no cause for wonder if in Homer contradictory things are said by different voices. For whatever things he himself says speaking in his own *prosopon* must be consistent and not in conflict with one another. But whatever he gives to other *prosopa* to say should be thought to be not his own words, but those of the persons speaking.

Athenaeus faults Plato for saying that Menelaus is a soft warrior, simply because Hector says he is, noting that "it is not true that if something is said in Homer, it is Homer who says it."[9]

Some inconsistencies cannot so easily be explained away. Odysseus in his narrative will portray the Cyclopes both as cruel savages who must toil as Polyphemus does, and as happy primitives in a fertile land that provides effortless abundance. Does this discrepancy suggest characterization of the speaker, or is the poet or speaker simply saying what he wants in each section without regard for what is said elsewhere?[10] Can this question be answered without an unjustified appeal to (unknown) authorial intention? We shall see a similar kind of inconsistent portrayal of both early humans in Lucretius, and, with considerable consequence for interpretation, the Italians in the second

---

[8] De Jong (2001) xiv. Porphyrius *Quaest. Hom.* p. 100, 4 Schrader uses the term λύσις ἐκ τοῦ προσώπου.

[9] Wine: *Il.* 6.265; Cyclopes: *Od.* 9.106–7, 275; general principle: Porphyrius *Quaest. Hom.* p. 100, 4 Schrader; Menelaus: *Il.* 17.588, Athenaeus *Deipn.* 5.178d. I have discussed these passages in more detail in O'Hara (1990) 123–7 and (1996d), with a call in the latter for more work on the problem, given the availability now of Erbse's indices. See briefly now Edmunds (2001) 74–5, and in more detail Nünlist (2003), who is working on a longer study.

[10] Scodel (1999) 45–7 (on *Od.* 9.106–15) and 181 (discussion in Antisthenes fr. 53).

half of the *Aeneid*. When Odysseus visits the Land of the Dead, he stands in one spot while shades come up to him, but later portions of his narrative would make more sense if he were traveling through the Land of the Dead rather than standing still. Similar uncertainties mark Vergil's picture of the underworld, perhaps in part in imitation of Homer.

Several scholars have tried to interpret rather than explain away the notorious dual forms used in *Iliad* 9.182–200 to refer to an embassy consisting of Odysseus, Ajax, Phoenix, and two heralds. It was unavoidable – and fairly reasonable – that Analysts would treat this as evidence that two different embassy stories, one with only two ambassadors, had been clumsily stitched together. Some scholars have tried instead to interpret the duals, suggesting that they serve to isolate Achilles' traditional foe Odysseus (Nagy), or treat Phoenix as so close to Achilles that his presence can be taken for granted (Martin), or that the error "results from underlying tensions and contradictions in the value system that is at stake in *Iliad* 9," where it is difficult to tell friend from enemy, so that both "Achilles and Homer slip into a mode of discourse which subtracts Phoenix from the embassy" (Nagler).[11] Nagler argues that both the *Iliad* and the *Odyssey* offer "representational inconsistency as a reflection of ideological uncertainty;" his reading of the poems might not convince every reader, but his general principles are interesting:

> All previous attempts to account for the irrational use of the duals have basically tried to explain the oddity away; the present approach attempts, by contrast, to explain why the oddity is there, and on a certain level must be there. The very inconcinnity of the scene is part of its message. To explain it away would be to participate in the masking of a critical ambiguity in the value system of which this poem is an ideal expression.

For the *Odyssey*, Katz has argued that contradictions in the portrait of Penelope – who seems both loyal to Odysseus, and ready for re-marriage – should not be explained away, but constitute "an indeterminacy of both narrative form and character representation."[12] Such problems have long nourished claims that our *Odyssey* has been stitched together from conflicting versions, but we might instead see how the problematic passages keep alive

[11] Nagy (1979) 49–55; see also Nagy (1992) 321; Martin (1989) 235–7, Nagler (1990).

[12] Katz (1991) 192. The claim in the review by Olson (1991) that "[a]cceptance of 'incoherence' and 'contradiction' ought to be the last resort of the serious unitarian critic" is both perfectly understandable, and completely unjustifiable.

the possibility that Penelope might conform to the example of Clytemnestra or Helen, so that we are kept uncertain about Penelope's intentions. Felson-Rubin's way of describing a similar reading of Penelope is to say the poet "assigns her roles in two incompatible types of plot: in Bride-Contest and Marriage-Avoidance."[13]

When Telemachus visits Sparta in *Odyssey* 4, the stories told by Menelaus and Helen about Helen's behavior at Troy "do not directly contradict each other, but . . . seem impossible as anecdotes about the same person at the same time in her life." Menelaus presents Helen as helping the Trojans, while Helen's story has her loyal to the Greeks; "the two examples may offer variant ways of imagining how the whole *Odyssey* will unfold." Scodel's reading finds the two stories equally plausible; Suzuki and others think that Menelaus' tale shows Helen's to be false.[14] Elsewhere, statements by characters that contradict the narrator appear to be false, but here the two characters' versions are to be compared, or we might say that they compete with one another. Competing stories about Helen, we shall see, abound in the Greek tradition, and may also occur in the *Aeneid*.

In *Iliad* 20.290–352, Scodel argues, the rescue of Aeneas from Achilles by Poseidon is deliberately inconsistent with the poem's main narrative.[15] Poseidon saves Aeneas even though he is otherwise pro-Greek (Vergil's Neptune will stress the oddity of this in *Aen.* 5.810–11). The episode both underscores Achilles' ignorance of the gods' plans, and also offers the notion that something Trojan will survive, while everything else in the poem suggests the utter destruction of Troy. The fates of both Hector and Achilles would be less moving if they were universal, Scodel suggests, but the Aeneas episode gives the story of Troy, in a sense, two endings: the dominant plot confirmed by the death of Hector and leading, through the death of Achilles, to the end of Troy, and a much less prominent one in which Aeneas inherits power, and something of Troy lives on.

Modern readings of the presentation of Penelope's character, and of the Helen and Menelaus stories, bring us close to an idea that will be prominent both in this chapter and later in the book: that of the poet alluding to variant versions of a myth. This may sound like the claims of the Neo-analysts

---

[13] Felson-Rubin (1996) 165, cf. too Scodel (1999) 150–3.
[14] Scodel (1999) 74–6 (whom I quote in the text); cf. Suzuki (1989) 67–70, Ahl and Roisman (1996) 39–42.
[15] Scodel (1999) 150.

mentioned above, except that it involves not clues that the poet has accidentally left, but instead deliberate allusion to an alternate version. We are not far removed from the idea of the remarkable novel described in Borges' story "The Garden of Forking Paths," in which multiple versions of events are all contained within the same text. Borges' narrator thinks that such a story never existed before, but there is an extent to which the "impossible fictions" of much post-modern narrative are anticipated by aspects of ancient narrative that have only recently begun to be appreciated.[16] The significance of these observations about Homer and other archaic and classical poets (to be discussed below) will become clear as this study proceeds. It has long been known that allusion to variant versions was important to the Alexandrian scholar-poets and to the Roman Alexandrians who used them as models. Scholars point to the classic examples in which Vergil or Propertius is describing one mythological character named Scylla or Atalanta, but makes unmistakable allusion to the other homonymous character, perhaps alluding to the work of earlier poets.[17] But readers of Alexandrian and Roman poetry need to know that allusion to varying and often incompatible versions is common in Homer, Pindar, and tragedy.

Examples abound: a small but telling one first. At *Iliad* 21.237 a simile in which a river "bellows like a bull" is "conscious acknowledgment of a variant tradition" in which the river actually becomes a bull (references for all these examples are collected in one footnote below). Ahl and Roisman have made a number of interesting suggestions about ways in which the *Odyssey* covertly alludes to other versions of myths than the one it is telling, e.g., stories of Odysseus' sons by Circe or Calypso. Edmunds suggests that in the prophecy of Tiresias in the Land of the Dead about Odysseus' death, "the *Odyssey* acknowledges, and repudiates, the variant represented by the Telegony." When it "places Helen and Menelaus in Egypt but on their return from, not on their way to, Troy (Book 4)," it may be that the *Odyssey* "recognizes

---

[16] Cf. (in another context) Winkler (1985) vii: "Borges and Nabokov have nothing on Apuleius," and see Eco (1984) 233–6, Ashline (1995), May (1995), and Dolezel (1998) (with classical comments on Dolezel by Edmunds [2001] 97–107), McHale (1987) esp. 33–40, 106–12 (where he briefly mentions the two endings for Fowles' *The French Lieutenant's Woman*). P. A. Miller (1994) 74–6 cites Borges' story in discussing Catullus' lyric collection. On re-evaluating inconsistencies in the Old Testament see the valuable observations of Sternberg (1985) and especially Alter (1981).

[17] Cf. Ross (1975) 62 on Propertius 1.1.15, Lyne on [Verg.] *Ciris* 54–91, Coleman on *Ecl.* 6.74ff., Barchiesi (1991) esp. 8, Hinds (1993) 14–16.

the variant" made popular later in which Helen spent the whole war in Egypt (see below on Stesichorus). It is important to note that we have clear early testimony about ancient awareness of Homer's technique here: Herodotus 2.116 explicitly claims that Homer "made clear that he also knew this story." Hephaestus says in *Iliad* 18.395–407 that when he was thrown out of Olympus by Zeus, he was cared for by Thetis, but in 1.590–4 he says that it was the Sinties who helped him; we may look on the Book 18 passage as an invention designed to stress Hephaestus' indebtedness to Thetis, for whom he is about to make the arms of Achilles, or we may complain that the inconsistency is of such magnitude that it is a "defect," an unwelcome intrusion into the poem of the intrinsic "variability" of myth.[18]

Other archaic poets, and the Greek tragedians, seem at times to revel in telling one version of a story and alluding to another. Griffith's classic discussion notes how in Hesiod *Theogony* 526–616 "two endings to the Prometheus story coexist, one leaving him suffering eternal torment from Zeus' eagle, the other bringing Heracles to the rescue." In *Works and Days* 167–73, "where our manuscripts all give us a straightforward description of the dead race of Heroes dwelling in the Isles of the Blessed . . . several papyri contain a modification of the account that includes Kronos as their king, and the tidy explanation that Zeus released him and gave him this honor" (if the passage is a later addition, the interpolator, of course, is the one producing the inconsistency – but doing so deliberately). Stesichorus' apparently innovative story of the phantom Helen who went to Troy still keeps the traditional story before our eyes, contrasting the innocent Helen with the guilty one almost as in the contrasting stories in *Odyssey* 4. In Pindar *Olympian* 1, the poet rejects the story of how Pelops was served as food to the gods, but makes effective use, as scholars have shown, of both the version he rejects and the version he champions; in *Pythian* 2 "Pindar completes the story of Ixion's rape of Hera before adding that it was only a cloud that he raped."[19]

The *Homeric Hymn to Apollo* seems to us as clearly as any ancient work to lack unity, to be either two poems patched together, or one poem with an incompatible extension tacked on. Yet the poem was almost certainly

---

[18] The bull: Nagy (1992) 325; Ahl and Roisman (1996); Tiresias: Edmunds (1997) 424; Helen in Egypt: Edmunds (1997) 423; Hephaestus: Scodel (1999) 39–40 (local motivation, requiring inattention), Edmunds (1997) 421–2 ("defect").

[19] Besides Griffith (1990) on all these (whom I quote three times), on *Olympian* 1 cf. Nagy (1990) 116–35, and Pratt (1993) 124.

produced, whether from scratch or from existing material, by a competent person or persons working in the classical, perhaps even the archaic period. It also contains – along with what seem to us such problematic features as the apparent farewell formula at 165–78, the contrasting lyric and epic narrative styles, and the different geographical and cultural focus of the Delian and Pythian halves – quite a number of unifying features.[20] We shall see below that Callimachus may have taken this two-part hymn as a model for his own two-section *Hymn to Artemis*. The *Homeric Hymn* indeed has features which some moderns find intolerable in a single poem, but this poem's features are unlikely to have seemed repugnant to its culture. The theory that imputes modern notions of unity and non-contradiction to classical poets, and then finds contradictions throughout the transmitted texts of ancient poets, must posit an ever-refreshed army of energetic, really stupid guys who kept splicing together single unified poems into self-contradictory new poems, in blissful ignorance of their culture's supposed dislike for such wholes.

Greek tragedy offers a number of factual or other inconsistencies. We must be very careful when analyzing inconsistencies in tragedy, as Tycho Wilamowitz argued long ago.[21] Some discrepancies, for example, must be caused by dramatic necessity, such as the placement of expository material in a dialogue between characters who must have already known this information. Aristotle famously cites Euripides' *Iphigenia at Aulis* for its inconsistency of character, since "Iphigenia the suppliant in no way resembles her later self" (15.9, 1454a31, Butcher trans.). Euripides may be making Iphigenia act the way he needs her to act in different parts of the play, but the discrepancy can also be interpreted, as in Rabinowitz's (1993: 39–40) discussion of Iphigenia's desire for and limited access to "subjectivity." Like Homeric epic, from which they doubtless learned the technique, tragedians also sometimes misdirect the audience to create suspense, surprise, or uncertainty. They probably wrote at first with the idea of a single, oral performance, in which comparison of early and late sections of a play depended on memory, so they could expect some degree of what Scodel calls "inattention," although the revivals

---

[20] Burkert (1979) suggests that the *Hymn* was put together for the "Delian and Pythian games" of 522 BCE, though others have put it much later. For unifying features cf. Clay (1989) 18ff. (noting that "certain crucial questions are raised in the first half but not satisfactorily answered until the end of the poem"), A. M. Miller (1986) (whose appendix tells the history of the unity question), Nagy (1979) 6–11.

[21] See Lloyd-Jones (1972). Waldock (1966) 11–24 discusses the "documentary fallacy" and Sophoclean criticism.

that began in the second half of the fifth century would eventually have had an impact upon playwrights' expectations. Scodel says that tragedians were "scrupulous" readers of Homer and of other tragedies (and that "Virgil read Homer through tragedy and through an exegetical tradition influenced by tragedy;" 1999: 133, 167–84). Sharp discrepancies such as those in the statements about prophecies in Sophocles' *Women of Trachis* or *Philoctetes* would surely be noticed or felt by some in the audience, and may reasonably be interpreted as authorial comments about the limitations of human knowledge, the tendency of characters to speak rhetorically and deceptively, or the growth in understanding of a character (Heracles, Neoptolemus) who understands a prophecy only late in the play.[22]

A radical notion of thematization produces Ahl's argument that in Sophocles' *Oedipus Tyrannus*, inconsistencies in the case against Oedipus (mainly the surviving witness' report that Laius was killed by more than one man) prove that he is an innocent victim of a frame-up job by Creon and Tiresias. Alternately we might view this problem in the light of the use of allusion to variants in epic and tragedy, to come up with this formulation: Sophocles' *Oedipus* tells the story of an Oedipus who did it, who is guilty, but *alludes* to a version in which, or to the possibility that, he did not do it.[23] Scodel argues differently that we must see the report of the surviving witness as a lie, and that so viewed this inconsistency is also "thematized," so that "human reluctance to speak the truth combines with the obscurity of the oracle to trap the hero."[24]

A number of plays allude to alternate and often incompatible versions of myth. Sophocles *Philoctetes* 570–97 presents, as a lie invented by Odysseus, the story that Odysseus and Diomedes have been sent to fetch Philoctetes from Lemnos; this is the plot of Euripides' earlier *Philoctetes*. Helen is often the subject of double versions; in Euripides' *Trojan Women* Helen argues that she is Aphrodite's victim, but Hecuba says that Helen's own weakness is to blame, and that neither the divine beauty contest nor Aphrodite's visit to Sparta ever happened. Griffith notes that "we have been given a 'double story' . . . with no touchstone of truth to help us choose between the contradictory versions." Scodel notes that in Sophocles' *Electra*, the differing versions of

[22] See Scodel (1999) 125–33, with further references, and on *Trach.* see also Heiden (1989).
[23] Ahl (1991); here I borrow from O'Hara (1996d), my review of Ahl and Roisman (1996), though I had fewer comparanda in tragedy then.
[24] Scodel (1999) 114.

the background to the sacrifice of Iphigenia provided by Clytemnestra and Electra "seem to function as alternative frames for the action" of the play; she compares the stories of Helen and Menelaus in *Odyssey* 4. Griffith and Halleran point to likely allusion to a variant myth in Aeschylus' *Agamemnon*, where the elders "break off their account of the sacrifice of Iphigenia at the precise moment where, in the alternative version, Artemis is due to substitute the doe." Griffith suggests that we are being reminded that the chorus' story may not be true, Halleran that "the brutal and irremediable fact of filial murder . . . is highlighted by the allusion to the road not taken." Elsewhere in the *Agamemnon*, Griffith finds allusions to the Helen-phantom story in the reference to "a 'phantom' *(phasma)* ruling in Menelaus' palace" (414ff.) and in the "lengthy reminder that Menelaus on his journey home from Troy has been diverted (617–80)," which points to the version in which he finds the real Helen in Egypt.[25]

From Plato to the modern era

This section will move quickly through Plato and Aristotle, pause to consider the whole history of "unity" (and the role in that history played by the Neoplatonists), and then touch on the modern era, with brief mention of Horace, Shakespeare and, doubtless surprisingly, modern physics. Treatment will be brief, but certain important ideas presented here will recur later in this chapter, and in subsequent chapters.

Three passages in Plato deserve special mention: the analysis at *Protagoras* 339–48 of a poem of Simonides; the discussion in the *Republic* of the problem of poetic imitation of varying voices; and the influential idea in the *Phaedrus* that a literary work should be like a living organism.[26]

The criticism of Simonides in the *Protagoras* is based in part on the poem's inconsistency. Ferrari sums up the problem:

> From the forty-line poem Protagoras selects the opening couplet, in which the poet avers how difficult it is to become a good person; he secures Socrates' agreement that the poem as a whole is a fine and "correct" piece; and then he produces a later couplet in which Simonides appear to

---

[25] Griffith (1990), Scodel (1999) 113, Halleran (1997).
[26] On Plato in general see Heath (1989), Kennedy (1989).

contradict himself by taking issue with the sage Pittacus for an apophthegm much the same as Simonides' opening lines.[27]

Since Socrates' defense of the consistency of the poem is to some extent insincere, and uses "somewhat shady tactics," Plato may be satirizing the inconsistency-hunting literary criticism of sophists like Protagoras. Plato might sympathize more with what Socrates says a little later on (in Ferrari's summary): "Treat poetry as argument, and you will quickly find that it only appears to have a voice, for your neighbor thinks the poet means one thing, you think he means another, and a new argument begins: not over what the poet says, but over what he means . . . (347c–8a)." Much of the long history of faulting inconsistencies or contradictions in poetry, I would suggest, flows from this kind of confusion between poetry and philosophical discourse – or perhaps we should say between literature and a particularly artless and prosaic kind of philosophical discourse, since Plato's own works are often complexly literary and at some levels inconsistent. Perhaps willingness to use inconsistencies is one thing separating poetic from certain kinds of philosophical discourse, and critical impatience with poetic inconsistency too often confuses the former with the latter.

In the *Republic*, some of the objections to poetry are based upon worry about the effects of drama and any narrative that includes speeches by characters. Because in both drama and epic poetry, Socrates is made to argue, the poet splits up his voice and often speaks in the voice of characters, the reader or audience or performing rhapsode has no clear guide to what is being said, and may be encouraged to imitate lesser or even wicked men (cf. *Rep.* 382c6–398b8). Thus poetry is not good for dialectic or argument or teaching or investigating virtue. In other words, because poetry does not present a single unified voice, it fails to present any single opinion on most matters discussed, and is thus problematic and unsuitable for the educational role it had been playing in Greek culture.[28] In the texts to be considered in later chapters, we will often confront the difficulty of interpreting texts in which what is said by different characters, or implied by different aspects of the

---

[27] Ferrari (1989) 99–103: 100 (below I quote from p. 102); cf. too Scodel (1986), Carson (1992).

[28] Cf. Ferrari (1989) 114–19, Murray (1997) 1–24, 168–84, Halperin (1992) (with further references), Laird (1999) 44–78, Edmunds (2001) 74–5. Ferrari (2000) offers the non-expert a window into recent discussion of voices in Plato himself; see also Blondell (2002).

texts, seems ambiguous or contradictory. Twentieth-century scholars often leveled charges of anachronism against readers who found "two" or "further" or "many" voices in a text, or who suggested that an audience or reader might legitimately sympathize with a villain or victim rather than with the hero, so that a text might present a plurality of voices and an inherent interpretive instability. But an awareness of such instability can be seen already in Plato.

Phaedrus 264c presents the famous passage in which Socrates suggests that every text (or perhaps just "speech") should be like a living thing (*zoon*). As Ferrari notes, however, "Socrates warns Phaedrus that this is the opinion of an 'ignoramus' in these matters;" and indeed Socrates "fails to consider the possibility" that the author whose speech he is analyzing "may have intentionally composed the piece in such a way as to produce an effect of haphazardness and spontaneity." Moreover, in composing the *Phaedrus* itself, "Plato himself is using the very technique of writing that he has Socrates ignore," for the dialogue "is deliberately disunified in its structure – more exactly, attains artistic unity only on a second order, by jarring its readers and urging them thereby to reconstitute the living creature from its scattered limbs."[29] Of course Plato's influence has often been mediated through his later interpreters, and it may well be the case that Neoplatonic stress on this principle led the way to Renaissance and early modern notions of strict unity (more on this below).

Aristotle should be mentioned for one idea that he does not in any extant text apply to poetry, but which many others have, and for his discussion of tragedy and epic in the *Poetics*.[30] The "Law of Noncontradiction" was mentioned briefly above in connection with Todorov's claim that it is the "cornerstone of all scholarly criticism." Aristotle in the *Metaphysics* says that "the most certain principle" of truth is that "contrary attributes cannot apply to the same subject at the same time and in the same respect," so that "clearly it is impossible for the same man to suppose that the same thing is and is not; for the man who made this error would entertain two contrary opinions at the same time" (IV [Γ] 1005b18–34, Loeb tr. by Tredennick). We probably cannot completely avoid applying this principle to fictional worlds as we do to the real world, but we should nevertheless think hard about the law's

[29] Ferrari (1987) 52–3; cf. Halperin (1992), with further references.
[30] On Aristotle I have been helped by Lucas (1968), Halliwell (1987) and (1989), Heath (1989), Hunter (1993) 190–5.

limited applicability to fictional worlds, and not yield to the easy temptation to treat poetry as sloppy philosophy.[31]

I have mentioned Aristotle's comments on inconsistency of character in the *Iphigenia at Aulis*. Two other sections of Aristotle's *Poetics* deserve mention for their influence throughout both antiquity and recent centuries, even if it may not have been our text of the *Poetics* that propagated the ideas in antiquity. One is the famous discussion of unity of tragic and epic plots, which builds upon Socrates' suggestion in the *Phaedrus* that a composition should resemble a living organism. Aristotle in Chapters 7–8 says that tragedy and epic should have a kind of "oneness" or unity, for each work should be the mimesis of a single action that is whole and complete, in which events follow one another out of necessity or probability rather than randomly. He says Homer wisely "made the *Odyssey*, and likewise the *Iliad*, to center round an action that in our sense of the word is one." The section concludes (Butcher trans.):

> As therefore, in the other imitative arts, the imitation is one when the object imitated is one, so the plot, being an imitation of an action, must imitate one action and that a whole, the structural union of the parts being such that, if any one of them is displaced or removed, the whole will be disjointed and disturbed. For a thing whose presence or absence makes no visible difference, is not an organic part of the whole.

In a later chapter focused on epic (23) he says that when properly constructed, epic too "will thus resemble a living organism in all its unity, and produce the pleasure proper to it."[32]

In *Poetics* 25, Aristotle discusses a topic that will receive considerable attention from learned Alexandrian poets and their Roman successors, namely the solving of Homeric problems – the practice of finding a solution (*lysis*) to scholars' complaints about a particular fault in Homer (*problema*). Doubtless here Aristotle summarizes lost discussions in treatises like his *Homeric Problems*.[33] Despite what he has said earlier about unity he recommends flexibility and a variety of methods, arguing sometimes that things that seem contradictory are not in fact so, and at other times that a poet may describe

---

[31] Cf. above, n. 16. See also Selden (1998), quoted below, n. 51, for ideas about Egyptian thought's different attitude toward "contradiction."

[32] For Callimachus and Aristotle see references below, n. 41.

[33] See Halliwell (1987) 176–80, Scodel (1999) 177–8, with further references.

things that are "impossible" (such as Achilles' pursuit of Hector), "if the end
of the art be thereby attained . . . that is, if the effect of this or any other part
of the poem is thus rendered more striking."

Aristotle, then, both presents a strong argument for a kind of organic unity,
and displays a moderately flexible attitude toward evaluating some apparent
breaches of unity. Aristotle's arguments about unity are important, but, I
would argue, are neither as dominant nor as helpful for the criticism of ancient
poetry as the twentieth century made them out to be.

The same may be said, to digress briefly and mention a Roman author
in this Greek chapter, of the comments on unity in Horace's *Ars Poetica*.
Horace denounces painters and poets who join unharmonious wholes together
to produce a grotesque monster with a woman's head, horse's neck, bird's
feathers, and a fish's lower half (*AP* 1–5). Artists' freedom, Horace says, in
language suggestive of Aristotle, must be limited by a requirement of unity
(*denique sit quodvis simplex dumtaxat et unum*, "in short, create what you
wish, as long as it is a single harmonious whole" 23). One need not swallow
whole Frischer's claim that the entire *Ars* is an obvious parody to see that there
is something odd about the opening of this poem, which "positively invites a
suspicious reading" in the way it denounces a fairly popular painting style,
and "indulges in the very playfulness and oddity that it supposedly censures"
(as does much of Horace's work, of course).[34] Horace thus gives voice to,
but stops short of clearly endorsing, the rule that poets should avoid making
use of inconsistencies.

Malcolm Heath's *Unity in Greek Poetics* (1989), mentioned briefly earlier,
is an interesting and valuable study, but perhaps because the book deals mainly
with Greek texts, and is often unconvincing in its main emphases and claims,
few Latinists have paid any attention either to his pages on Latin poetry or
to his general argument.[35] This book should not be ignored, however, for
Heath does show that many of our assumptions about unity are imposed
on classical texts, and that numerous ancient authors state a preference for
stylistic variation instead of monotony.[36] A reading of Heath and his reviewers

---

[34] For "suspicious:" Oliensis (1998) 199, "indulges:" Sharrock (2000) 18; cf. too Heath
(1989) 63–4, Frischer (1991) 68–85, and (more broadly) Armstrong (1993).

[35] On Heath (1989) see now Fowler (2000a) 38–9, 70–1, and Sharrock (2000).

[36] Heath smuggles in along with that demonstration, however, his claim that ancient authors
are not interested in thematic unity – as if they had to make a choice between stylistic

suggests that modern, inflexible definitions of poetic unity, and the whole tendency to find fault with texts that are inconsistent in any way, may stem from late antique Neoplatonic misreadings of Plato, and the developing idea that each work of literature should have a single unified *skopos*.[37] If one could identify the biases and flaws in Heath's argument, and isolate them from the great learning and intelligence to be found in his book, it is possible to imagine how someone (not me!) could write a history of the concept of unity in Western poetics. Such a history might explain how suggestions about unity in Plato and Aristotle were emphasized and made stricter by the Neoplatonists and others, and perhaps given a great boost by the spread of both monotheism and Christianity – indeed twentieth-century critics discussing the unity of this or that poem often became as exercised as fourth- or fifth-century Church Fathers debating the concept of the Trinity. Neoplatonism, monotheism, and Christianity may have played a vital role in promoting, or at least making the world hospitable to, the notion of single-focus unity or univocality that reigned among critics for so long.

Some versions of the latter stages of a history of unity have recently been written. Jonathan Bate, in *The Genius of Shakespeare* (1998), has intriguingly suggested that nineteenth- and early twentieth-century critics misunderstood some plays of Shakespeare because they had odd notions of unity which the plays did not fit. According to Bate, the key development that made us better able to handle ambiguity more recently came when William Empson began as an undergraduate to study English instead of math, science, and the new physics of Heisenberg et al., because the new physics suggested to him that we should look at texts in a both/and way rather than the either/or way that critics had been doing. The more broadly ranging 1997 study of William Everdell, *The First Moderns*, claims that "discontinuity" is the basic concept of "modernism," and he traces its appearance, beginning in the 1870s, in mathematics, physics, music, painting, and literature.

variety and thematic coherence. (In a sense, then, Heath's book on unity is flawed because of its lack of unity.) Heath's own assumption that digressions, for example, are expected both to provide variety and also to be *thematically* irrelevant, is not supported by the ancient sources he quotes.

[37] On Heath see n. 35 and cf. (each with further references) Ford (1991), Halliwell (1991), Schenkeveld (1992), and Lamberton (1991), who notes, "Clearly the dialogues of Plato posed special problems of interpretation for Platonists who took seriously Platonic scruples about mimesis and poikilia."

Variety and variants in Alexandrian poetry

This section will discuss poets who exerted considerable influence on the Roman authors to be examined in the following chapters. Callimachus, Theocritus, and Apollonius seem to have brought to new prominence the use of varied voices, innovative construction of the parts of a poem, and allusions to incompatible variants. Working with, but distinguishing themselves from, archaic or classical models, the Alexandrians stressed variety of style, often even within the same poem, and they sometimes accomplished this variety by means of an embedded narrative or description, and not only in what we call epyllion or mini-epic. As scholar-poets, some Alexandrians worked on Homeric texts or problems, or engaged in the scholarly classification of genres, and most preferred to mix genres in their own work.[38] Their scholarship nourished the allusive or intertextual aspects of their poetry, and imitation of multiple models often produced what has seemed to some to be the impression of disunity. Their ideas on unity seem to play with earlier formulations – perhaps even specifically with the Aristotelian notion of unity. The one extant Alexandrian epic, the *Argonautica* of Apollonius of Rhodes, offers four books of episodic adventures with a particular focus on the aetiological, and has often been thought to feature "disunity" of a sort, or to play with Aristotelian notions of unity, and to offer a fractured notion of both character and narrative.[39] Goldhill argues that a Hellenistic poet's "self-conscious adoption of a persona (or more than one persona) in a poem develops a multiplicity of points of view (similar perhaps to a dramatic text) with no authoritative viewpoint; and provides a demonstration of the variegated nature of reality as

[38] In general on the Alexandrians as scholar-poets see my references at O'Hara (1996a) 22, and add Selden (1998), Nelis (2001) 382–402 with further references, and Fantuzzi and Hunter (2004); on mixing of genres see esp. Thomas (1999) 246–66 = (1996). On the text of Homer see the interesting suggestions of Hexter (1994) about how the "cumulative and often contradictory commentary" on ancient texts may have presented to the "post-Aristarchan scholarly reader" a "polyvocal" text in which conflicting views are presented side by side; cf. briefly too Hexter (1992) 364 n. 21, although we must not assume that the original Hellenistic commentaries seemed as polyvocal as our variorum-style scholia. Alexandrian scholarship also must lie somewhere in the background of our bits of surviving theoretical as opposed to practical evidence from antiquity: see the material from O'Hara (1990) discussed above at n. 9.

[39] Hunter (1993) 3–7, 12, 59–60, 150–1, 172, 190–5; cf. Hutchinson (1988) 94–7, 104–6 (on "disjointedness" and "discontinuity," some, he thinks, only apparent), Nelis (2001) 386–9 with further references.

perceived by the Hellenistic poets."[40] Callimachus' most famous poem, the *Aetia*, is an elegiac collective-poem with certain aspects of unity, but a greater devotion to variety. The *Aetia* begins with a famous and influential prologue, discovered only in 1927, in which the poet asserts that foes have murmured against him "because I have not accomplished one continuous poem in many thousands of lines on kings . . . [or?] heroes." Key words here, both "one" and "continuous," may be in dialogue with Aristotelian ideas about unity – or their use by less nimble critics than Aristotle[41] – although we must be cautious since this quoted, compendious, negative charge makes it hard to see what parts of the charge Callimachus is accepting or rejecting.[42] The *Aetia* might well be described as a poem that is neither "one" nor "continuous," and may or may not be an attempt to take a position different from that of Aristotle's recommendations about epic. As learned scholar-poets who were remarkably well informed about differing versions of myths, the Alexandrians were also fond of playing with references or allusions to mythic variants, so much so that we have often thought they originated the practice.[43] This notion, however, must all be revised in the light of the work on Homer noted above, and Alexandrian practice must be seen as a change in emphasis rather than as the introduction of startlingly new techniques.[44]

---

[40] Goldhill (1986). Goldhill uses the broader term "Hellenistic" rather than the narrower "Alexandrian;" I shall use both terms somewhat inconsistently, and "Alexandrian" more often (stressing the poetics of Callimachus and Apollonius, to which I assume Theocritus subscribes even when not writing at Alexandria), but "Hellenistic" when citing or discussing scholarship that uses that term. For references on the distinction see O'Hara (1996a) 21 n. 80.

[41] Cf. Hunter (1993) 190–5, Heyworth (1994) 74 n. 60, Heath (1989) 56–9, Cameron (1995) 342–3 and 441, where Cameron would distinguish between the *Aetia*, in which he admits Callimachus might be "pursuing a deliberate aim of unhomeric disunity," and the *Hecale*, which "deploys in miniature just those unifying techniques that set the *Iliad* and *Odyssey* apart from Cyclic epic – and Apollonius."

[42] Hunter (1993) 190–1 is right to say that Callimachus makes it unclear whether the charge is something that he thinks is unfair, or something of which he is proud. The translation of *Aet.* frag. 1.3–5 at Cameron (1995) 339, "because (they claim) it is not one continuous poem I have written on the deeds of kings or heroes of old in many thousands of lines," makes it a little too easy and clear.

[43] Besides the examples discussed below, cf. the scholars quoted above at n. 17, as well as Horsfall (1991b) 35, Hunter (1989) 21, and now Fantuzzi and Hunter (2004) *passim*, esp. 49–60.

[44] My argument here is similar to what I suggested about etymologizing at O'Hara (1996a) 41.

My brief comments will look first at two pairs of poems by Callimachus and Theocritus; the section (and the chapter) will end with some simple examples from Apollonius of Rhodes.

An inconsistency as much of form and style as of content marks Callimachus' *Hymn to Artemis*. The relationship between lines 183–268, on Artemis' cult-shrines, and 1–182, on her development from a cute child to an adult deity, has long seemed problematic. The last third of the poem tends to be slighted, or described as an unfortunate learned postscript or addendum.[45] Recent responses have been more generous and insightful, arguing that Callimachus favors a looser type of unity here as in the *Aetia* (Bornmann), or that Callimachus deliberately seeks variety by imitating and adapting Homeric narrative in 1–182, then Hesiodic aetiological catalogue poetry in 183–268 (Griffiths). We discussed earlier the *Homeric Hymn to Apollo*, whose distinctive Delian and Pythian sections made modern scholars think they were composed separately. Callimachus' *Hymn to Artemis* "makes extensive references to *both* parts of the *Homeric Hymn*, Delian and Pythian," including a prayer (136–7) which resembles the apparent closural formula in *Hymn to Apollo* 165–78, so it has been suggested that Callimachus "clearly sees" the two parts of the *Homeric Hymn* "as a unity."[46] If we take into account, however, rather than dismiss, the responses of generations of readers to the Homeric and Callimachean *Hymns*, we might say that Callimachus saw the *Homeric Hymn to Apollo*, with its two separate sections but certain unifying features, as a fitting model for his own *Hymn*, with its two separate sections and even more unifying features. This reading means we avoid saying that Callimachus did not notice the distinct features of the two parts of the *Homeric Hymn*. It also means that we can see Callimachus endorsing a different kind of unity than twentieth-century critics usually praised.[47]

---

[45] Cf. the fine summary of scholarship in Griffiths (1980) 134–5 and Uhrmeister and Bing (1994).

[46] Uhrmeister and Bing (1994).

[47] I have combined the insights of Bornmann (1968), Griffiths (1980), and Uhrmeister and Bing (1994), but should make clear that Bing and Uhrmeister criticize Bornmann's idea that the looser kind of unity of the *Aetia* is what we should expect in a *Hymn* by Callimachus. Cf. too Fantuzzi and Hunter (2004) 30–1, 364–5, Haslam (1993) 113–15 on how the ends of Callimachus' first three *Hymns* play games with the reader, and Barchiesi (1999) 125 on how "reading each poem in the context of the book [of Callimachean *Hymns*] has the effect of juxtaposing clashing or even irreconcilable views of divinity."

Theocritus' *Idyll* 22, the *Hymn to the Dioscuri*, presents similar challenges to our notion of unity; the poem has rightly been said to embody "twoness."[48] It presents two narratives, 27–134 and 137–213, which differ in tone, style, and even moral outlook, with the brothers Castor and Pollux gently chastising a wrongdoer in the first, then in the second mercilessly killing a man who criticized them.[49] Naturally scholars posited that the two sections had separate origins; the most scornful description is Gow's: "Having by him a poem or fragment on the Dioscuri and Apharidae, T[heocritus] pulled it out of the drawer, added Kastor's speech, scribbled a duel out of the *Iliad*, and clapped the whole into place."[50] Another familiar scholarly reaction is to emend: Wilamowitz posited a lacuna with change of speaker, in order to allow one of the brothers to defend their actions. More recently scholars have described the differences between the sections as deliberate and functional, and a result of both the general Alexandrian fondness for variation, and a desire to follow different models in different parts of the hymn. Thomas argues that "The impression of disunity establishes itself . . . precisely because the poem in a sense is a demonstration of generic multiplicity." Links between the hymn's two parts also suggest that their contrasting features must be a deliberate creation, and as Hunter notes, the "twoness" of the *Hymn to the Dioscuri* is appropriate to the unique "twoness" of the brothers. But what should we do with the contrasting morality suggested by the two stories? Since the Dioscuri are the sons of Zeus, Hunter suggests that the differing moral stances of the two sections show differing and, to mortal minds, difficult aspects of the divine. Thomas and others argue that "heroism itself is denigrated" in the second part of the *Idyll*; Haslam has offered a less reverential reading of many aspects of Callimachus' *Hymns* along these lines. Griffiths, in a reading consistent with the principles later enunciated by Heath, argues that there is no thematic unity because the poet is interested in style and not in thematic matters.[51]

---

[48] Cf. Griffiths (1980) 129–32, Sens (1992) and (1997), Thomas (1999) 252–60, Hunter (1996) 46–76; for a traditional discussion of unity see Laursen (1992).

[49] See the summary in Sens (1997) 14, and also Cameron (1995) 431–3.

[50] Gow (1942) 16, quoted by Thomas (1999) 252.

[51] Thomas (1999) 253 = (1996) 232, Hunter (1996) 59, Griffiths (1980) 129–32, Sens (1992) and (1997); both Thomas and Griffiths point to similarities between the technique of this poem and that of the singing contest. Note too the challenging idea of Selden (1998) 349–50 that Hellenistic poetry, especially that of Callimachus, reflects "Egyptian

Part of the formal complexity of Callimachus' *Hymn to Artemis* and Theocritus' *Hymn to the Dioscuri* is signaled for the reader by the use of different models. In other poems the relationship to earlier literature involves incompatible variant versions of myth. Callimachus' *Hymn to Zeus* offers two passages in which an alternate myth is evoked and rejected, but the rejection is ambiguous, and the rejected version remains as plausible as the selected one. The first involves Zeus's place of birth: the speaker notes that some say Zeus was born in Crete, some in Arcadia, and asks Zeus which of the two has lied.[52] The next words, "Cretans always lie," seem to decide in favor of Arcadia, but in fact muddle things more. The words echo the famous paradox of the Cretan Epimenides, but if a Cretan always lies, then a Cretan who says Cretans always lie must also be lying. Further, the words here are spoken by Zeus, who could be another lying Cretan. The initial impression that Callimachus is rejecting the Cretan birth yields to a more basic uncertainty about which version is correct. Later, Callimachus' speaker explicitly rejects the story of the lots drawn by Zeus, Poseidon and Hades to determine who will rule Olympus, the sea, and the underworld (59–63). Callimachus rejects this story as implausible, saying that no one would ever draw lots for unequal prizes like Olympus and the underworld, but Haslam has noticed the sham seriousness of this objection, which is then followed by Callimachus' famous and revealing comment "may I tell lies that the one hearing them would believe" (64). Like Pindar in *Olympian* 1, who both tells and incompletely rejects the story of Pelops, and Hesiod in the *Theogony*, who mentions the Muses' ability to fashion "lies like the truth," Callimachus calls attention to the fictionality of both his own and other poets' constructions. There may even be a direct link between Pindar and Callimachus here, given the influence of Pindar on Callimachus, and of *Olympian* 1 on Callimachus' *Hymn to Zeus* – though this connection has not been mentioned in most recent discussions of the speaking voice in the *Hymn to Zeus*.[53]

---

thinking" which "eschews the 'either/or' for a 'both/and' rationale that admits a plurality of divergent actualities within the same existent, even when these stand in contradiction."

[52] I owe much to recent discussions of the *Hymn to Zeus* by Bing (1988) 76–7 n. 42, Hopkinson (1984), Goldhill (1986) 27–30, Lüddecke (1998), Depew (1993) 72–3, Haslam (1993) 115–17, Barchiesi (1993) and (1997) 181ff., Thomas (1999) 220–4; the last two have talked about this *Hymn*'s influence on Latin poets.

[53] Thomas (1999) 9, 70ff., 274, with further references, and suggesting (274) that Callimachus may have dealt, somewhere, "with the infamous Pindaric zetema concerning the way Pelops lost his shoulder." Selden (1998) 349–50, quoted above, n. 51, is discussing

Callimachus thus explicitly mentions, and pretends to reject, two mythic variants incompatible with the versions being endorsed by his speaker. Theocritus' *Idyll* 18, the short *Epithalamium of Helen*, also allows the reader to think of two incompatible versions of myth, but does not mention one of them at all. Theocritus, although he and his learned readers know the stories about Helen, writes an epithalamium for her wedding to Menelaus whose surface ignores the problems that lie ahead for the couple. Two factors encourage a reading that focuses on the innocent Helen: the first is that Egypt, where presumably Theocritus is writing, is where in the "phantom" story the innocent Helen waited out the Trojan War. The second is that Helen received cult in Egypt, and was associated with the Ptolemaic queen Arsinoe, and so some readers of this poem may have been comfortable with a totally positive reading of Helen. Thus critics such as Cameron claim that "like the Attic dramatists, Hellenistic poets could surely count on readers tuning out inappropriate or inconvenient alternative versions."[54] But how exactly, I would ask, would this work? Does it not depend on the assumption, so handy to critics throughout much of the twentieth century, that a literary audience was almost a single organism, whose uniform reactions could be predicted or described with unerring accuracy? Instead the weight of the Iliadic and Odyssean stories of Helen, the long, rich tradition of authors who evoke conflicting stories of Helen in the same poem,[55] and the way in which so much Hellenistic and especially Alexandrian poetry depends on its readers'

Callimachus' *Coma Berenices*, but his ideas could be relevant to the *Hymn to Zeus* as well.

[54] Cameron (1995) 435.

[55] See above; cf. also Rosenmeyer (1997) 142 on the reference to Helen in Sappho fr. 16:

[T]he lack of a specific reference to the seamy side of Helen's story does not necessarily mean that we are not meant to think of it. Myth is saturated with meaning, intrinsically allusive even if the full details are missing; it is enough for Sappho to allude to Helen, Menelaus, Paris, and the sea-voyage to Troy. How can we not imagine the consequences, how Homer told the story, how Helen will eventually sail back with the husband she is in the process of abandoning? The very name of Helen functions as an allusion to Homer's epic. The lyric text reveals that it is not its own contemporary, that it cannot constitute a self-contained whole. With one brief allusion to Helen, an entire epic cycle is evoked, other worlds, other texts, a counterpoint for Sappho's lyric ellipses. Neither Sappho nor Helen can be *contained*, but expand to include countless variations on their stories, looking simultaneously to the past and to the future.

See also the apt quotation by Halleran (1997) 140 of the fourth-century comic poet Antiphanes fr. 189 K–A, who complains that tragic poets have it easy because they

knowledge of earlier poetry, make it almost impossible to imagine that some of Theocritus' readers would not be thinking of the darker future that awaits Helen and Menelaus. It is, after all, only a chorus of Spartan girls who make the claim – fairly conventional for a wedding song – that the bride will belong to the groom forever (in Chapter Two we shall see a similar claim in Catullus 64 by the "Fates," whom one would expect to be more authoritative). And so some readers speak of the dramatic irony that results from the singer's position in time, before the seduction of Helen by Paris.[56] The irony would be similar to that felt in many of Ovid's *Heroides*, which Barchiesi (1993) has called "Future Reflexive Allusion" (more on this too in the next chapter). This ironic reading contrasts the surface optimism of the poem with a covert but powerful pessimism. It is also possible, however, to argue, as Hunter does, that the poem offers the reader two fully incompatible readings, one, a "Spartan" or "Dorian" or Ptolemaic reading that focuses on the idyllic wedding and blots out all thought of a dark future, the other, a reading that focuses on the irony of the dark future that awaits the couple.[57] It is not true, Hunter argues, "that Theocritus imagines that we will forget this other Helen," for "the obvious ironies of the poem keep her insistently before us." Each reader must decide how to respond to the choices offered by the text, and yet each decision produces a reading that is somehow too simple, and must ignore some aspect of the poem.

We close with some examples from Apollonius of Rhodes. Apollonius is often quite serious about offering two incompatible ways of reading,[58] but my focus here will be on a few simple allusions to mythic variants inconsistent with his main narrative, allusions which are most often more smoothly integrated into the text than some of the examples we have seen above. Apollonius

> makes visible the process of selection between variants, either by referring to a rejected version in the course of telling the selected one or by

can rely on the audience knowing the characters in their plays: "Say Oedipus and the audience knows everything . . . If a comic character, say a Chremes or a Pheidon, leaves out something he's hissed off stage. But that's perfectly all right for a Peleus or a Teucer."
[56] Cf. Hutchinson (1988) 187–8, with further references.
[57] Hunter (1996) 163ff., endorsing and building upon a suggestion of Stern (1978) that the poem epitomizes ambiguities in Helen's character in its two halves.
[58] Besides the scholars cited in n. 39 above, see Feeney (1991) 57–98, esp. 81–3, 88–9, and Clare (2002) *passim*.

combining previously competing versions . . . No single explanation will account for every case: some may be put down to sheer academic fun, others . . . to a desire to use as many poetically interesting situations as possible; many have a vital role to play in the poem.[59]

When Aeetes in 3.375–6 angrily says that the sons of Phrixus joined up with the Argonauts in Greece, his charge does not fit what Apollonius has narrated, but is consistent with earlier versions of the myth. At 3.1071–4 Medea says Circe lives on an island, and Jason repeats the word island in 1093, but Apollonius' Circe lives on the coast (3.311–13); "Medea's ignorance is characterised by making her adhere to a piece of Homeric geography which her own poet has rejected" (Hunter). At 1.609–32 and 1.793–833, we are given two explanations why there are no men on Lemnos: first the narrator tells us that the Lemnian women have killed them, then we hear Hypsipyle tell Jason that they have all moved to Thrace; it is easy to see that the latter version is a lie.[60]

In none of these examples do the variants intrude upon the text; it has been said that Apollonius' method is to "work up a single vast conglomerate which takes account of all (or many) of the existing antecedents."[61] One example fits less smoothly, at least in some interpretations: Hera at 4.784–90 seems to say that she has helped the Argonauts get through the Wandering Rocks, even though the Argo will not pass through the Wandering Rocks until 4.922–67, where it is Athena and the Nereids (acting for Hera) who save them. Many have wanted to emend the lines, or make the verb "saved" mean "could save," but since Hera's words match what is said about the Argonauts and the Wandering Rocks in *Odyssey* 12.66–72, it is tempting to see this as a literary joke about an alternate version,

> making Hera say to Thetis, in effect, "Well, I hardly need to repeat how I saved the Argonauts from the Wandering Rocks: you know your Homer as well as I do, and it's all in there."[62]

---

[59] Hunter (1989) 21, from whom this paragraph borrows much.

[60] Nelis (2001) 387, Fusillo (1985) 170–1.   [61] Horsfall (1991b) 35.

[62] Green (1997) 324–6, who surveys other solutions; cf. also Hinds (1993) 18 n. 18, and Nishimura-Jensen (2000) 310 with further references. Zissos (1999) shows that Valerius Flaccus' *Argonautica* does to Apollonius what Apollonius did to Homer: Valerius refers to details of the Argonautic myth not consistent with his own version of the story, but most often in line with the Apollonian version.

Our final example will offer a transition to the next chapter. In Apollonius, the Argo is not depicted as the first boat, but the poem contains two passages that have been seen as allusions to the tradition in which it is: 1.547–52, where the gods watch the ship's launch and the nymphs "marvel," as nymphs will marvel in Catullus 64, and 4.316–22, where shepherds who have never seen "sea-faring ships, at any rate" (the qualification suggests that they may have seen smaller craft) are afraid of the Argo.[63] These allusions, if felt at all, are subtle; to confront head-on the problem of mythological reference to the first boat we must turn to Catullus.

---

[63] Hunter (1989) on 340 says Apollonius "plainly" alludes to the first-boat tradition here; Gilchrist (n.d.) argues that he is "commenting on a live issue when his text shows that the Argo could not be the first ship."

CHAPTER

2

Catullus 64: Variants and the virtues of heroes

Theseus knew he owed his life and his country's freedom to Ariadne's courage, and he knew he could not leave without her. Some say he asked Minos for her hand in marriage, and that the king gladly consented. Others say she stole onto the departing ship at the last minute without her father's knowledge. Either way, the two lovers were together when the anchor lifted and the dark ship sailed away from Crete. But this happy ending is mixed with tragedy, as stories sometimes are. For the Cretan captain of the vessel did not know he was to hoist white sails if Theseus came home in triumph, and King Aegeus . . . spied the black sails coming over the horizon. His heart broke at once, and he fell from the towering cliff into the sea, which is now called the Aegean.

William Bennett, The Book of Virtues

quis ille? "who is that speaking?"

Apuleius, The Golden Ass, 1.1

Catullus 64, the epyllion or miniature epic often called the *Peleus and Thetis*, is not really an epic, but some definitions of epic would exclude four of the five works examined in this study; we must appreciate, rather than lament, the fact that most Roman epics were not written by authors who spent their whole careers working in the genre. Doubtless this fact helped make generic experimentation almost the norm for Roman epic. The *Peleus and Thetis* is our first fully extant example of Latin mythological hexameter epic, but the crucial role of the poem in the Roman epic tradition is often overlooked. The influence of Catullus on Augustan poetry and of Catullus 64 in particular on both Vergil and Ovid is clear, extensive, and significant, and includes questions of style, structure, content, theme and ideology; it is no exaggeration to describe "Augustan poetry as a natural growth in the soil prepared by Catullus."[1] Catullus 64 can be seen as setting the standard for later poets in at least two respects: the persistent habit of starting a poem with a striking inconsistency, and the tendency to play with chronological problems and mythological variants.

The first ship, and the earlier ship

Discussion in recent years of the start of Catullus 64 has revealed its allusions to Euripides, Ennius, Apollonius, and Callimachus; how the poem's initial focus on the voyage of the Argonauts misleads the reader about the poem's subject-matter; and the way the first few lines serve notice that questions like "who speaks?" and "what version?" will be important throughout the poem.[2] The poem is now often seen "as a work of competing perspectives whose authority is repeatedly called into question," as critics view it in the tradition of the Hellenistic poets' deliberate fragmenting of the poet's voice "into a multiplicity of citations, different levels of enunciation, and conflicting or ambiguous attitudes," to cite the formulation of Goldhill mentioned in the last chapter.[3] Such a poetics of fragmentation or conflicting perspectives has obvious relevance to a study of poetic inconsistency. This chapter will begin with the problem of the "first boat" in Catullus 64, then will treat the figure of the speaker in the poem, the generic and other expectations raised by the start of the poem and by the start of the insert on Theseus and Ariadne, and the song of the Fates and the figure of Achilles.

The poem's opening lines seem to describe the Argo upon which the Argonauts are riding as the world's first boat (1–15):

---

[1] Ross (1975) 2. Catullus 64 is not discussed in Feeney (1991) (as I pointed out in O'Hara [1993b]), Goldberg (1995) (deliberate; see p. v), or Keith (2000) (even though she discusses both *virtus* [see below, n. 27] and a number of characters influenced by Catullus' Ariadne and Polyxena). For the quotation from Bennett (1993) used as an epigraph above see below, n. 32.

[2] See Thomas (1982b) = (1999) 12–32, Zetzel (1983), Gaisser (1995), Clare (1996) 60–5, and Theodorakopoulos (2000) 121–5.

[3] "Competing perspectives:" Gaisser (1995), "multiplicity of citations:" Goldhill (1986); see also Williams (1968) 227–8 and Theodorakopoulos (2000).

Peliaco quondam prognatae vertice pinus
dicuntur liquidas Neptuni nasse per undas
Phasidos ad fluctus et fines Aeeteos,
cum lecti iuvenes, Argivae robora pubis,
auratam optantes Colchis avertere pellem
ausi sunt vada salsa cita decurrere puppi,
caerula verrentes abiegnis aequora palmis.
diva quibus retinens in summis urbibus arces
ipsa levi fecit volitantem flamine currum,
pinea coniungens inflexae texta carinae.
illa rudem cursu prima imbuit Amphitriten.
quae simul ac rostro ventosum proscidit aequor,
tortaque remigio spumis incanuit unda,
emersere freti candenti e gurgite vultus
aequoreae monstrum Nereides admirantes.

At one time pines born on the Pelian peak
are said to have swum through Neptune's clear waves
to the waters of Phasis and the land of Aeetes,
when select young men, the strength of Argive youth,
hoping to take away from Colchis the golden fleece,
dared to run in a swift ship over the salty straits,
sweeping the blue sea-surface with oars of fir.
The goddess who keeps hold of citadels in the heights of cities
herself made for them the chariot that flew by the light breeze,
joining the pine framework to the curved keel.
That ship first stained the inexperienced sea with its running.
And as soon as it cut the windy sea with its beak,
and the waves, twisted by the rowing, grew white with foam,
faces emerged from the white swirl of the strait,
watery Nereids looking in wonder at this marvel.

The marveling of the Nereids at this *monstrum* underscores the singularity of the event; they are amazed to see this first boat. One of them, Thetis, is so amazed she will eventually wind up married to one of the Argonauts, and the rest of the poem describes the wedding of Peleus and Thetis, with an extended description of the coverlet on the marriage bed. That coverlet tells the story of Theseus and Ariadne, and is introduced with these lines (50–4):

> haec vestis *priscis* hominum variata figuris
> *heroum* mira *virtutes* indicat arte.
> namque fluentisono prospectans litore Diae,
> Thesea cedentem *celeri cum classe* tuetur
>
>   . . . Ariadna

This coverlet, decorated with figures of mortals of *olden days*,
depicted the *manly deeds* (*virtutes*) *of heroes* with amazing artistry.
For looking out from the loud-resounding shore of the island of Dia,
Ariadne watched Theseus departing *with his swift fleet*.

A boat is always useful for getting to and from an island, but Catullus calls attention to Theseus' ships in 53 with the phrase *celeri cum classe*, "with his swift fleet." He also stresses chronology by referring to Theseus and Ariadne, by means of a transferred epithet, as *prisci*, "people of the olden days."[4] In the space of 54 lines, then, Catullus has described both the first ship, and an earlier fleet. What should we make of this?

We must first verify that we have read the text correctly, because the text and interpretation are uncertain at some points. If we are going to suggest that inconsistencies in a text should be interpreted, we need to know whether they have been caused by textual corruption or other problems in the production of texts. A textual critic of American literature, Herschel Parker, has collected sobering examples of elaborate theories worked out to interpret inconsistencies in Twain, Melville, Crane, Fitzgerald, and others, for which he can prove, using diaries and other documents, that the inconsistencies were introduced by lazy revisions, poor or puritanical editing, or even typesetting errors. Classicists may well think of Sebastiano Timpanaro's discussion of "the Freudian slip," and his contention that many of the errors that Freud described as signs of repressed unpleasant memories (including the famous misquotation of *Aen.* 4.625) are instead the kind of simple mistakes of banalization, haplography, or simplification familiar to anyone who has worked with either the manuscripts of classical texts or the proofs of journal articles.[5]

---

[4] Treating *priscis* as a transferred epithet makes the figures depicted like the παλαι-γενέων . . . φωτῶν, "men born long ago," of *Arg.* 1.1, but perhaps the effect of a transferred epithet should not be completely obliterated: to some extent these may also be "old figures of mortals." On *priscis* see also below, n. 8.

[5] Parker (1984), Timpanaro (1976); in favor of interpreting some but not all inconsistencies (or "puzzles") in modern novels: Sutherland (1996), (1997), (1998). On modern fiction cf. also Chapter 1 n. 16.

The inconsistency in Catullus 64 resists attempts to emend it away, I believe, but the possibility of textual corruption should not be ignored. The word *prima* in line 11 does not appear in all manuscripts, and some scholars have offered emendations or supported other readings, some in order to remove (they think) the first-boat problem. Lines 11–12 are also difficult to construe: the antecedent of *quae* in 12 is uncertain, and some have argued that it must be Athena, and not the ship as I have it above, so that what is being said is that it is not the first ship, but somehow the ship's first sailing.[6] But even without *prima*, or without *prima* modifying the ship, too many details suggest that we are indeed seeing the first ship: the Argonauts are bold (*ausi sunt*), the Nereids are startled, the words used to describe the ship (chariot, run over, running, "little palms" for oars) are borrowed from land travel or elsewhere, and the sea is described as "inexperienced" and as being stained, dyed, or even violated (*imbuit*). Even the most recent proponent of removing *prima* (in favor of *proram*) thinks we are still dealing with the first ship.[7]

Other stratagems for eliminating the inconsistency fall short of being convincing:[8] Catullus describes the Argo as the first ship, then goes on to describe earlier seafaring. Possibly this contradiction is something Catullus did not care about. Many critics have seen it as a blunder, or insignificant error: the young and romantic poet's ability to handle narrative without bungling it is thought to be as limited as his ability to handle independent-thinking older women.[9] This option too deserves consideration, for poets can make

---

[6] Cf. Quinn (1970) on 11, refuted by Jenkyns (1982) 104 n. 18, and see Thomson (1997) on 11; see below on the first-ship/first-sailing ambiguity in Eurip. *Androm.* 865.

[7] Heyworth in Harrison and Heyworth (1998) 105–6.

[8] Weber (1983) 264 n. 3 uses *priscis* to refute both the idea that the coverlet predicts the future, and the idea of Thetis and the busy Argonaut Peleus being engaged to be married for long enough for Theseus' Cretan adventure to take place and quickly get embroidered into the coverlet; he gives bibliographical references for both suggestions. The idea that the coverlet predicts the future, also argued in an unpublished paper by F. Williams (which I thank him for discussing with me by electronic mail), and mentioned by Theodorakopoulos (2000) 126 n. 26 and Martindale (2005) 98, can be saved by imagining that *priscis* is focalized through the speaker or readers and not the contemporary viewers of the coverlet. But nothing in the text points in this direction. Cf. Martindale (2005) 98: "Catullus 64 simultaneously encourages and resists a unified reading, teasing with paradox."

[9] Blusch (1989) 122 simply asserts that "Der Mythos hat keine Zeit." Theodorakopoulos (2000) 126–9 discusses intertextuality and the first-boat/not-first-boat problem, and

mistakes, just as films can have "continuity errors."[10] Weber and Gaisser, however, have shown that Catullus deliberately creates and calls attention to this problem; he "flaunts" the inconsistency, to use Wheeler's word for Ovidian chronological problems, and "draws our attention to the contradictions that he has manufactured," as Gaisser puts it.[11] The importance of finding the author's fingerprints all over the chronological problem should not be underestimated, for it suggests to me that for this poem at least, we should not be eager to use the inconsistency to deconstruct the poem without regard for the apparent intentions of the author – as though he had tried and failed to be consistent. Catullus is thus an interesting starting point for our survey of Roman poets, because although it may be true that the nature of language or literature can make any text inconsistent regardless of the intention of the author, Catullus seems to offer evidence of deliberate manipulation of inconsistency. Other readers, I realize, might wish to attribute even errors like this to unconscious forces working upon the poet, and there may be some arbitrariness in where I come down on this question. In later chapters we will find some clear examples like this where the poet calls attention to an inconsistency, and others in which it is not clear what conscious and unconscious processes may have produced an inconsistency.

In part Catullus is playfully alluding to an Alexandrian scholarly debate about mythological chronology. The relative chronology of Theseus and the Argonauts depends on Medea, whom Jason meets as a young woman at Colchis, and by whom the young Theseus is almost killed when she is an older woman receiving asylum in Athens, shortly before the Cretan adventure in which Theseus meets Ariadne.[12] But Apollonius of Rhodes has Jason talk to Medea about Theseus and Ariadne's story as something that happened

suggests that "the lying and cheating of Apollonius' Jason becomes Catullus' obviously and deliberately shaky 'truth'" (129).

[10] See e.g. Givens (1996) and websites like www.slipups.com. For possibly interpretable inconsistencies see Traube (1992) 37–8 on *Indiana Jones and the Temple of Doom*, and Taylor (1995) on the notorious beach sunset (rare in eastward-looking Vietnam) in *The Green Berets*.

[11] Gaisser (1995) 605; cf. Batstone (1993) on Poems 16 and 49: "Catullus meant to write these unsolvable riddles." For Wheeler see Chapter 5 on Ovid.

[12] Gilchrist (n.d.), Clare (1996) 61. Colum (1921) 219–21, my daughter's "children's version" of the story of the Argo solves the problem in this way: Medea helps the Argonauts, including the young Theseus, then "Medea, the wise woman, counseled [Theseus] to go to Athens" to find his father; there an unnamed "evil woman, a witch," tries to kill Theseus.

once upon a time (*Argonautica* 3.997–1108, esp. 997 δή ποτε). Callimachus' *Hecale* (frs. 232–4 Pf. = 3–8 Hollis) seems to have featured the asylum story, in which the Argonauts must be earlier than the story of Theseus and Ariadne. Catullus 64 has an extensive and significant intertextual involvement with the *Argonautica*, as we have noted, but the *Hecale* is also important for the poem, in part because "for Roman poets the *Hecale* may have had a special position as one of the earliest, finest, and most substantial specimens of the epyllion."[13] More specifically, when Aegeus describes Theseus as "recently returned to me" (*reddite . . . nuper mihi*, 217), Catullus presents an allusion to and perhaps even a "virtual paraphrase" of the phrase "you have come back unexpectedly" in the *Hecale* (παρὲκ νόον εἰλήλουθας, fr. 234 Pf. = 8 Hollis).[14] Both phrases refer to Aegeus' recognition of his son after his arrival in Athens, which saved him from Medea's attempt on his life. In Catullus 64 Medea has been brought to the reader's mind numerous times, and then in line 217 Catullus points to the very scene in Callimachus' *Hecale* that causes the most chronological problems: like many of the poets discussed in the last chapter, he borrows from or alludes to incompatible versions of mythology. Allusions to Callimachus work along with the reference to the figures of Ariadne and Theseus as *prisci* and the prominence of the words *celeri cum classe*, to make it hard for the reader to miss the inconsistency. These aspects of the poem make it doubtful that Catullus either simply did not care about chronology, or was pursuing one set of poetic goals in the first few lines of the poem, and others in the first few lines of the description of the coverlet.

Like later poets such as Ovid, who will play chronological games with the Argo myth and with other stories, Catullus thus seems to be deliberately alluding to two incompatible versions of the Argo myth. Gaisser describes several ways in which the opening of the poem stresses the poet's choice between variant versions; with the problem of Jason's "first ship" and Theseus' earlier

---

[13] Hollis (1990) 32. On Callimachus and Poem 64 more generally: Cat. 64.111 *nequiquam vanis iactantem cornua ventis*, resembles a verse some attribute to Callimachus: πολλὰ μάτην κεράεσσιν ἐς ἠέρα θυμήναντα (fr. 732 Pf., fr. 165 inc. auct. Hollis); cf. Gaisser (1995) 599. Thomas (1999) 4–5, 89–100 suggests a Callimachean model in the *Victoria Berenices* for the ecphrastic structure of Catullus 64; cf. Thomson (1997) 390–1. Thomas (1982b) = (1999) 12–32 discusses Callimachean and other influences on the start of 64. Klingner (1964) 196–7 suggests a Callimachean version of the Phyllis and Demophon story (cf. fr. 556 Pf.) as a possible model for Ariadne's speech at the shore.

[14] Weber (1983) 265; cf. Gaisser (1995) 604–5, Skinner (1994) 147 with references and (brief) broader reflections.

ship, instead of following one version and alluding to another, Catullus seems
to be following two incompatible versions, so that both variants are impossibly prominent in the poem.[15] Here it may be important to recall that the Argo
as first ship was probably not a classical Greek myth at all, but developed in
the Hellenistic or early Roman period, possibly as a result of a creative or
perverse misreading of words in Euripides' *Andromache* 865 that could be
taken to refer to the first ship, or to the Argo's maiden voyage.[16] Apollonius
can be seen, as Gilchrist puts it, as "commenting on a live issue when his text
shows that the Argo could not be the first ship: he is both contributing to the
study of relative chronology, and pointing to a preference in the interpretation
of the word πρωτόπλοος in Euripides' *Andromache*." Gilchrist comments
further that the "only implausibility left" is one that would be "apparent to
any reader of Callimachus or Euripides, who would know the story of Medea
and Theseus: but this is not in Apollonius' text." Such a reader, however, is
created or insisted upon by Catullus, who calls to mind both Apollonius and
Callimachus, as well as the Jason and Medea story as told by both Euripides
and Ennius.

That such readers actually existed in antiquity is suggested by the number
of times later poets play with chronological impossibilities, or allusion to
incompatible variants, including some that involve the Argo.[17] Over eighty

[15] Gaisser (1995) does not describe the chronological problem in this way, but attributes it
to aspects of the poem she describes with two metaphors: that of the labyrinth and that of
the bending of time (cf. pp. 587, 602, 605, 608). The latter seems too anachronistically
Einsteinian or Roddenberrian to be satisfying. Thomson (1997) on 52 says that Catullus'
description of the island makes clear that "two divergent accounts" of the setting of the
desertion of Ariadne by Theseus "have been fused together."

[16] I draw here from Jackson (1997) and Gilchrist (n.d.) (which I thank Dr. Gilchrist for
sending me).

[17] For Ovid, see below in Chapter 5 for Wheeler's reading of *Met.* 6.721, which calls the
Argo the first ship despite earlier seafaring in the poem, and for Ovid's other chronological impossibilities. For the Argo and Medea cf. too Hinds (1993) on Ovid *Heroides* 12,
and Zissos (1999) on the *Argonautica* of Valerius Flaccus. Feeney (1999) puts Ovid's
violations of chronological order in the context of recent Roman attempts, by Cornelius
Nepos, Atticus, Varro, and others, to order the events of mythology and history. Catullus
knew Nepos' work; Poem 1.6 says Nepos dared to "unfold/explain all of time in three
volumes" (*omne aevum tribus explicare chartis*), which suggests that he tried to harmonize mythological chronology. Catullus may have known early work by Atticus and
Varro, though their best-known work probably appeared after his death. It is thus tempting to see the chronological impossibility of Poem 64 as a reaction by a poet against the
work of historians on myth.

years ago Pasquali, arguing against those who suggested that Catullus 64 must be a translation of a Hellenistic poem, suggested it was an adaptation (not a slavish translation) of *two* Hellenistic models, which would then also account for the chronological discrepancy between the frame and the description of the coverlet.[18] Even this may have been an overstatement, but Catullus' limited deliberate use of two Hellenistic models for mythical chronology juxtaposes two incompatible traditions about the Argo and about the chronological relationship between the Argonautic expedition and the story of Theseus and Ariadne.

The aesthetic response, and the narrator

How we should respond when a poet juxtaposes incompatible mythological variants is a difficult question, which this chapter can only begin to answer. I start by describing and combining (despite their incompatibilities) two recent types of approach to this poem and to much learned poetry. Both scholars who concentrate on Alexandrian learning and allusions as a source of delectation separate from thematic interpretation, and those who disdain Alexandrian poetics but focus on the luxurious aesthetic qualities of Catullus 64 and its status as a "masterpiece," would recommend that we not take the "content" of the poem seriously, but should enjoy its beauties, its experiments in style, its self-consciously virtuoso adaptation of earlier sources.[19] This option deserves serious consideration, both here and in the following chapters. We must be aware that many Romans may have sought in poetry, and found in it, aesthetic pleasures both linguistic and formal, without much regard for what was being said. This is the problem of "aesthetic" or "formalist" in contrast to what may be termed "thematic," "interpretive," "ideological," "moralist," or "political" readings of a poem, mentioned in the previous chapter's description of the work of Malcolm Heath. This choice is usually not thought to be an option for Lucretius (though it should not be ruled out even for him), but is a question asked at times for Vergil and Ovid, and one that may be rephrased to

---

[18] Pasquali (1920) esp. 18–23.

[19] Heath (1989), Jenkyns (1982), Griffiths (1980); Fitzgerald (1995) deals with some of these issues but is not part of this movement. Cf. the responses (in general, not on Catullus 64) of Fowler (2000a) 29–30 (with the ironic "Thank God for Callimachus"); Hinds (1987a) and (1992), and often in the writings and reviews of Richard Thomas and James Zetzel. Martindale (2005) has now argued for an aesthetic approach to Roman poets that would complement, not exclude, ideological or political readings.

apply to Lucan. During Catullus' lifetime, after all, the Epicurean philosopher and poet Philodemus feels compelled to argue against "euphonists" who
argued that "good poets excel and they alone endure on no other account than
the sounds."[20] But this approach, sometimes implicit in learned articles that
ignore thematic matters, and at other times aggressively promoted in a way
scornful of other approaches (with claims that "nobody except professors
reads *that* way"), is far from fully satisfying, for it cannot be said to have
exhausted the poem's potential, and seems false both to a great deal of the
evidence for the historical function of poetry in antiquity, and to this poem's
apparent extensive concern with issues of fidelity, justice, betrayal, heroism,
and truth or falsity.

We must also consider the way in which the poem seems to play with the
position of the narrator, and his relationship to the truth or falsity of what he
is reporting. Somewhat like Callimachus' allusions in the *Hymn to Zeus* to
variant stories of Zeus' birth, Catullus' strong use of incompatible variants
serves to undercut the authority of the speaking voice – not the poet behind
the creation of the poem, but the voice of the speaker – and to call attention
to the fictionality of the work. The speaker of Catullus 64 first revels in the
idea of the heroic age (*o nimis optato saeclorum tempore nati | heroes*, 22–3),
but then the poem breaks the plausibility of the fiction for the reader, who is
forced to confront the constructedness and unreality of the poem, if not of
Greek heroic mythology itself. Unlike in Callimachus' *Hymn*, however, the
speaker of Catullus 64 is never, as it were, let in on the joke, never says "may
I lie persuasively" as Callimachus does in the *Hymn*, so that the breaking
of the illusion would serve to buttress, rather than undercut, the authority of
the speaker. Catullus' speaker never wavers from his devotion to the heroic
age, even as the poem calls attention to its fictionality – never says *haec
mihi fingebam* or "such things did I imagine" the way Tibullus 1.5 does, or
describes his devotion to the heroic age as something he once (*quondam*) felt,
but now (*nunc*) does not, as other Catullan poems do. Readers on the other
hand can see that if there are two factually incompatible versions of reality,
one or both of them must be wrong, and must simply have been made up. We
can have both a first boat, and an earlier boat, because neither story is true.

In some ways what I am suggesting, without quite wishing to put all my
eggs in this basket, is close to the modern notion of the naive narrator, and the

[20] Philod. *On Poems* 1.83; see Janko (2000) 279 (whose translation I quote) and index s.v.
"euphonists;" cf. O'Hara (1997) 246.

ancient notion of inconsistency as a marker of characterization: the "solution from character speaking" discussed in the last chapter. "Who speaks" in Catullus has been a topic of some discussion lately, both in many discussions of his shorter poems and in Gaisser's study of Catullus 64, but Gaisser is more concerned to describe other voices heard later in the poem. I am attracted to the notion that the chronological inconsistency of the first-boat problem helps open up a separation or gap between the poet – the creator of the work or the implied author or "hidden author" of the poem – and the unnamed speaker of the poem.[21] The learned poet crafts allusions to variant versions; the romantic speaker of the poem yearns for the heroic age, and remains, to the very end of the poem, blissfully unaware of the problems with his notion of the heroic age.[22] This is not a solution to every problem in the poem, and recently Paul Allen Miller has sagely warned of the dangers of using "persona theory" to produce a reading of another longer poem, Catullus 68, in which all problematic aspects of the work can "be seen as part of a rhetorical strategy" on the part of the poet, "designed to illustrate the shortcomings of the speaker." There is danger too, however, in assuming that in Catullus 64 or 68 the speaker's errors give us unmediated access to the real-world poet's own conflicts and uncertainties, in ways of which the poet is unaware.[23] In Catullus 64 the elaborately crafted chronological impossibility calls attention to the issue of fictionality, and breaks the "reality effect."[24] Similarly,

---

[21] Cf. e.g. Skinner (1989) on Cat. 10, Winkler (1985) on Apuleius, Conte (1996) on Petronius, and below in my final chapter on Lucan. On the *persona* cf. Edmunds (2001) 63–82, though see also P. A. Miller as cited in n. 23 below, and now the skeptical views of Clay (1998) and Mayer (2003). On "confusion" between the poet's voice and that of Ariadne at some points in 64 see DeBrohun (1999), esp. on the reference at 64.150 to the Minotaur as Ariadne's (full) brother, seen by some as an inconsistency.

[22] Cf. Janan (1994) 108 on 64.22: "How is one to take *nimis optato* in this line – as 'very much wished for' or 'too much, excessively wished for' age? The decision demands a choice between an age of heroes that either was truly heroic or was overrated."

[23] P. A. Miller (2004) 50–2, with further references. Miller's example of a scholarly lecturer who claimed that it was deliberate that all of his slides were upside down would not quite work for Catullus 64 or even 68. These poems were written a bit more carefully than the average academic lecture; Catullus 95.1–2 describes Cinna's poem *Smyrna* as having taken nine years to write.

[24] Cf. Scodel (1999) 14 on how our poem differs from archaic and classical Greek epic and drama:

> Some narratives are deliberately inconsistent or unverisimilar [. . . and] offer inconsistencies or violations of verisimilitude that make the mimetic world impossible. They

O'Connell (1977: 755) has noted how "the poem has a curious way of stating an opinion about something, then implicitly contradicting the opinion in the narration." O'Connell mentions especially the contrasts between *heroum virtutes* ("manly deeds of heroes") and the following narrative, and between the prophecy of the Parcae about the happiness of Peleus and Thetis and what the text says about Achilles. To these, in order, we now turn.

The manly virtues of heroic epic

The narrator's investment in the truth of the heroic age, and the way that the poem challenges the reader's ability to stay with him, suggest that the inconsistency about the first boat is not merely "playful," and that issues of the truth or falsity of myth and of the reliability of the narrator should be an important part of our experience of the poem. We need now to consider another type of inconsistency that begins to come to the reader's mind at the same time as the question of the first boat; we are concerned now with features of Catullus 64 that may be called thematic inconsistencies. The coverlet is said to describe the "manly deeds of heroes" (*heroum . . . virtutes*, 51), but the great exploit on which the coverlet focuses is Theseus' abandonment of Ariadne, after her own betrayal of her family. Accordingly many scholars have noted that the coverlet seems to portray not any positive sense of *virtus* but instead the faithlessness or lack of *fides* Catullus laments so bitterly elsewhere. *Virtus* as "admirable manly courage" is not completely absent from this section of the poem, as Theseus' *fervida virtus* inspires his attempt to save his countrymen from the Minotaur, but this is a small part of the long description, occurring in a father's lament that his son's *virtus* is taking him

break the frame. When Catullus emphasizes that the Argo was the first ship . . . and then describes a tapestry that shows Theseus sailing away with his fleet, the mimetic level temporarily collapses – unless the implied reader is inattentive, which seems unlikely. The technique relies on the audience's expectation that the mimetic world will be self-consistent and possible, since the effect is lost otherwise. Such anti-mimetic thematization is common in post-modernist literature, but is not used in archaic and classical Greek, except in comedy, and perhaps by Euripides.

Eco (1984) 233–4 argues that it is impossible for a narrative to construct a world in which contradictory claims are both true ("such a world is in fact *quoted*, but is it not *constructed*"), except in "science-fiction novels and avant-garde texts" whose effect "is just that of producing a sense of logical uneasiness and of narrative discomfort." Cf. McHale (1987) 33–6, and also my Chapter 1 n. 16.

44

away from him.[25] Some have sought to explain or defend Theseus' actions as consistent with tough Roman military values, and the poem itself seems open to this kind of reading, but it offers little encouragement for it, despite the speaker's apparent pleasure later in the poem in relating the Parcae's predictions of the exploits of Achilles. It may be helpful here, however, to consider certain aspects of the Roman context, and to try to imagine what expectations the beginning of the poem, the genre, and the phrase *heroum virtutes* would create for at least some Roman readers.[26]

Catullus' only hexameter narrative begins with praise of the age of heroes, and allusions to the poetry of Ennius and Apollonius. Hexameters describing *heroum virtutes* must also resonate with the notion of "glorious deeds of men" as the proper subject of epic song (κλέα ἀνδρῶν, *Il.* 9.190, *Od.* 8.73), and with Apollonius' announced topic of "glorious deeds of men born long ago" (παλαιγενέων κλέα φωτῶν, *Arg.* 1.1), which also must have influenced Catullus' *priscis figuris*.[27] At Rome *virtus* and praise of great deeds were prominent in Ennius' *Annals*, and then central to the image of Ennius promoted during Catullus' lifetime by Cicero; the Scipionic epitaphs of the third and second centuries BCE also show verse being used to praise *virtutes*.[28] We

---

[25] Cf. 218–19 *quandoquidem fortuna mea ac tua fervida virtus | eripit invito mihi te.* Lines 73–85 are the most "heroic," describing how Theseus came to Crete to risk his own life to save fellow Athenians from the Minotaur.

    One way of evading the plain meaning of *heroum virtutes* is to take the phrase as meaning simply "myth" or "high poetry;" Syndikus (1984) 139 cites Cic. *De Or.* 2.194 *heroum veteres casus,* but that phrase itself also has a particular and very different negative meaning; *non heroum veteres casus fictosque luctus velim imitari* = "I would not wish to portray the bygone misfortunes and legendary griefs of heroes" (translation adapted from Sutton's Loeb).

[26] For stimulating thoughts on the Roman reader, and useful warnings against oversimplification, see Edmunds (2001) 39–62.

[27] This paragraph owes much to Wiseman (1974) 36–7, Conte (1986) 141–6, White (1993) 78–82, Goldberg (1995) *passim*, Fantuzzi and Hunter (2004) 90–2, and Keith (2000) 5–6, who notes (without mentioning Catullus 64) that "Just as Greek epic examines the panhellenic ideals of manliness (*andreia*) and military prowess (*aristeia*), Latin epicists from Ennius to Statius scrutinise the conventions of Roman *virtus* ('manliness'). . . ."

[28] The poetry of Ennius himself may have been much more complex than this (cf. Goldberg [1995] 111–34), but for his reception cf. the inscription mentioned at Cic. *TD* 1.34 (= Enn. fr. 45 Courtney; Ennius "recorded the great deeds [*facta*] of your ancestors"), as well as fr. 29 Courtney (only Homer could properly praise Scipio). The Scipionic epitaphs praise one Scipio for his great wisdom and many *virtutes* and say he was never surpassed in *virtus*; another epitaph speaks in the first person to suggest that by his *mores* another

must think too of the small resurgence at Rome of panegyrical or historical epic, albeit much of it by "second-rate" poets (White [1993] 79), including Archias' epics for Marius and the Luculli, Varro of Atax on Caesar's *Bellum Sequanicum*, and Cicero's quick work on an epic on Caesar's exploits in Britain in 54. Near the time in which Catullus may have been writing the *Peleus and Thetis*, Cicero in 62 BCE also discusses the relationship between *virtus* and poetry in his speech in defense of the poet Archias. Cicero stresses poetry's value to the state, and its role in propagating the *virtutes* of the best men, and inspiring the pursuit of *virtus*; citing for comparison the statues and images which played a major role in Roman veneration of their ancestors in funeral processions, he argues that poetry can provide "an image of our counsels and virtues" (*Pro Arch.* 30: *consiliorum . . . ac virtutum nostrarum effigiem*).[29]

In Catullus 64, both the early praise of the heroic age, and the announcement that the coverlet will depict the *heroum virtutes*, create the expectation that Catullus' hexameter poem will praise the virtues or heroic deeds of great men – men of the olden days perhaps, but great men nevertheless. That the poem is mythological need not have stopped Romans from expecting a typical Roman attitude towards *virtutes*, as we learn from Braund's discussion of the "historical dynamic" of "writing a Roman *Argonautica*" such as that of Catullus' near-contemporary Varro of Atax.[30] The expectations created in some Roman readers by the phrase *heroum virtutes* would thus make for the strongest and sharpest contrast between the material in the coverlet and the introductory verses 50–4. It would not have been surprising, for example, if the words *heroum virtutes* had introduced more adventures from the Argonautic expedition. The introduction to the work sets us up, then the poem moves almost violently in another direction – not too surprising a move, I suggest, from a poet who has been working in lyric, elegy, and a version of iambic.[31] It might be suggested that this proves either that the poem has more

Scipio has added to the *virtutes* of his clan; see the texts in Ernout (1957) 12–21, and cf. Goldberg (1995) 61–5, Van Sickle (1987), Thomas (1998) 283–4.

[29] Elsewhere in the speech Cicero speaks of how literature publicizes the *virtutes* of great men (15), and would be useless and unread if it did not (16). Poor Cicero of course never got anyone to write on his own consulship, and had to do it himself; cf. Goldberg (1995) 135–57.

[30] D. Braund (1993).

[31] Cf. the way in which Catullus 11 begins with lines that praise heroic deeds – this time literally the accomplishments of "great Caesar," then abruptly changes direction with

serious moral concerns than some have claimed, or that writing a largely aesthetic poem which begins by arousing expectations of praise of heroic *virtutes* must have its political consequences. The contrast also serves further to undercut the reliability of the narrator, who should be understood as making the affirmative claim that the coverlet demonstrates *heroum virtutes*.[32]

Death and the optimistic wedding song

So far we have seen problems of mythological variants and clashes of values; the wedding song for Peleus and Thetis sung by the Parcae or "Fates" at 323–81 involves both. The same narrator or speaker who says the coverlet displays *heroum virtutes* also describes the marriage of Peleus and Thetis, near the start of the poem, as "fortunate, happy" (*taedis felicibus*, 25). The Parcae's Song at the wedding goes into great detail to suggest that the union will be unsurpassed for concord (334–6) and will be a "happy union" (*felix foedus*, 373), and that the bride's mother will have no cause to worry about her daughter quarreling with her husband and sleeping apart (*discordis maesta puellae | secubitu*, 379–80) or about the prospect of not having grandchildren (380). The narrator then refers to their song as *felicia . . . carmina* (382–3). Predictions of future happiness, concord, and children are conventional for wedding songs, but here they must collide violently with the reader's knowledge of most other versions of the myth of Peleus and Thetis, which say that when Achilles was still an infant, Peleus and Thetis quarreled and separated permanently; one particularly conspicuous version of this story was in *Argonautica* 4.[33] Scholars have seen numerous possible allusions in Catullus 64 to the pair's breakup, both in general (the model of the relationships of

the words *non bona dicta* in line 16. Many recent readings of the shorter poems focus on their ambiguity or disunity (cf. especially Selden [1992] and Batstone [1993]) or the fractured picture of the speaker, whether in individual poems or in respect to the figure of the Catullan lover more generally. Theodorakopoulos (2000) 118 (with further references) speaks of similarities between "the labyrinthine strategies" of Cat. 64 and "the often fragmented and incoherent persona of Catullus the lover in other poems."

[32] For a Theseus and Ariadne story that literally promotes "virtue" in the way Cicero wanted, cf. the desertion-free version of the story published in *The Book of Virtues* by a U.S. political figure: Bennett (1993) 466, in the section on "courage," quoted as an epigraph to this chapter; he seems to be using a version by Andrew Lang.

[33] Survey in Gantz (1993) 1.230–1, noting that the *Iliad* at times seems to imply a normal home life for Peleus and Thetis, but also depicts Thetis in the sea with her father and sisters. Sources that clearly depict the breakup are in the *Iliad* scholia, fragments of Hesiod (as discussed by Philodemus), Sophocles, Lycophron, and Apoll. *Arg.* 4.869–79.

Theseus and Ariadne and of Jason and Medea) and in more specific terms.[34] We are in a situation somewhat comparable to that of readers of Theocritus 18's epithalamium of Helen and Menelaus, or of the several of Ovid's *Heroides* that are set before, and yet seem to allude to, well-known future events, using the technique Barchiesi has called the "Future Reflexive," as noted in the previous chapter's discussion of Theocritus' epithalamium. What we have in Catullus is different from what we find in the *Heroides*, however, in flatly denying those future events, in what might accordingly be called the "Future Reflexive Contrary-to-Fact."[35]

It might be possible, of course, for us to put aside thoughts of these other myths – as some scholars urge us to do with Theocritus 18. After all, the narrator claims that the Parcae's prediction of future happiness for Peleus and Thetis is one "which no future age will accuse of perfidy" (*carmine, perfidiae quod post nulla arguet aetas*, 322); he stresses this point also in calling them "truth-speaking songs" (*veridicos . . . cantus*, 306) and the Parcae themselves call their song a "truth-speaking oracle" (*veridicum oraclum*, 326). It is startling, however, that this poem so deeply implicated in numerous intertextual relationships here almost literally asks us to read it in isolation.[36] Courtney insists that "Catullus went out of his way to make these authorial statements, and . . . we must simply accept them at face value."[37] We must

More than one child is mentioned only in versions that have Thetis put one child after another into a boiling cauldron to see if they are mortal (they are).

[34] Cf. Clare (1996), Konstan (1977) 81–2, who sees allusion to the breakup in the tortured and ambiguous Latin of 379–80, Hunter (1991) ("there is no doubt that we are cued in, not just to the *Argonautica*, but specifically to Apollonius' version of the story of Peleus and Thetis"), Morwood (1999), and Townend (1983), who notes that in the myth of the wedding of Peleus and Thetis Eris or Discordia makes her appearance (with or without the apple that is securely attested only later) "precisely at the point where Catullus breaks off his account;" he does not stress as I might the relevance of the myth of Discordia to Catullus' words *concordia* (336) and *nec mater discordis maesta puellae* (379).

[35] Barchiesi (1993) = (2001) 105–27; some aspects of the "contrary-to-fact" are implicit in some of Barchiesi's comments about ironic allusion to future events. For Theocritus and Helen, see my Chapter 1 at n. 54.

[36] Cf. Fowler (2000a) 121 on how in recent studies of intertextuality, "even when explicitly denied or changed, aspects of source-texts may be present under erasure, ready to be 'flipped' into prominence by a strong reader." See also the comic poet Antiphanes ("Say Oedipus and the audience knows everything . . ."), and Rosenmeyer's discussion of Helen in Sappho fr. 16, both in my Chapter 1 n. 55.

[37] Courtney (1990) 114; on whether these are in fact "authorial statements" see below. Cf. too Todorov (1977) 61 on Odysseus' lies: "invocation of the truth is a sure sign of lying."

indeed certainly give them full consideration. But our considerations must account for another aspect of these lines. The narrator's remarks about truthfulness also remind us of another alternate myth, this time about a treacherous song sung at the wedding of Peleus and Thetis. In some versions this song was sung by Apollo, who, Aeschylus has Thetis complain, had prophesied a happy motherhood for her, when in reality he was to be the killer of her son; she laments that she "thought that the divine mouth of Phoebus would not lie."[38] Homer alludes to the same tradition when in *Iliad* 24.62–3 Hera says that all the gods were present at Thetis' wedding, including Apollo, who "with your lyre dined among them, friend of evils, always faithless" (αἰὲν ἄπιστε, using the Greek word closest to *perfidus*).[39] Catullus in characteristic Alexandrian fashion alludes to this version of the story by having Apollo stay away from the wedding (299–302), by saying that no one could accuse the Parcae's song of perfidy (321–2), and by referring to "truth-speaking songs" and "truth-speaking oracle." Both contrast with Hera's charge of faithlessness in Homer and Thetis' regret that she believed Apollo to be truthful in Aeschylus.

So far we have described how a reader might react to the question of alternative myths about whether Peleus and Thetis will enjoy the concord of a happy marriage. Next, however, we must consider the rest of the song of the Parcae, which dwells on the brutality and early death of Achilles, and so suggests not *felicitas* but unhappiness for both Thetis and Peleus, despite the always curious fact that immediately after describing the death of Achilles and its aftermath, the Parcae say "*wherefore* join together in the love you've longed for" (***quare** agite optatos animi coniungite amores*, 372) and then describe the *felix foedus* in which the bride's mother will never have to worry about grandchildren. The song does describe heroic martial accomplishments, to be sure; more so than in the coverlet we are dealing with *heroum virtutes* (cf. *egregias virtutes claraque facta* in 348, and *magnis virtutibus* in 357 and 323). But along with these exploits, the song also alludes to the death of the couple's only son Achilles (362–74):

> denique testis erit morti quoque reddita praeda,
> cum teres excelso coacervatum aggere bustum
> excipiet niveos perculsae virginis artus.

---

[38] Fr. 284 Mette = 350 Nauck or Radt, from Plato *Rep.* 383a–b. Here I repeat some of O'Hara (1990) 46; cf. Pasquali (1920) 20–1, Williams (1968) 226, with further references; see now also Thomson (1997) on 301–2.

[39] *Il.* 24.55–63; cf. Scodel (1977).

currite ducentes subtegmina, currite, fusi.
nam simul ac fessis dederit fors copiam Achivis
urbis Dardaniae Neptunia solvere vincla,
alta Polyxenia madefient caede sepulcra;
quae, velut ancipiti succumbens victima ferro,
proiciet truncum summisso poplite corpus.
currite ducentes subtegmina, currite, fusi.
quare agite optatos animi coniungite amores,
accipiat coniunx felici foedere divam,
dedatur cupido iam dudum nupta marito.

A final witness will be the booty given to death,
when a rounded tomb heaped up with a lofty mound
will receive the white limbs of a maiden struck dead.
Run leading the weft-threads, run, spindles.
For as soon as chance will have allowed the weary Achaeans
to loose the Neptunian bonds of the Dardanian city,
a high tomb will be wet with the gore of Polyxena,
who, falling to a two-edged sword like a sacrificial victim,
will collapse at the knees and let drop her headless body.
Run leading the weft-threads, run, spindles.
And so come and join together the love you've hoped for;
let the husband receive the goddess in happy union,
now at last let the bride be given to the eager bridegroom.

Here we must recall that the Roman word *felix* applied to the pair by both the speaker and the Parcae (25, 373) means not simply "happy" or "lucky," but also "fertile" both as applied to farming and by extension to human beings: in the next generation of poets *infelix Dido* will be both ill-fated and lamentably childless. An earlier section of Catullus 64, we recall, featured Aegeus' grief-stricken thoughts of the death of an only son.[40] For Thetis we might also think not of happiness, but of the Homeric notion of her as "ill-fated mother of so great a child" (δυσαριστοτόκεια, *Iliad* 18.54). For Peleus we think of how the Iliadic Achilles says his father surpassed all men in wealth, and was given a goddess as a bride, *but* that the gods added evil to this, since his only son

---

[40] Cf. Thomas (1982b) 107 n. 41: "in Roman poetry the premature death of a sole child is attended by an unequalled sense of pathos and loss" (he is discussing Catullus' Aegeus and Vergil's Evander).

would die far from him (24.534–42). Similarly Pindar *Pythian* 3 describes Peleus as supremely happy among mortals for marrying Thetis, *but* unhappy in the end *precisely* because of the death of his only son at Troy. We might still try to ignore these misgivings, following Courtney's advice that "Catullus went out of his way to make these authorial statements" about the prophecy of the Parcae being true, and so "they cannot be disregarded; we must simply accept them at face value." But are these actually *authorial* statements? The gap opened earlier in the poem between the learned poet, who knows that the notion of Argo as first ship is in conflict with the depiction of the earlier sailing, and the speaker of the poem, who does not, is operative here, and moreover is both confirmed and widened.

The option of heeding the speaker's wish that we not question the veracity of the song also seems complicated, if not completely forestalled, by the way that the Parcae describe the future of Peleus and Thetis' son Achilles. The Parcae's words remind all readers of his early death, but make no reference to his death that his parents – the internal addressees of their song – could understand. This distinction has not been sufficiently appreciated by most earlier studies, although the essential point was made briefly by Newman.[41] Numerous readers have commented on the oddity of a wedding song that talks about the early death of the couple's son, and especially about the bizarre logic of that line 372 which immediately follows the allusion to the death of Achilles: ***quare*** *agite optatos animi coniungite amores.*[42] In context, the song makes better sense to its internal audience if we realize there is no clear reference to Achilles' death.

After describing how Achilles will cut down the Trojans like a reaper and clog the Scamander with corpses (352–60), the Parcae say in 362, *denique*

---

[41] Newman (1990) 223: "Achilles' birth is prophesied, but, as in the story of Ariadne, the narrative is skewed toward the tragic. The baby yet to be born will be the ally of 'the third heir of *perjured* Pelops' (346), and his bloodthirsty victories will end with the slaughter of the injured Polyxena. But Polyxena was slaughtered to appease the spirit of the *dead* Achilles, though the Sisters carefully skirt round that unpleasant truth (*morti quoque reddita praeda*, 362; they fail to say whose *mors*). The whole happy prophecy, on closer analysis, turns out to be fraught with foreboding, the canonization of a serio-comic horror."

[42] Cf. Townend (1983) 29 n. 16: "the very reference to the hero's death is strikingly inappropriate before he has even been born," Kinsey (1965) 926: "the preceding lines give, if anything, reasons against the marriage," and the scholars cited by Bramble (1970) 26 n. 3; add Godwin (1995) on 372: "*quare* is breathtaking," and Martindale (2005) 95: "powerful and weirdly discordant *quare*."

testis erit morti quoque reddita praeda, which I have translated literally as "a final witness will be the booty given to death." Readers know (or soon figure out) that this is a reference to Polyxena being sacrificed on the tomb of the dead Achilles, and the word *morti* here is usually translated as "to him after his death," as though it were the equivalent of *ei mortuo*. But we should stop and think how much we need to supplement the Latin to get that meaning. There is no word to specify whose death this is, as Newman notes. This might be a reference to booty Achilles offered to someone else (Patroclus?) at death, until the subsequent lines begin to talk about a virgin's death. There is in fact no clear need to see that the Parcae are talking about anyone's death (except for the virgin's): the word *mors* is occasionally used to mean "corpse" and to us who know the myth *morti* must mean "to him when dead," but without that knowledge the line would more naturally suggest "booty offered to death" or even "to Death." The dative *morti* need not imply reference to a person, for the "dative of goal" often occurs with nouns for "death."[43] What we usually do with this line is to look ahead to the next few lines about Polyxena, supply the full story from our knowledge of the myth, and then use the full myth as a kind of "translation trot," which allows us to force *morti* to mean *ei mortuo*. In some sense we are thus "cheating" as readers, just as our poorer Latin students do when they try to make a Latin sentence fit what they have read in a translation. Readers are being reminded of the death of Achilles, but his parents at their wedding are not. In 366–7, there is no mention that Achilles is not among the Greeks who sack Troy: what is being concealed from his parents is that Achilles will die young at Troy, before accomplishing what he set out to do. We are dealing with not only the characteristic ambiguity of oracles and prophecies, but more specifically the pattern of "death and the [deceptively] optimistic prophecy" that I first observed in the *Aeneid*. In the *Aeneid*, numerous prophecies "predict success in some activity, or future happiness, while conspicuously omitting or only obscurely hinting at the

---

[43] See Hofmann-Szantyr (1965) 100 and Görler (1985) 266; cf. *Aen.* 2.85 *demisere neci*, 5.691–2 *infesto fulmine morti, | si mereor, demitte*, 11.197 *multa boum circa mactantur corpora Morti* (where some see an archaic abl., but cf. Gransden [1991] ad loc. and now especially Horsfall [2003] ad loc., whom I thank for discussion of this point), and the phrase *ollus leto datus est* quoted by Varro *LL* 7.42 (cited by Ellis on the Catullan line). Weber (1969) provides a handy survey of expressions for "kill" in Latin hexameter, among them *demittere morti/leto/neci/Orco, dare leto/neci, praebere leto*. Modern readers would not think of Death unless they see *Mors* with a capital M, but Romans would write both Death and death in all capitals: see Feeney (1998) 88.

death of one individual that will somehow qualify or destroy that success."[44] For the internal audience, Peleus and Thetis, and apparently for the naive narrator of Catullus 64, the song makes no clear reference to the death of their son, since they do not know the myth of Polyxena as we do. This reading, which appeals to the "solution from character speaking" discussed in the last chapter, and posits that characters are being deceived, is one way to make sense of "wherefore join your love" in 372, and the succeeding lines about "grandchildren," which sound intolerably odd after a reference to their son's death.

So the song which the narrator pronounces as trustworthy in fact deceives, opening up a gap between the perspectives of the internal audience and the reader regarding the Song of the Parcae, a gap comparable in some ways to the gap between the experience of the wedding guests who view the two-paneled coverlet and that of readers of Catullus' much more detailed version of the story, as Gaisser has described so well. A gap also widens between the naive or ignorant speaker on the one hand, who seems genuinely to believe that the marriage will be happy – in keeping with his view that the heroic age is superior to his own – and the learned poet and reader on the other. It now also becomes more significant that we have been reminded at 298–302 of the "treachery" of Apollo in other versions of the wedding. At first it seemed as though the poem were distancing the song of the Parcae from that of Apollo, but what the Parcae say to Peleus and Thetis about their future concord, and about their son's deeds at Troy, makes their song as deceptive as Apollo's would have been, and in fact repeats the pattern of that story. Furthermore, although we may refrain from thinking about external information about the myth when trying to believe the Parcae's claim that the marriage will be happy and full of concord, we have had to call upon our knowledge of the myth of Polyxena to help us understand *morti quoque reddita praeda* in 362, at any level.

The announcement that the song of the Parcae will be true and will never be accused of "treachery," then, serves first to distance the song from, and then to link it with, the treachery of Apollo's prophecy in the alternate version. It also helps make an issue of the truthfulness or treachery of the song, and reminds us of claims of treachery elsewhere in the poem, most notably in Ariadne's speech of reproach to the absent Theseus. Treachery thus emerges as a theme in the whole poem. There is a parallel between the coverlet,

---

[44] O'Hara (1990) 9 and *passim*; cf. now Leigh (1997) 88.

whose introduction says it will tell of *heroum virtutes* but whose content depicts treachery, and the epithalamium, whose introduction says it will not be accused of treachery and whose surface meaning tells the parents it is about their son's great virtues and deeds (*egregias virtutes claraque facta*, 348). The relationship to the Song of the Parcae of both the narrator, who announces that the song will never be accused of the treachery of which I have just accused it, and the marrying couple Peleus and Thetis, is similar. As *Iliad* 24 and the passage from Aeschylus suggest, the Parcae's predictions to Peleus and Thetis will one day seem as empty and deceptive to them as the words of Theseus seem to Ariadne. And yet the narrator of the poem seems to be completely taken with this version.

At what is in some sense the start of Latin narrative mythological epic, then, in a poem which exerted extensive influence on authors like Vergil and Ovid, we see the poet follow two contradictory models in the mythic tradition, one in which the Argo is the first ship, and one in which Theseus and others sailed earlier. He also begins the poem by investing his narrator with unbridled admiration for the heroic age, implicitly promising a poem far different from what actually follows in the text; each of the next four chapters will discuss poems whose openings feature similar misdirection. Later, both the narrator and the Parcae's song ask us to ignore the literary tradition to which the poem alludes insistently throughout, when they promise that the marriage of Peleus and Thetis will be happy, harmonious and fruitful. The Parcae's song then alludes to the death of the couple's only son Achilles, but in a way that only we as readers can understand, and then only if we appeal to the literary tradition that we have been asked to ignore. My reading posits that these inconsistencies and their effects are all under the control of the poet, which seems to me to be the most reasonable explanation for what I have found in this poem, but others may wish to attribute them to forces beyond the poet's control. My next chapter will describe a Lucretius largely (but possibly not always) in control of the inconsistencies in his poem and their effects, so this question will recur, and the chapters on Vergil and Ovid will consider a wide variety of inconsistencies and possible explanations for them.

3

Death, inconsistency, and the Epicurean poet

From hindsight, it is easy to reject the philosophical opening of the poem as untrue or inadequate. Yet how does one know on a first reading that Ovid is *not* committed to the orthodox view that he is presenting? Part of his strategy, I suggest, is to win the reader's assent to a comforting picture of the work and then to reform it.

Stephen Wheeler, A Discourse of Wonders

desine fata deum flecti sperare precando
"Stop hoping the fates of the gods can be swayed by prayer"

The Sibyl, Vergil, Aeneid 6.371

MAYNARD:	It reads, "Here may be found the last words of Joseph of Arimathea. He who is valiant and pure of spirit may find the Holy Grail in the Castle of uugggggggh."
ARTHUR:	What?
MAYNARD:	". . . the Castle of uugggggggh."
BEDEVERE:	What is that?
MAYNARD:	He must have died while carving it.
LAUNCELOT:	Oh, come on!
MAYNARD:	Well, that's what it says.
ARTHUR:	Look, if he was dying, he wouldn't bother to carve "aaggggh." He'd just say it!
MAYNARD:	Well, that's what's carved in the rock!

GALAHAD: Perhaps he was dictating.
             Monty Python, "The Search for the Holy Grail"[1]

Like Catullus 64, Lucretius' *De Rerum Natura* is often omitted in studies
of Roman epic, but recent scholarship has demonstrated both this poem's
engagement with the epic tradition, and subsequent epic poets' interest in
the notion of philosophical epic. It is also useful to discuss Lucretius here,
because the difficult questions with which this chapter deals will benefit
from being looked at in the context of other epics, and will also recur later
in this study: philosophy vs. poetry, first and second readings of the start of
a poem, the extent to which the gods do or do not control or interfere in
human affairs, and – as my third epigraph indicates – the question of whether
inconsistencies in a poem should be attributed to a poet's inability to polish
a poem before death. Lucretius seems to have died either without putting
final polish to his poem, or, according to the major study by Sedley (1998),
without making extensive planned revisions. Throughout this book we have
to deal with the problem to which my chapter title alludes, namely that either
in appearance or reality Lucretius, Vergil, and Lucan died with their poems
to some extent unfinished.[2] The list can be expanded to include Catullus, if
he indeed keeled over of a broken heart immediately after making his latest
datable reference, and Ovid, who tells us in *Tristia* 1.7 that his exile meant
that the *Metamorphoses* lack final polish. For Lucretius, somewhat ironi-
cally for an Epicurean who proclaims that *mors nil est ad nos*, death has
had a major role in the reception of his poem. It must be true either that he
died without fully revising his poem, or that he had largely or completely
finished it, but something about the poem, combined with the doubtless fictional story of his death preserved in Jerome, allowed scholars room for
endlessly elaborate theories about how Lucretius would have changed the
poem had he lived longer (*correcturum nisi mors occupasset* or "he would
have corrected this if death had not taken him first," as one ancient source says
about Vergil).[3] Others today seek to improve our transmitted text by arguing,
as Deufert does, that all imperfections in Lucretius' text are the result of

---

[1] For Wheeler on Ovid see below in Chapter 5, for Vergil's line and the way it bothered
Dante, see Chapter 4 n. 38.

[2] Cf. Ahl and Roisman (1996) 16 on the "escape hatch for the critic of the *Aeneid* or the
Pharsalia" created by the death of Vergil and Lucan with their poems "left unrevised."

[3] Aulus Gellius 10.16.11, quoting Julius Hyginus; cf. Chapter 4 n. 1 and the start of Chapter
5 where I quote Ovid *Tristia* 1.7.40.

later interpolators, whom he credits with 368 lines, or about 5 percent of the extant text.[4] Both Deufert's interpolation hunting, and the more common "archaeological" or "genetic" approach that seeks to uncover changes that Lucretius made or was planning to make while writing the poem, focus great attention on passages that appear inconsistent. Some of these same passages have been the object of attention from two other kinds of critics: both those who since at least the nineteenth century have argued for an "Anti-Lucretius in Lucretius," and those in more recent years who see poetic or rhetorical strategy in these same passages. All these passages will benefit from being examined in the context of what other epic poets do with inconsistencies.

This chapter will discuss the proem to the first book of the *De Rerum Natura* in some detail, then the larger context of inconsistencies in Lucretius, which includes the old theory of the "Anti-Lucretius in Lucretius," then the relationship between the proems of Book 4 and 5 and the rest of their books, and finally Lucretius' depiction of early humans.

Asking for help from a god who does not care

Lucretius' Epicurean epic begins with an invocation of the goddess Venus, who is called "mother of the race of Aeneas, source of pleasure for men and gods" (*Aeneadum genetrix, hominum divomque voluptas*, 1.1), and the cause of generation among plants and animals (3–30). Because she "alone governs the nature of things" (*rerum naturam sola gubernas*, 21), the poet asks her to be his ally in the composition of his poem (*te sociam studeo scribendis versibus esse*, 24), to grant eternal charm to his words (*aeternum da dictis, diva, leporem*, 28), and to use her influence on Mars to pacify both land and sea (29–40), because Lucretius and his addressee Memmius cannot with equanimity give proper attention to the poem when their *patria* is troubled (*patriai tempore iniquo*, 41). Then he explains why this is so (44–9):

> omnis enim per se divom natura necessest
> immortali aevo summa cum pace fruatur
> semota ab nostris rebus seiunctaque longe;
> nam privata dolore omni, privata periclis,

---

[4] Deufert (1996); cf. the review of Gottschalk (1999), and also my Chapter 4 n. 11 and O'Hara (2005b) 20.

ipsa suis pollens opibus, nihil indiga nostri,
nec bene promeritis capitur nec tangitur ira.

For the nature of the gods must enjoy complete peace
for all time, removed far from our affairs;
for the nature of the gods, free from all pain and danger,
is completely self-sufficient, does not need us,
and is not won over by our merit, or touched by anger.

He then seems to speak to his addressee, saying, "As for the rest, apply to the
true explanation your full attention, and a mind that is discerning and removed
from cares" (*Quod superest, vacuas auris animumque sagacem | semotum a
curis adhibe veram ad rationem*, 50–1). The main problem here is reconciling
lines 44–9 with 1–43, but as with Catullus 64, we have to discuss the text
before we can talk about an inconsistency, and it must be admitted that there
are some odd features of these lines. The first fifty lines, for example, mention
no human being to whom the imperative commands of 51 could be directed,
unless we think that either the mention of Memmius or the description of
the gods implies a human addressee. It may be that Lucretius' style is by
nature rough or archaic enough for this solution to be valid,[5] or perhaps lines
have been lost before 50, or after 43. We might also emend 50 – or emend the
line in some new and different way, since the text in every modern edition
is the result of emendation of a faulty transmitted text – to restore the name
Memmius.[6] For our purposes it is enough to grant that there may well be
something odd or faulty about the last few lines of 1–51.[7]

But the major problem is that 1–43 and 44–9 present radically different
views of the gods. The first lines, at least on the surface, depict conventional

---

[5] On how Lucretius' style sometimes has misled textual critics see Friedlander (1939) and
Elder (1954), with earlier references.

[6] The manuscripts present the unmetrical *quod superest, ut vacuas auris animumque*. The
word *sagacem* at line-end in most texts today comes from an apparent citation in Schol.
Veron. Verg. *Geo.* 3.3, but some have thought that the scholiast conflates *DRN* 1.50 and
4.912, and choose instead to restore some version of Memmius' name to the line, e.g. *quod
superest, Memmi, vacuas auris animumque*. Courtney (1987) suggests that Memmius'
name appeared in an earlier line now lost. Discussion with references at Deufert (1996)
38–9.

[7] For the slight oddity of *enim* in 44, which must reach over the *nam* clause in 41–3 back
to 29–40, see Friedlander (1939) 372 and other scholars cited by Gale (1994a) 215–16,
who is skeptical; cf. too Fowler (1989a) 128. Smith (1982) supplements the English:
"[I pray to you for peace,] for . . ."

mythological Olympian gods who may have human children, and interfere in human affairs in response to human prayers. In 21, Venus is said to control nature, and in 38–40 she is asked to prevent warfare. Lines 44–9, by contrast, are closely adapted from the first of the "Principal Doctrines" of Epicurus, and depict Epicurean gods removed from and disinterested in human affairs, who are not captured by our services, and so are not likely to listen to our prayers, or our requests that they help us with our poems, or make the world peaceful. In the seventeenth century, Cardinal de Polignac, in his long poem *Antilucretius*, "turned to his prayer to Venus to show that Lucretius has 'forgotten himself' in invoking the very gods he would destroy (5.35–6 . . .): *Deinde vocet demens quos tentat perdere Divos, / Immemor ipse sui.*" Bailey, who omitted the lines in his original Oxford text but then argued for their restoration in his later edition with commentary, spoke of the "hopeless inconsistency of the verses with what precedes." More recently Monica Gale asks, "If the gods are remote and indifferent to human concerns, why does Lucretius invoke a goddess who is represented as active in the world, and pray to her for peace and for assistance in composing his poem?" David Sedley puts it in the strongest terms: "It would scarcely be an exaggeration to say that he spends the remainder of the poem undoing the damage done by the first forty-three lines."[8]

At one time most scholars dealt with this inconsistency by trying to explain it away or remove it in some way or another; we can categorize many of these strategies as falling under one of two "options" – options that I will be rejecting, but not without adopting some of their more attractive features in order to describe a third option that has been gaining in popularity in recent years.

Option one is to "Epicureanize" the invocation to Venus, and stress the subtle ways in which 1–43 are consistent with Epicurean philosophy when understood allegorically or symbolically. This is a kind of Unitarian approach, to borrow that word from Homeric criticism: you explain away the inconsistency. We may say, for example, that Lucretius attempts "to fashion an Epicurean divinity, Venus, who would take the place of Stoic Zeus," and so, when properly understood, Venus actually "stands for the Epicurean belief that the gods have nothing to do with the world."[9] Those who would reject

---

[8] On de Polignac: Clay (1983) 234–6 (whom I quote), Johnson (2000) 88–94; other quotations: Bailey (1947) 601 (citing Giussani); Gale (1994a) 208, Sedley (1998) 16.

[9] Asmis (1982). For the argument that Lucretius never argues against the Stoics see Furley (1966) and Sedley (1998) 62–93, who gives references for those like Schmidt who would

this reading because they think Lucretius never argues against the Stoics might still believe that Venus represents one or more of a number of acceptable Epicurean concepts: "Venus, then, is a multi-faceted figure, symbolizing the onset of spring; the creative forces of nature; pleasure; and natural law liberated from divine rulers."[10]

Option two is to delete 44–9, which is to do what Analysts did to the *Iliad* and *Odyssey*: you cut away the inconsistency. This maneuver has a long history; as early as the year 1512, the verses were omitted on the theory that they had been added as marginalia in someone's manuscript "in order to show that the invocation to Venus clashes with the Epicurean doctrine of the gods inaccessible to all human influence."[11] The lines are indeed repeated in 2.646–51, after the description of the *Magna Mater*, and many have thought they belong only there, whence they were copied into the margin of Book 1. That the lines should be deleted was once argued by most editors, although many now accept them; a wide range of respected scholars still advocate cutting the lines.[12]

Neither of these options is impossible, but they are both inadequate and unnecessary.[13] Explaining away the inconsistency is inadequate because it works only when you read the prologue again after having read and been convinced by the whole poem. How can we have a didactic poem whose prologue can be understood only by those in the know, those who do not need teaching?[14] If ordinary readers, to whom Lucretius is trying to explain Epicureanism, encounter Book 1 in a linear fashion without preconceptions, they must be expected to find a contradiction between 1–43 and 44–9. Conte

---

disagree; add Long (1997) 136, Campbell (1999) and Fowler (2000b) 140, who notes that contemporary readers would inevitably be thinking of Stoicism as they read the *DRN*.

[10] Gale (1994a) 222.

[11] Friedlander (1939) 369; cf. Clay (1983) 231, Deufert (1996) 32–3 and 40.

[12] Brown (1988), Courtney (1987) and (2001), Deufert (1996) and the review by Gottschalk (1999), Hutchinson (2001); Cole (1998) would delete 46 and 48, or regard 31–40 and 44–9 as a doublet.

[13] Sedley (1998) 1–34 attributes the problem to use of a source incompatible with Epicureanism, in this case not the willful juxtaposing of inconsistent sources played with by Hellenistic or neoteric poets, but the poet's almost overpowering desire to follow one poetic source, Empedocles, because he is an important predecessor in the genre of didactic epic, even though many details of his teachings will have to be denounced later on; see below in text.

[14] Kleve (1966) 90.

discusses Lucretius in terms of the reader who is "docile" – both docile and easy to teach[15] – but that is not the only kind of reader imaginable: think of Cicero, for example, one of few contemporaries who we know for a fact read this poem. Nothing about the *De Rerum Natura* suggests that Lucretius is preaching to the choir. The numerous allegorical or symbolic readings used to soften the conflict between 1–43 and 44–9 require a reader who is not merely docile but in fact already *doctus*, already taught. There is a paradox here in that the more learned modern scholars become in respect to Epicureanism, the more removed their experience of the poem becomes from that of the ordinary Roman reader of the poem. (I realize this formulation is somewhat self-serving to me as a non-philosopher, but I think the claim is legitimate.)

The problem is similar to the mythological "cheating" in Catullus 64 discussed in the last chapter. Just as readers of the Parcae's obscure allusions to the death of Achilles in Catullus 64 can use their mythological knowledge to supplement the Parcae's ambiguous words and strip them of their obscurity, so too readers who know that Lucretius' poem is a defense of Epicureanism are understandably tempted to read that Epicureanism back into the first forty-three lines. This is a perfectly appropriate description of second and subsequent readings of the lines, after the whole poem has been read, and much of this scholarship is of great value. But it will not do as an explanation of how the lines work on a first-time reader.[16] Deletion of the lines is also inadequate, because even if these lines appear only in Book 2, there is still an inconsistency between the basic meaning of the first forty-three lines and basic tenets of Epicurean philosophy that will soon be explained in the poem. Some have downplayed this problem by saying that Epicurus sanctioned prayer to the gods (seeking I suppose a kind of ancient version of what is now called "the relaxation response"), and we indeed must be

---

[15] Conte (1994) 24; I say "both docile and easy to teach" because Conte uses "docile" in the original Italian (1991:35). On Conte here cf. too Edmunds (2001) 59–61.

[16] Gale (1994a) 211: "Having once offered the reader the honeyed cup of the proem, however, Lucretius proceeds to substitute the medicine of Epicurean philosophy. When the reader looks back at the proem from the vantage-point of the *edita doctrina sapientum templa*, he is forced to reassess its meaning." On first and subsequent readings, cf. on Apuleius Winkler (1985) index s.v. "reader: comparison of first- and second," on Ovid Wheeler (1999) index s.v. "reading: experience of 'first reading,'" and also below, Chapter 4 at n. 4 on Jupiter's prophecy, and Chapter 6 on reading Lucan's praise of Nero a second time.

careful not to follow the Epicureans' ancient foes in exaggerating their lack of interest in religious practice.[17] But surely Epicureans would not pray to a mythological god they believed was in control of nature (*gubernas*, 21) in the hopes of stopping war or getting help with a poem.[18] Much of the dissatisfaction with the lines comes from nineteenth-century obsession with repetition as an index of interpolation, but in fact neither in Lucretius nor in Homer is it true that only interpolators, and never the original poet, repeat whole passages of verse. Modern intolerance for repetition is at the heart of much dissatisfaction about Lucretius, but as an Epicurean poet writing in an epic tradition started by Homer, Lucretius has ample motivation for such repetition.[19] And apart from that roughness around the edges, lines 44–9 do work well in their context.[20] They also are cited in authors as early as the third or fourth century, and are equipped in our manuscripts with a "capitulum" or heading derived from Epicurus, so any interpolation would have to have taken hold quite early.[21]

A third way: from Venus to Epicurus

The suggestion that Lucretius is making use of inconsistency here and elsewhere, for rhetorical purposes, has been made by a number of scholars in recent years, and in certain circles has become the consensus view. The non-Epicurean feel of the Hymn to Venus can be seen as part of Lucretius' strategy for identifying with the reader, so as to be able to move the reader from his Roman religious beliefs, which Lucretius is going to suggest are wrong, towards Lucretius' Greek, philosophical, Epicurean teachings.[22] Clay suggests that the poet "is reluctant to introduce the reader without an adequate

---

[17] On Epicurus and prayer see Obbink (1996) 396–8 and index s.v. "prayer;" Summers (1995) argues that Lucretius is more hostile to religious practice than Epicurus.

[18] The word *gubernas* is rightly stressed by Clay (1983) 87 and Sedley (1998) 16 n. 65, though the problem is softened a bit if we understand the *natura* which Venus is said to control to be not our "nature" in its entirety but the process of "coming into being" (cf. *nascor*) which even an Epicurean could say is controlled by the goddess of sexual desire.

[19] On repetition see Clay (1983) 183–96, Gale (1994b) 5–6; *contra* Deufert (1996) 27–31 and *passim*.

[20] See esp. the arguments of Friedlander (1939) 376 and Bailey (1947) 603.

[21] Bailey (1947) 601–2, citing Lactantius, the scholia to Statius, Servius, and Nonius.

[22] Clay (1983) 82–110 and 212–25, anticipated in part by Kleve (1966) and others, but with different emphases; see also Summers (1995).

philosophical background to Epicurus for fear that he will think that he is entering into an ungodly and criminal way of looking at the world (1.80–82)" and so "*De Rerum Natura* opens with a scene that could please and attract any reader." But soon we see "[t]he rapid and abrupt movement from the surface of the proem to its submerged themes" which "has jolted and jostled many of Lucretius' more careful and critical readers." In other words

> Lucretius prays for peace . . . and [then] . . . introduces a foreign conception of divinity which destroys the very motivation for prayer . . . We are present here at the collision of two worlds: that of Roman religion, which supports the belief that Venus could ever have willed to make Memmius glorious and successful in all his endeavors (1.26–27) and the remote world of Epicurus' teaching concerning "that which is blessed and imperishable." . . .[23]

The similar formulation of Minyard suggests that,

> having prayed to a Venus which the Romans understand as a force in nature and history, alluded to Memmius's duty to *communis salus*, and then declared the material basis of reality and the absence of providence from the world, Lucretius leads his perhaps shaken but surely aroused reader through a devastation of the civic inheritance by striking at what he considers its core, the category named *religio*.

Gale, although uncertain whether 44–9 should be retained, cites Cicero's remarks about capturing the good will of the reader or audience in a proem, and finds it plausible that 1–49 should deliberately present "two contradictory images of divinity." Sedley refers to 44–9 as an "Epicurean corrective" of what has preceded, and notes that "the sudden reversal is too characteristic of Lucretius to be lightly dismissed." Summers says that Lucretius

> couches his invocation in strikingly religious terms because that is what a Roman expects to hear. Religious language retains its value for Lucretius as a kind of vernacular observation on reality; it is simply the way a

---

[23] Quotations from Clay (1983) 98, then 94–5; see also 218: "the reader as we find him at the threshold of the poem is first a Roman, attracted to an unknown argument by the appeal of a familiar and congenial divinity and praised for his own accomplishments and race."

Roman communicates about the universe, and it is too deeply a part of the Romans' shared cognitive experience to disregard.[24]

Gale cites the recommendations of Cicero's rhetorical works, but no one has looked at this problem in the light of what other Roman epicists do at the start of poems. It is difficult to compare the *De Rerum Natura* and Catullus 64 at any great length, given the differences in subject-matter and size, but we should recall that Catullus 64 begins with extensive misdirection about its subject-matter, literary models, and ideological complexity. Catullus gestures first in the direction of Medea and the Argonauts, before settling on Peleus and Thetis, and then surprising us with Ariadne and Theseus. He also begins with a reverential attitude towards the heroic age and the *virtutes heroum* that is radically modified a few dozen lines into the poem. We shall see in succeeding chapters that Ovid, Lucan, and Vergil both in the *Georgics* and *Aeneid* begin with extensive misdirection as well. Ovid, as the quotation from Wheeler used above as an epigraph indicates, begins his poem with a philosophical account of creation by a rational unnamed god, before turning the world of his poem over to his own irrational and randy Olympian gods. Lucan begins with praise of the emperor Nero, but eventually his poem will denounce Caesar and Caesarism. Vergil presents a more gradual development or modification of ideas from *Aeneid* 1; many of the expectations set up by the speech of Jupiter to Venus will be modified by the end of the poem, and a similar technique has been described in recent work on the *Georgics*.

The not-quite-yet-thoroughly-Lucretius in Lucretius

This newer rhetorical approach to the problem of inconsistency in Lucretius must also be put in the larger context of the impression some readers have long had, especially in the last several centuries, that Lucretius was somehow fighting against himself, or unsure of his quasi-atheistic beliefs: this is the old theory of the "Anti-Lucretius in Lucretius." We have mentioned the way in which de Polignac focuses on the Hymn to Venus as a sign of the poet's inconsistency, but the problem is surely not an early modern invention. Hardie has argued that Vergil *Georgics* 3.242–83 "implicitly criticizes Lucretius by juxtaposing two passages widely separated in the *De Rerum Natura*," namely

---

[24] Minyard (1985) 37, Gale (1994a) 217, Sedley (1998) 27, Summers (1995) 49.

the Hymn to Venus and certain portions of the discussion of sex and love in *DRN* 4. "By introducing elements from [the end of *DRN* 4] into a section of the *Georgics* which takes the Venus-proem as its primary model, Virgil may be said to be using Lucretius against himself."[25] In the mid-nineteenth century the problem was given classic expression in Patin's "L'Anti-Lucrèce chez Lucrèce." In a sense we could say that this French scholar deconstructed the poem, for he took this materialist, anti-religious poem and found in it what we might call "traces" of a more spiritual, religious outlook, against which the poet struggles with only partial success.[26]

We can now explain that the passages on which these readers have focused are indeed inconsistent with Lucretius' beliefs, but are related to his poetic or rhetorical technique, as Lucretius either works with contradictions within Epicureanism or uses inconsistency as a deliberate poetic device.[27] Years ago De Lacy wrote of a basic inconsistency at the heart of Epicureanism, between the urge to take care of one's self and the urge to have and help friends. Some of the philosophical underpinnings of his study have been criticized, but there is some soundness in the basic idea that there is a tension between the fervor of the poem and the claim that it is written in serenity. Epicureans, of course, did not write explicitly philosophical poetry, passionate or otherwise, and Epicurus to some extent seems to have discouraged even a serious interest in poetry. Recent work has cautioned us not to accept too readily all of the Epicureans' opponents' ideas about their hostility to poetry in all forms,[28] but there is nothing in the prior tradition to prepare us (or the first Roman readers) for Lucretius. Poetry generally involves the emotional manipulation of readers; at the very least poets must consider how the emotions are involved in readers' response to their work. Time and time again Lucretius will, in describing his readers' likely attitude toward a religious festival, or the fear of death, or the wonder of the sky overhead, vividly portray the emotions that have led the reader to hold some incorrect belief, and then provide an Epicurean corrective. Clay explains:

---

[25] Hardie (1986) 163, who suggests (165) that Vergil's "technique of writing deliberately contrasted and apparently irreconcilable passages is . . . heavily indebted to Lucretius (in whom it was one of the factors inviting the construction of an 'anti-Lucrèce chez Lucrèce')."

[26] On Patin (1868) see Clay (1983) 234–8 and Johnson (2000) 123–7.

[27] Cf. De Lacy (1957) and the discussion of De Lacy by Long (1997), and Anderson (1960) and the discussion by Mitsis (1993).

[28] See esp. the essays in Obbink (1995).

Lucretius can transport himself into a world of beliefs that are entirely unlike his own, but this is the world of his reader. There are, of course, some readers who cannot easily pass from their world to his. In their attachment to what is familiar and congenial in the world of *De rerum natura* they fill the poem with contradictions in their inability to mark its transitions.[29]

Indeed the focus on the role of the *reader* in most recent criticism of Latin poetry, as opposed to an earlier focus on an author's intention, has been a key factor in our ability to think not of a poet torn between two belief systems, but of a reader being moved from one belief system to another. So too Mitsis (1993) has argued that

Lucretius is not a poet afflicted with doubts and conflicting allegiances; rather, he is employing a rhetorical strategy that deliberately exploits these two types of responses from his readers. Both compassion and detachment serve his purposes because both bind readers either to the poet or to the addressee, and thus to the particular terms in which he offers his arguments and instruction.

Another influential recent discussion of this phenomenon is that of Segal, who describes Lucretius' attempts to allay readers' anxieties about death, and the risks that Lucretius takes in subjecting his work to the tension between emotional poetry and the calm science that underlies it. In Segal's view, Lucretius takes these risks because our fear of death is not as easily overcome as Epicurus suggested. Lucretius tries to be more persuasive and effective than the master, by fully confronting this problem, and by shifting between a subjective compassionate voice that sympathizes with our fear of death, and an objective, scientific voice that calls us away from it. Segal wants to "listen to the dialogue, sometimes the polyphony, among these voices."[30] On this reading the choice of poetry as a medium for philosophical argument becomes more than just a use of honey-on-the-cup (to cite Lucretius' own metaphor) or even a poetic tour-de-force: "the range and nuance of feeling and the images and associations that only poetry can evoke enable him to explore dimensions of the fear of death that the prose writings of Epicurus could not touch." Lucretius thus seems to think that the argument needs poetry's superior ability to involve readers or auditors emotionally.

---

[29] Clay (1983) 238; cf. too now Martindale (2005) 194.   [30] Segal (1990) 46–7.

Many other "inconsistent" passages in the poem can be explained in this way.[31] We must be careful, however, not to overestimate the problem-solving power of the new focus on rhetorically planned inconsistency. Indeed Don Fowler (1991), after describing how "the dominant tendency of modern Lucretian criticism has been to stress rather how poetry and philosophy can be made to work together in the poem," has suggested that while it is certainly possible to explain away tensions in Lucretius, we might want to ask ourselves whether it is necessary to do so, and whether in fact a poet can be – to put it in the terms of this study – in control of his inconsistencies to the extent that these new readings of Lucretius assume. Fowler notes that

> The stress (over the last 30 years) has been on the *control* of apparently disturbing elements. But recent literary theory has made this concept of "control" problematic: what keeps these elements in their place? Why can't one flip the *DRN* as well as the *Aeneid*? What about a dark "two-voices" view of Lucretius for a change?

I tend to think that Lucretius is usually in control, but Fowler's question is a valid one.[32] At times critics seem to think that identifying a poet's rhetorical strategy or goals is the same as identifying how the poem in reality does work rhetorically on its readers, as though all rhetorical or poetic strategies were immediately successful (unlike, say, military, political, or courtship strategies). We tend to assume that this poet whom we love has been successful, and then work backwards from that posited success to come up with an explanation of how it has been achieved, almost like a high school chemistry student "fudging" an experiment to achieve the desired result, or we might think again of the poor Latin student struggling to find, in the Latin text to his left, the English translation open on his right.

This illegitimate assumption should be of special concern to us when it is claimed that the poet's strategy involves careful and precise manipulation of "the reader" – by which is generally meant each and every reader in a diverse readership – through a complex set of reactions, such that the reader's response to the text unfolds like the workings of a Rube Goldberg contraption,

---

[31] I do not think this can be said of Lucretius' apparently unfulfilled promise at 5.155 to talk at greater length about the gods; see (most with further references) Costa (1984) on 5.155, Smith (1982) 390 note b, Gale (1994a) 224 n. 71, Sedley (1998) 154.

[32] Cf. too Reckford (1995) 32–3: "anthropomorphic gods are not easily put to rest in an Epicurean poem – they do not always stay where they are told; and Venus as goddess of sexual passion, can be quite uncontrollable."

or thousands of dominoes arranged to fall in sequence. Dominoes fall in place much more predictably than do human emotions; in using poetry to manipulate an emotional response to issues such as the fear of death, Lucretius may be in the position of those he describes in Book 5 as using wild animals in warfare: what you are trying to control can turn on you in unpredictable ways.

I have described how the move from the Roman, religious, myth-centered Hymn to Venus to the scientific, Greek, rational explication is supposed to work on a reader, but we must not overlook the possibility that many readers may not have responded in this way. I have mentioned Cicero as a possible hostile or less than "docile" reader of the poem, in terms at least of its philosophy. The famous letter in which Cicero discusses Lucretius (*Ad Quintum fratrem* 2.9.3) says that he was reading the poet along with Empedoclean writings of one Sallustius, and Furley and Sedley have described numerous detailed Lucretian borrowings from Empedocles. We should ask whether it is possible to begin a poem with many echoes of Empedocles, then hint that he is wrong on a number of points, then politely but firmly denounce him several hundred lines later, and have all of your readers drop Empedocles exactly when you want them to.[33] In Lucretius the poet's traditional concern for literary immortality may also clash with the philosophy's insistence that nothing but the atoms lasts forever. Recent analyses suggest that a reader's concern for immortality becomes modified and corrected during the course of the poem, but it is possible that the real, rather than intended, result of the poem's statements about literary immortality was to fire others with desire for it, regardless of the qualifications later in the poem.[34] Similarly, it may be that in *Georgics* 2.490ff., Vergil's "series of frightening images (the abyss

---

[33] Cf. above, n. 13. Is it possible that Lucretius is to be held responsible for the interest in Empedocles shown by poets of the next generation like Vergil and Ovid? See Hardie (1995) esp. 214 n. 48, Hardie (1998) 31 n. 12, Farrell (1991) index s.v. "Empedocles."

[34] Clay (1983) 237 argues that "The prospect of the poem's eternal charm (1.28), of Mars' eternal wound (1.33), and of Ennius' eternal verses (1.121) comes to be qualified when seen *sub specie aeternitatis*," and Segal (1990) 183 that "Lucretius suggests a dynamic movement within the poem from the poetic persona who can still be carried away by the thrill of fame" towards "the persona who in the last scenes of the work can confront death in its unrelieved horror." By contrast Edwards (1993) improperly bends over backwards to limit how readers might respond to the *DRN*: *aeternum da dictis diva leporem* in 1.28, he says, "admits of two constructions," either "let my poem manifest this grace eternally" or "shed the grace, which you possess eternally, upon my poem," and then he ignores the first possibility completely.

of Acheron, the cosmic revolution) suggests tactfully that Lucretius' poetry ends up endangering its very own goal of reassurance."[35] In more general terms, Phillip Mitsis has raised questions about Lucretius' tendency to speak to his reader as though to a child, and about "the theoretical appropriateness and effectiveness of such an authoritarian stance in the specific case of Lucretius's poetry" since "No reader is forced to persist in a reading of the poem regardless of its poetic enticements."[36] We must not become so enamored of our ability to describe the poet's strategy that we simply assume that the strategy has been successful.

Rules for poets and proems in *DRN* 4–5?

The move to cut lines 44–9 from Book 1 reflects the irresistible urge critics have felt to improve our text of the *De Rerum Natura* through excision of supposed interpolations, rearrangement of the transmitted text, and descriptions of the changes Lucretius would have made had not death overtaken him. What has been called the "archaeological" approach has been losing appeal in recent years, but may receive a boost from the recent learned study by David Sedley.[37] Sedley's claims about aspects of Books 4 and 5 allow us to discuss the archaeological approach (which he calls the "genetic account of the poem") as it relates to inconsistency in Lucretius. Supposedly inconsistent passages, and the assumption that the poet could not have wished for any sections of his poem to be inconsistent, have always played an important role in theories of how the *DRN* could have been improved. This section will look briefly at passages in Books 4 and 5 that Sedley has seen as signs of incomplete revision.

---

[35] Conte (1994) 7; so too Gale (2000) 187 sees Vergil as exposing the inconsistency of Lucretius' simultaneous detachment and passion.

[36] Mitsis (1993).

[37] Before Sedley (1998), cf. Gale (1994a) and Brown (1987a) 7–9: "the whole 'archaeological' approach to the poem's composition has turned out to be a sterile exercise. In the absence of external evidence, the light it has thrown on the genesis of the poem and the spiritual development of Lucretius is feeble at best and it has detracted from interpretation of the poem itself. Ultimately, we can never know how much restructuring, revision, and addition took place during the poem's composition or how much, if any, remained to be done. As far as structure goes, the existing cross-references and interconnections conform with the present design . . . which undoubtedly embodies Lucretius' final conception. It is thus more constructive to look for logical and aesthetic continuity in the poem as it now exists than to waste effort on the phantom of its origins and growth."

The start of Book 4 has always attracted the scholar interested in improving Lucretius' text. The first twenty-five lines, which proclaim the novelty, difficulty, and utility of Lucretius' poetic task, are virtually repeated from 1.926–50, and constitute the largest continuous repetition in the poem. Many scholars once supposed 4.1–25 to be an interpolation, but in recent years others have explained the function of the repetition and how well the passage works in both places.[38] Lines 26–53 then sum up what has preceded and introduce what will come next in the poem ("since I have taught . . ." 26; "now I shall explain," 29), but 26–44 and 45–53 seem to be "doublets," or alternative passages, either of which could have been meant to continue the introduction to Book 4. Further, 45–53, in summing up what has gone before, refer only to material from Books 1–2, which has led some to think that 45–53 survive from a time when Book 3 did not precede Book 4, and others to suggest that we must tinker with the text of 26–53.[39]

So far, so good; the transmitted text of Lucretius is far from flawless. Sedley goes further, however, and his arguments will, if accepted, do much to rehabilitate the archaeological approach to the poem.[40] He argues not only that 45–53 predate and thus do not belong with the present text of Book 4, but also that 26–44, although they *do* reflect Book 4's current position after Book 3, do not match up with the current contents of Book 4. Lines 26–44 must therefore postdate the current contents of Book 4, and so Sedley concludes that Lucretius planned to make extensive revisions to Book 4. What Sedley thinks he has proven for this book then encourages him to seek (and find) similar signs of planned revision for Books 5 and 6. What I would like to suggest is that in a study of Lucretius otherwise filled with solid evidence and philological rigor, Sedley has allowed too large a role to be played by rigid notions of consistency and inconsistency, and that his conclusions about planned extensive revisions of Books 4, 5, and 6 are based on extremely ambiguous evidence.

Sedley's argument follows from his valuable demonstration that Lucretius largely follows one Epicurean text, *On Nature*, and his argument that the poet went through a two-stage process of first following the order of *On Nature*,

---

[38] See esp. Gale (1994a); for claims that the lines are interpolated in Book 4 see Deufert (1996) 81–96, with references.

[39] Gale (1994a) and others would rearrange rather than delete; Martin's Teubner text moves 45–51 after 25, brackets 49–51, and puts 52–3 after 30.

[40] Sedley (1998) 148–65.

and then rearranging some material to fit his own needs. For Book 4, his focus is on one thirteen-line sentence (29–41):

> nunc agere incipiam tibi, quod vehementer ad has res
> attinet, esse ea quae rerum simulacra vocamus,
> quae quasi membranae summo de corpore rerum
> dereptae volitant ultroque citroque per auras,
> atque eadem nobis vigilantibus obvia mentes
> terrificant atque in somnis, cum saepe figuras
> contuimur miras simulacraque luce carentum,
> quae nos horrifice languentis saepe sopore
> excierunt ne forte animas Acherunte reamur
> effugere aut umbras inter vivos volitare
> neve aliquid nostri post mortem posse relinqui,
> cum corpus simul atque animi natura perempta
> in sua discessum dederint primordia quaeque.

> Now I shall begin to treat for you a topic especially relevant to
> this matter, namely the existence of that which we call the images of
>   things,
> which, like skins snatched from the outer surface of things,
> fly here and there through the breezes,
> and which meet us and frighten our minds both when we are awake
> and when we are sleeping, when we often see amazing shapes
> and the images of those who have died,
> which as we languish in sleep often wake us in fear,
> but we should not think that somehow souls escape from Acheron,
> or that shades fly around among the living,
> or that something of us is able to be left after death,
> when the body and the soul itself have resolved themselves into
>   their atoms.

Sedley calls this Lucretius' "preview of the book's contents," which "tells us emphatically that the book's main purpose is to dispel the fear of ghosts." After the demonstration in the third book "that the soul is mortal and death not to be feared," then "book IV's account of psychic functions will complement this by showing that encounters with 'ghosts' are not evidence that something of us does after all survive death." But "what we actually find on the topic of ghosts in book IV is a mere 11 lines (757–67)."[41] Not only, Sedley argues, has Lucretius announced that he will devote the book to fear of ghosts, but he *needs* to do this to make his argument coherent:

> None of the important questions is addressed. Are the images of the dead which invade our dreams ones which emanated from those same people before they died, even centuries ago? Or are they images which our minds pick out merely because they bear some resemblance to those people? And how are waking visions of ghosts – referred to explicitly in the proem – to be explained? These are important questions for an Epicurean to be able to answer.

To Sedley it thus seems "self-evident that book IV is not in the final state which Lucretius envisaged for it at the time when he wrote its revised programme of contents."

This is an attractive and seductive explanation, but we need to recognize how contingent and arbitrary much of this argument is, and the extent to which things that are contingent and arbitrary are being presented as factual. The assumptions made here are typical of much scholarly analysis of texts, but need to be challenged; they show how one learned and sensitive critic's way of categorizing a passage can lead to a sense of inconsistency, and the longing for a differently organized, more consistent text. Do 29–41 really offer a "preview of the book's contents"? Another reader might feel that lines 29–32 introduce the notion of *simulacra*, then lines 33–41 discuss that aspect of *simulacra* that ties them most closely not to what is coming up in Book 4, but to what has preceded in Book 3 – an entire book devoted to combating the fear of death.[42] More specifically, do the lines promise that the book will

---

[41] Sedley (1998) 149.

[42] So Brown (1987a) 14 suggests that as he begins to discuss *simulacra* in 4, "Lucretius calls special attention to [visions and dreams of the dead] in the introduction not because the whole theory of simulacra is subservient to the explanation of phantoms but because he wishes to engineer a smooth transition from Book Three to Book Four and seizes the opportunity to protect his former conclusions against a possible objection." Cf. Hardie (1988) 73 on how "the first example of such delusive images discussed in book four by Lucretius, one chosen to establish a link with the subject-matter of the previous book, is *simulacrum* as image of a dead person; Lucretius returns to this type of delusion briefly at 733–4 . . . In the course of the book he adverts to a much wider range of misleading *simulacra* . . ." Dalzell (1982) 207–29 notes the tendency of Lucretius' proems to highlight certain themes regardless of whether they are actually prominent in the book that follows.

focus on "fear of ghosts?" The purpose clause in 37, which must reach back to depend on the main verbs *agere incipiam* in 29, suggests that continuing to combat fear of death is one purpose behind writing the book, but there is little in 29–41 that suggests that the whole book will focus on the shades of the departed. It is unwise to demand from a poet such a correspondence between the introduction to a book and its contents, which amounts to establishing rules for poets, which they are unlikely to have obeyed. Poets are free to put at the start of a book whatever material they think will work there to create the effects desired. They need never show all their cards at every moment, and of course we have seen how Lucretius chose to start Book 1. Sedley's up-to-date research on Hellenistic philosophy and the newest fragments of Empedocles and Epicurus, I suggest, has been yoked to old-fashioned and largely discredited methods developed for finding fault with the "unity" of countless classical texts.

More broadly, Sedley's sense that Lucretius' argument about death is incomplete without more discussion reflects his own dissatisfaction with the argument of Book 3. This is not sufficient grounds for alleging that the poet planned to refocus Book 4, in effect to make it a second book about whether any part of us escapes death. Book 3 has dealt with this argument already, and Book 4 instead has other important things to accomplish, namely to explain the function of *simulacra* and illusions in numerous aspects of human life, including but not limited to dreams of the dead (757–67), and including especially the crucial role of illusions and *simulacra* in erotic passion (1058–1287). Given Sedley's knowledge of Lucretius and Epicurus, I would be hesitant to match my sense of the poem against his, except that I am reading the poem we have, while Sedley is claiming that the poet had planned a massive re-focus and rewriting of Book 4. What of the present book could survive this rewriting? There is nothing in 26–44 about sex and love, and little in 1058–1287 about fear of ghosts; would anything from the famous discussion of erotic passion survive Sedley's rewriting?[43] For many readers this is one of the most interesting and significant parts of the poem, and – to return to the argument of the preceding paragraph – the lines are no less effective and significant for being almost a complete surprise to the reader.

Finally, we may note that when Sedley faults the current text of Books 3 and 4 for devoting too little attention to fear of ghosts, and says that "none of

---

[43] Erler (1997) 85: "the depreciation of the passion of love . . . happens within the main theme of Book IV – how to deal with images and how to evaluate them correctly."

the important questions is addressed," he is demanding that the poet provide an extensive argument that does not appear in any extant text attributed to Epicurus, although he cites passages in Diogenes of Oenoanda and in Lucretius that *may* point to an Epicurean precedent.[44]

Sedley has similar complaints about the supposedly unrevised state of Book 5, where he faults "the sequence of topics," since "lines 509–770, on astronomy, constitute a surprising interruption between two phases of the history of the world, coming as they do after the development of the cosmos itself but before the emergence of life and civilisation." Again the key is the proem, this time to Book 5, which "places the astronomy at the end, *after* the history of civilisation;" and Sedley argues for a planned "transposition of the astronomical passage to the end of book v," which "would have eliminated the unwelcome interruption in book v's history of the world, and led to a smooth continuity between the end of v, on astronomy, and the primary content of vi, the remaining cosmic phenomena." This scenario is plausible, and less radical than the proposal for the wholesale rewriting of Book 4, and in Lucretian terms we might imagine that somewhere there is a parallel world in which this did happen. But it depends on a requirement of consistency between the topics in a proem and the order in which they appear later in the book – a requirement that would lead us to find fault with the beginnings of three of the six books as they now stand: that of 4 for stressing ghosts and not mentioning sex and love, that of 5 for mentioning astronomy and other topics in an order different from the order in which they will later appear, and that of 6 for making no mention of the plague at Athens which dominates the end of the book. Sedley's claim that the astronomy section does not work well in its present location is also arbitrary and easily countered, as it has been in a review of Sedley's book which argues that although the section on astronomy does interrupt the narrative, still the order of topics suits Lucretius' purposes well.[45]

Early man, and the usual suspects

I end with brief discussion of a different kind of argument regarding the next section of Book 5, the account of the history of early mankind that begins in 771. Earlier we saw some ways in which Lucretius' poem might seem ambiguous or open to alternative readings despite the poet's apparent wish that certain

---

[44] Sedley (1998) 149.   [45] Campbell (1999).

passages be read in only the way most complementary to his argument. In his history of early mankind, Lucretius seems genuinely ambivalent about one issue, as Farrell (1994) has shown, with the ambivalence expressed through some textual inconsistency that scholars have labored mightily to remove or explain away. Inconsistencies of logic and chronology in Lucretius' account have long been attributed "to the poem's unfinished state, to the poet's odd personality, to problems of textual transmission, and to various other causes: i.e. to the usual suspects."[46] In 780–820 Lucretius first claims that only "soft" conditions could have allowed life to begin and then thrive, but then in 925–1010 he argues the human race needed to be "hard" to survive. One solution to this problem has been to read human beings out of the first passage, either by emending the text, or by reading the words *mortalia saecla* in 791 and 805 to mean not "man and other living things" but "living things other than man." This can only be done by "cheating," or reading in a decidedly non-linear way, in a maneuver we have seen in the previous chapter's discussion of the Polyxena passage of Catullus 64: you read the whole passage, decide what you want the earlier part of it to be saying, and then argue that since the words *mortalia saecla* can sometimes have a restricted meaning, then they do here – even though there is no signal to the reader to read the words in this way. Farrell sensibly proposes instead that we accept what we have: two pictures of the life of early humans, one in which the environment is lush and nourishing, and one in which primitive humankind faces harsh and difficult conditions, with Lucretius' presentation carefully developed to create the ambivalence.[47] Farrell argues that

> An attentive reader at least should acknowledge the text's pointed ambiva-
> lence. The views presented in the two paragraphs that deal with the *novitas
> mundi* are too purposefully opposed to reflect a simple failure of reasoning

---

[46] Farrell (1994) 82.

[47] Farrell (1994) 89 (next quotation is also from 89). It is not merely, as Costa (1984) 110 suggests, that "traces of the 'Golden Age' theme, or at least phraseology, survive in the occasional references to the earth producing food *sponte sua*;" such a claim stems from precisely the kind of critical assumptions that my study is trying to expose as illegitimate and inadequate. Campbell (2003) 11 and 180–3 suggests that Lucretius is working with the "memes" of pre-history and of the Golden Age, using Richard Dawkins' term for, in Campbell's words, "generally accepted background ideas . . . that tend to exist and evolve as if they have a life of their own independent of any writer." His Lucretius knows that "accretions of meaning will still attach to each [Golden Age] theme from its former context," and adjusts his presentation accordingly.

or an imperfect collocation of sources. Rather, they disclose the poet's explicitly ambivalent conception of the earth's (and humankind's) original state.[48]

This ambivalence resembles one that we have seen in Homer, where the Cyclopes, because of the poet's or speaker's desire to make certain points, are portrayed both as cruel savages who must toil as Polyphemus does, and as happy primitives working a fertile land that provides effortless abundance.[49] As at the start of the *DRN*, where scholars have wanted to remove the statement of Epicurean principles that seems to clash with the Hymn to Venus, and in later books that Sedley faults for not matching up with his version of their prologues, we do not in Lucretius' history of mankind need to emend or distort the text, if the poet is using techniques used throughout Greek and Roman literature.

In the next chapter we shall see a similarly inconsistent portrayal of Italy in the *Georgics*, and the Italians in the second half of the *Aeneid*. To Vergil, then, we now turn.

[48] Farrell (1994) 88.   [49] Scodel (1999) 45, 181; cf. above, Chapter 1 at n. 10.

4

Voices, variants, and inconsistency in the *Aeneid*

In the *Aeneid* we read that Aeneas will have a son in old age, and that he has only three more years on earth; that Helen both openly helped the Greeks enter Troy, and (if Vergil wrote that passage) that she cowered in hiding in fear of punishment; that Aeneas' Trojan son Ascanius will be the ancestor of the Alban kings, and that his half-Italian son Silvius will be; that Theseus escaped from the underworld, and that he is still there; that the Italians were peaceful before the arrival of the Trojans and that they were warlike; that Aeneas is fighting on the side of Jupiter, and that he is like a monster fighting against Jupiter; that Palinurus fell from Aeneas' ship the day before Aeneas met him in the underworld, and that he fell three or four days before; that Aeneas will impose customs on the Italians he conquers in Italy, and that the Italians will keep their own customs; that Jupiter both predicted and forbade the war in Italy, and that he both was impartial and gave help to one side; that the golden bough will yield willingly and easily or not at all, but then that it yields only hesitantly to Aeneas.

The *Aeneid* clearly lacked Vergil's final polish when he died in 19 BCE, for it is the only extant hexameter poem with unfinished lines (it has fifty-eight), and biographical and scholarly tradition soon began to assert both that the poet was planning three years of revisions to his poem after the trip to Greece on which he died, and that it was possible to identify certain passages that he "would have corrected, if death had not intervened."[1] Inconsistent

---

[1] Aulus Gellius 10.16.11, quoting the Augustan Julius Hyginus. For basic discussion, see Squillante Saccone (1987) and Horsfall (1981) = (1990); Griffin (1989) surveys the material.

passages have long been a favorite object of study by those interested in the "development" of the *Aeneid*, and the theories about how Vergil would have revised his poem, had he lived longer, have been even more numerous, complex, and confident than those that have been advanced for the *De Rerum Natura*. This chapter will argue that such confidence is misplaced, and that several external factors, as well as close examination of the text of the *Aeneid*, suggest that many inconsistent passages in the poem should not be emended or explained away, but should be interpreted, as they indeed have been in some recent scholarship. The external factors, over which we will not linger long here, include the healthy skepticism with which scholars have looked at the biographical tradition of Vergil lately, which renders it almost useless as support for arguments about revising the poem.[2] The long tradition of the apparent use of inconsistencies in classical and especially Hellenistic and Alexandrian poetry, and the inconsistencies in Catullus 64 and the *De Rerum Natura* discussed in the preceding chapters, should also contextualize our response to such passages in the *Aeneid* (as should material in later chapters on Ovid and Lucan). Most telling, however, should be the recent demonstration of the extent to which the *Georgics*, though completed several years before Vergil's death and in no sense lacking his final revisions, also make use of inconsistencies; these we shall discuss a bit below.

This chapter will discuss inconsistencies in prophecies, the extent to which the fully polished *Georgics* still contains passages that conflict with one another, allusions to mythological variants, the complex picture of the underworld of *Aeneid* 6, and the indeterminacy of the war in Italy of *Aeneid* 7–12, especially as expressed in allusions to the myth of gigantomachy.

Optimistic and other prophecies

As noted at the start of my Introduction, a central argument of my study of prophecy in the *Aeneid* (O'Hara 1990) is that some discrepancies between what is said in prophecies in the poem, and what either happens or is predicted to happen elsewhere in the poem, are not signs of Vergil's inability to revise the *Aeneid* before his death. Rather these inconsistencies are indications that

---

[2] See Horsfall (1995) 20. For the development of the *Aeneid* see the intelligent but unconvincing arguments of Günther (1996), with the reviews of Horsfall (1997) and Hardie (1999); the book you are now reading is like those Günther castigates at 81 n. 220. More discussion is featured in the Introduction to Horsfall (2006).

characters within the *Aeneid* are being deceived, and that readers may be deceived as well, or at least offered conflicting possibilities for interpretation. I began with Jupiter's speech at 1.256–96, in which he consoles Venus for Aeneas' troubles by predicting for her the future glories of the Roman race. Jupiter's prophecy to Venus has been called "a summary of the whole plot [of the *Aeneid*], which makes possible a correct understanding of the poem from the beginning."[3] A first-time reader might expect this to be the case, but consideration of the "whole poem" shows that it is not. Several details are in conflict with, and therefore an inadequate introduction to, the rest of the poem.[4] Lines 263–5 seem to present a sort of summary of Books 7–12:

> bellum ingens geret Italia populosque ferocis
> contundet *mores*que viris et *moenia* ponet,
> tertia dum Latio *regnantem* viderit aestas . . .

> He will wage a great war in Italy and crush fierce
> peoples and give *customs* and *walls* to men,
> until the third summer will have seen him *reigning* in Latium . . .

These lines are an inadequate or even deceptive summary of the war in Italy in both general and specific terms. In general, Jupiter, who the commentator Servius rightly tells us is trying to console Venus, makes the war sound easy, simple, and triumphant: Aeneas will simply crush these fierce peoples. More specifically, Jupiter's prophecy omits mention of, and is in conflict with, the crucial compromise worked out between Jupiter and Juno in Book 12, in which the Trojan and Italian peoples will merge, with the Trojan name dying out. Line 264, "he will give customs (*mores*) and walls (*moenia*) to men," must be compared with Jupiter's words to Juno in 12.834–7:

> sermonem Ausonii patrium *mores*que tenebunt,
> utque est nomen erit; commixti corpore tantum
> subsident Teucri. morem ritusque sacrorum
> adiciam faciamque omnis uno ore Latinos.

---

[3] Büchner (1955) col. 1343 (my translation); cf. Murgia (1987) 51: "Such a trustworthy prediction [as Jupiter's prophecy] is needed as a control on more ambiguous predictions later in the poem."

[4] I briefly outline here the argument of O'Hara (1990) 132–63; see also Lyne (1987) 79–81, and on misleading prophecies by Jupiter and others see Mack (1978) 55–84. On first and second readings see my Chapter 3 n. 16.

The Ausonians will keep the language and *customs* of their fathers,
and the name will stay as it is; contributing only to the stock
the Trojans will subside. I shall add the sacred customs and rites,
and shall make them all Latins, with one language.

Jupiter says that "The Italians will keep their customs," with the same word *mores* used as in Book 1. This compromise is a key development in the conclusion of the *Aeneid*, towards which much of the second half of the poem has been pointing, but there is no hint of compromise in Jupiter's words to Venus. Earlier in Book 12 Aeneas says he does not seek to reign in Latium (*regna*, 189) and that his men will build separate walls for him (*mihi **moenia** Teucri | constituent*, 193–4). This passage is inconsistent with the most reasonable meaning of Jupiter's prediction that Aeneas will reign in Latium (*regnantem*, 265), and that he will impose walls on men (264, *moresque viris et **moenia** ponet*). Jupiter's words in Book 1 look as though they should refer to building walls for the men he has conquered, not merely for his own men – although of course what Aeneas says in Book 12 may be questioned either as high-minded goals that will not be met, or as rhetoric.[5] The rest of Jupiter's prophecy continues to present a picture for Venus that omits the compromise of Book 12, from the stress on Aeneas' Trojan son Ascanius in lines 267–71, with no mention of his Italian son Silvius (who *is* mentioned in the underworld speech of Anchises in Book 6), to the emphasis on the Trojan-ness of the Caesar who is described in lines 286–90.

The compromise of Book 12 is thus completely absent from Jupiter's prophecy. I have argued that it is important to realize that many speakers of prophecies in the *Aeneid* speak rhetorically, and sometimes deceptively, telling their audiences what they need or want to hear. The difference between the views presented in Books 1 and 12 may be thought of as a kind of development: the view of the Romans as an essentially Trojan people that Jupiter presents to Venus yields to Book 12's more complex views of the different forces, qualities, and heritages, both positive and negative, that make up the Roman state. But other aspects of these inconsistencies put us in a more uncertain position, because if Jupiter is deceiving Venus and perhaps the reader about some of these points, might this not call into question his veracity more generally, including his most basic claim to have granted

---

[5] Cf. Lyne (1983) 197 = (1990) 329. Some readers may choose not to read *viris* in 264 with both *mores* and *moenia*.

the Romans "empire without end" (*imperium sine fine*, 279)? The *Aeneid*'s prophecies thus put the reader of the poem in the same position as the characters who receive deceptively optimistic prophecies; this uncertain position for the reader is one of the things that deliberate inconsistency can create in a poem.[6] When the source of the deception is Jupiter, whose moral force and authority have been for many readers the anchor of a stable and comforting reading of the poem, that kind of reading begins to look anachronistic and flawed.[7]

Jupiter's prophecy to Venus also specifies that Aeneas has three more years of life.[8] This detail is in conflict with another part of the poem, but in such a way that we cannot be certain of the truth, since it refers to events beyond the end of the *Aeneid*. In the great prophecy in the underworld in which Anchises tells Aeneas about their future Roman descendants, the first person that Anchises identifies is the son Lavinia will bear to Aeneas in "old age:" "Silvius, of Alban name, your posthumous offspring, | whom your wife Lavinia will raise in the woods for you | late, after a long life" (*Silvius, Albanum nomen, tua postuma proles,| quem tibi longaevo serum Lavinia coniunx | educet silvis*, 6.763–5). Like Odysseus, informed by Tiresias in the underworld in *Odyssey* 11.134–7 that he will die in old age, Aeneas is told that he will be "long-lived" (*longaevus*), in contradiction to the whole tradition about Aeneas, as well as what is said elsewhere in the poem. In *Aeneid* 6, the subtle prediction of a long life for Aeneas is part of the encouragement given in Anchises' prophecy; Servius appropriately refers to the words *quem tibi longaevo* as a *consolatio*. Anchises' words can be defended by referring to unparalleled but not impossible meanings of the adjective *longaevus*, but the Odyssean parallel argues against this solution, and it is hard to escape the feeling that in the underworld Aeneas is being deceived. We can take a

---

[6] This notion of the "interpreting character" is developed more in O'Hara (1993a) than it was in O'Hara (1990). See O'Hara (1990) 126–7 and Müller (2003) 371–4 (with further references) for the fascinating passage in which Augustine, after Rome is occupied by Gauls in 410, has Vergil stress that the *Aeneid*'s false promise of *imperium sine fine* was made not in his own persona, but through the false persona of Jupiter: *Non ex persona mea dixi rem falsam, sed Iovi imposui falsitatis personam* (*Serm.* 105, 7, 10).

[7] On unacknowledged modern (mis-)assumptions about the role of Jupiter see especially Schmidt (2001) 167 on "illegitimate application of Judeo-Christian thought, where God is both almighty and the supreme good and his will a moral command. Does that really apply in the *Aeneid*?" See also below at n. 65; on Jupiter, Johnson (1976) is still crucial.

[8] Again I repeat arguments presented with more detail in O'Hara (1990) 91–102.

positive view of Jupiter's words, and say that Aeneas has only three years of life left, but will become a god, as Jupiter tells Venus. Or we can recall the way in which Dido's curse calls for Aeneas to fall before his time, and lie unburied in the broad sand (*sed cadat ante diem mediaque inhumatus harena*, 4.620). The wording could even point to some combination of these two alternatives: a grim death followed by apotheosis, as in the case of Julius Caesar, or (at least in Lucan) of Pompey.

A number of other inconsistent passages in prophecies may be mentioned more briefly. In 3.388–93, Helenus says or implies that the omen of the white sow will mark the site of Aeneas' future city, while Tiberinus at 8.42–8 seems to say it is Ascanius' city of Alba Longa; both versions have sources in the tradition, Horsfall reminds us, but the discrepancy is still odd.[9] Tiberinus also says that Aeneas should not worry, because all the anger of the gods has yielded (*neu belli terrere minis; tumor omnis et irae | concessere deum*, 40–1); this claim is not true, as we have just seen Juno summon Allecto from Hell in Book 7, but it fits the pattern of deceptively optimistic prophecies. So too does the prediction to Aeneas by the shade of Creusa at the end of Book 2 that "happy times" (*res laetae*) await him in a Western land (780–4).[10] In Book 3, the Harpy Celaeno predicts to Aeneas that the Trojans will not reach their destination before they have to eat their tables (3.254–7). But when in Book 7 this prophecy is harmlessly fulfilled as the Trojans eat table-like bread, Aeneas says that his father Anchises, and not the Harpy, made a prophecy to him about eating tables (7.122–7). Horsfall (2000: 112) suggests both that "the variation in Virgil itself follows the good Hellenistic usage of alluding to more than one version of the story narrated," and also that the problem can be explained away or rationalized by assuming (following the practice of Homeric scholia and Servius) that an epic poet may allude to earlier events which he has not depicted, and so at some time "Anchises unravelled the latent ambiguity of Celaeno's prophecy." Others might wish to read this passage in Book 7 more psychologically, and say that Aeneas has mis-remembered, has suppressed the dark episode involving the Harpy and attributed the prophecy to his father. The text is not clearly marked.

---

[9] Horsfall (1981) 146.

[10] On Tiberinus see O'Hara (1990) 117, on Creusa, 88–9 (with references), and also Mack (1978) 57–8.

The best poem of the best poet

That the *Georgics* are a complete, fully revised Vergilian poem that still contains certain kinds of inconsistencies must be considered by anyone wishing to understand the other Roman poems studied in this book. The contrasting moods and tones of different sections of the *Georgics* have long been obvious, and different sections contradict one another quite explicitly. In 2.458–60, farmers have a fortunate life, in which the earth pours forth **easy** sustenance (*o fortunatos nimium, sua si bona norint,* | *agricolas! quibus ipsa . . .* | *fundit humo **facilem** victum iustissima tellus*). Conington noted long ago that "the tone of the present passage is certainly opposite to that which prevails generally in the *Georgics*, where the laborious side of the farmer's life is dwelt on." The sharpest contrast is with Jupiter's dispensation at 1.121–2: "Jupiter himself wanted the path of the farmer **not to be easy**" (*pater ipse colendi* | ***haud facilem** esse viam voluit*).[11] This poem both hails Italy as a "Saturnian land" (2.173) with connotations of the Golden Age, and also clearly shows that the world of the poem is that of Jupiter's Iron Age; we shall see below that there is a similar ambivalence about Italy in the *Aeneid*. In one section of *Georgics* 2, Italy is a land of constant Spring (*ver adsiduum*, 2.149) which has no snakes (2.153–4); in the rest of the poem Italy has four seasons and plenty of snakes (2.214–16, 3.414–39). Ross and Thomas have argued that Vergil uses poetic "error," or even "lies," to make thematic suggestions in these passages and throughout the poem, chiefly to undercut, they argue, the more optimistic passages.[12] In *Georgics* 3 (as noted in the last chapter), Vergil criticizes Lucretius by juxtaposing allusions to the Hymn to Venus and the discussion of sex in *DRN* 4. Hardie also points to Vergil's own contrasting pictures of sexuality in the Praise of Spring in *Geo.* 2.323–45 (where we see a "moderate and creative

---

[11] The problem with 2.458ff. has been noticed by scholars as diverse as Conington (1963) = (1883–4), Wilkinson (1982) 75–6, Thomas (1988), Mynors (1990). The amusing attempt by Cramer (1998), writing, like Deufert (1996) whom we saw in the last chapter, under the influence of Zwierlein (1999), to make the *Georgics* fully consistent by excising 200 lines or 10 percent of the text, is as good a demonstration as I could imagine of the inconsistency of the poem. On Zwierlein's recent Ph.D. students see O'Hara (2005b) 20.

[12] Cf. Ross (1987) passim, esp. 109–28, "Laudations and the Lie," and also Thomas (1982a) 76–7 and (1988). Fowler (1988) is skeptical about Ross's claim that the grafting at the start of *Geo.* 2 is to be thought of as impossible, but see Gale (2000) 212–14 on grafting ("pure fantasy"), although at (2000) 71–2 and 216 she criticizes the use of the term "lie" by Ross and Thomas.

picture," viewed "in the positive light" of Lucretius' proem to Venus) and in 3.242–83 (on love as *furor*), and suggests that "this technique of writing deliberately contrasted and apparently irreconcilable passages is . . . heavily indebted to Lucretius."[13] Farrell has briefly suggested that imitation of different models in *Georgics* 1.118–258 "causes Vergil's argument to shift back and forth between ostensible hope and despair, between seeming acceptance and rejection of the notions of providence, between apparent agreement with or dissent from the views of now one source, now another."[14]

Earlier scholars tended to ascribe this shifting of mood and philosophy to Vergil's inability to integrate his Hesiodic or other source material successfully, or his lack of interest in consistency.[15] But now Gale, building on the work of Hardie, Perkell, and others, has strongly argued that the *Georgics'* allusions to earlier authors are often deliberately and challengingly inconsistent. Some allusions to Lucretius, for example, seem to support a Lucretian or Epicurean view of the world, but others clearly refute or problematize such a view, at times through allusion to contradictory intertexts in Hesiod and Aratus.[16] Even adjacent passages can be inconsistent, as in the famous double *makarismos* of 2.490–4, which seems to assert allegiance to the beliefs both of Lucretius and of those whom Lucretius scorned. Gale argues for "a way of reading the *Georgics* . . . as a polyphonic text in which different 'voices' of the didactic tradition are brought together but not harmonized into a seamless whole." Of particular interest for the present study – and not just for this chapter – is Gale's demonstration that "Virgil tends to open each book [of the *Georgics*] with a relatively optimistic and unproblematic view of the relationship between human beings and the gods, which is gradually complicated as the poem proceeds and a range of different perspectives is offered to the reader." We may compare with this feature of the *Georgics* the relationship between what Jupiter tells Venus in *Aeneid* I, and what is said later in the poem, as well as the openings of the other epics under study

---

[13] Hardie (1986) 165; cf. above, Chapter 3 at n. 25.   [14] Farrell (1991) 187.

[15] See the (critical) discussion of Perkell (1989) 113 and (1992). Heath (1989) 62–3 and Griffiths (1980), whose views on Greek poets are discussed in Chapter 1, say that passages in the *Georgics* differ in tone because the poet of the *Georgics* loves contrast, and has little interest in thematic unity, or even thematic content. Contrast Miles (1980) 62: "apparent contradictions in the poem are so forcefully drawn, sharply contrasted, and fundamental that they cannot be dismissed simply as part of a rhetorical strategy," and Batstone (1997).

[16] Gale (2000) *passim*; the quotations below are from pp. 11, 58.

here. The role of the *Georgics*, then, as a fully polished and revised poem by a mature poet that still contains numerous inconsistencies, seems to be an important "control" that should limit scholarly confidence about our ability to identify parts of the *Aeneid* Vergil would have "corrected had not death intervened."

A garden of forking paths?

With prophecies, the notion that one (or both) of two predictions might be false or deceptive in some sense can help us "save" the consistency of the overall narrative. We often cannot respond that way, when Vergil follows the precedent of Hellenistic poetry and Catullus 64 (and, as we have now learned, classical Greek practice as well) by alluding to, or, in a more challenging practice, actually following contradictory mythological variants; we have already seen some of these in our discussion of prophecies. Over twenty years ago Horsfall observed that "if we turn to the 'classic' inconsistencies" so often discussed by those who have claimed the *Aeneid* lacks polish, "it is striking how often both versions are established and traditional."[17] At *Aeneid* 6.718, to start with a simple and untroubling example, in Anchises' words to Aeneas in the underworld *quo magis Italia mecum laetere reperta* ("so that you might rejoice with me on finding Italy [with me?]"), Servius (on 1.267) sees an allusion to versions in which Anchises lived to make it to Italy, but the subtle allusion does not really break into the text. In 11.16, when Aeneas uses the word *primitiae* or "first fruits" as he stands over the body of Mezentius, Vergil is doubtless alluding to a version of the Mezentius story in which the Etruscan king earned the ill will of the gods by demanding the first fruits of the harvest from the Rutulians.[18] When in 4.420–3 Dido refers to her sister

---

[17] Horsfall (1981) 145. Cf. again the claim by Herodotus 2.116, mentioned in Chapter 1, that though Homer rejected a certain version, he "made clear that he also knew this story." See Zissos (1999) with further references for allusions to other versions in Valerius Flaccus' *Argonautica* and other poets. For the title of this section cf. the discussion of Borges in the Homer section of Chapter 1.

[18] See Macrobius *Sat.* 3.5.10, Gotoff (1984) 196 n. 17, Horsfall (2003) 16. Other examples: the ill-fated attempt in *Aen.* 3 to found a city on Crete, which results from Anchises' misinterpretation of the oracle from Apollo, may be in part a problem of variant versions; see Williams on 3.107, but see also now Horsfall (2006) on this part of *Aen.* 3. In that same part of Book 3 Vergil has Anchises imply that Zeus is from Crete (3.104), with allusion to Callim. *Hymn to Zeus*, discussed above in Chapter 1; in *Aen.* 8.573, Mayer

Anna's special relationship with Aeneas, this is at least an allusion to the story in Varro and other sources in which Anna, and not the chaste Dido, has a relationship with Aeneas; Hexter has made the interesting if not fully convincing argument that the presence of other versions of the Dido story haunts Book 4.[19] Allusions to variants also mark Aeneas' narration of the fall of Troy in Book 2. Vergil's depiction of the death of Priam is clearly challenging: Priam is killed at the altar inside his palace, but at the end of the story his "huge body lies on the shore" (*iacet ingens litore truncus*, 557). Vergil combines two incompatible versions, as commentators note, one in which Priam is killed at the altar of Zeus, another in which Pyrrhus drags him from the palace to Achilles' tomb by the shore. We are even "given advanced warning of the variant – the dragging is made a part of the main narrative: *altaria ad ipsa trementem traxit* (550–51)."[20] Part of what Vergil may be doing here is assimilating the death of Priam to that of Pompey, as Servius and others have suggested, but the effect is jarring, especially in Aeneas' narration. In the tradition, Priam was killed in two different places, but in a narrative that often (but perhaps not always) invites us to read it as realistic, should he not be killed in one place?

In some texts, as we have seen, inconsistencies may be used to undercut the credibility of a speaker. Some have questioned aspects of Aeneas' narration in Books 2–3, modeled as it is on that of the great liar Odysseus whose dishonesty Aeneas denounces so firmly in Book 2, but Vergil does not seem to give clear signals that Aeneas' credibility is undercut in this way.[21] Aeneas' narrative of the Fall of Troy is, however, somewhat inconsistent with aspects of Deiphobus' narrative of the same events in the underworld in Book 6. Aeneas says "that the Greek fleet used a fire signal to alert Sinon to open the horse (2.257–9); Deiphobus says that it was Helen who sent a signal to the Greeks ([6.]518–19)." This seems more of a mythological variant than a mythological contradiction, since more than one signal can have been given

---

(1988) argues, Evander appeals to Jupiter as a fellow Arcadian, reproducing (albeit five books apart) the uncertainties of the *Hymn*.

[19] Hexter (1992), with bibliographical references.

[20] Norwood (1954) 25; cf. Austin (1964) ad loc., and now Dyson (2001) 88–9, with further references. I thank Neil Coffee for information here.

[21] Ahl (1989) argues for a skeptical reading of Aeneas as narrator; see also below, n. 25, Carnes (2001) on the presentation of Neoptolemus, and Hexter (1989–90) on how readers should respond to puzzling and inconsistent details in *Aen.* 2, especially inconsistencies that undercut the words of Sinon.

at the sack of Troy, but the whole sense of Deiphobus' narration feels different
from Aeneas' (both men of course tell of some events that happened when
they were asleep).[22] Even within Book 6, Aeneas tells Deiphobus the version
of Deiphobus' end that he has heard, and Deiphobus corrects him at length:
here one mythological variant is rejected, as a kind of commentary on the
untrustworthiness of *fama* or "report."[23] Deiphobus also describes Helen as
actively helping the Greeks, in sharp contradiction to the separately transmitted "Helen passage" editors now print (generally in brackets) at 2.566–88;
Servius says that the contradiction with Book 6 was one of Vergil's posthu-
mous editors' reasons for removing the passage. If Vergil did write the Helen
passage, in which Helen cowers in fear of the Greeks instead of helping them
as she does in Deiphobus' story, then Vergil would be taking his place in a
long tradition of poetic variants on the Helen story, as we have seen in Chapter
One: *Odyssey* 4 (to which, Bleisch shows, Vergil makes specific allusion in
Aeneid 6), Sappho, tragedy, and Theocritus.[24]

Another allusion (or set of allusions) to a variant tradition involves the
versions in which Aeneas betrayed Troy: if Aeneas were a traitor this would
of course completely contradict the whole of Book 2. The only clear allusion
to this tradition comes in the words of Turnus, who at 12.15 calls Aeneas the
"deserter of Asia," which suggests at least that Turnus is familiar with the
story; there is no real narrative inconsistency here. Some, including Servius,
have seen the variant also in 1.488, where Aeneas sees himself depicted
among the Greek leaders in one of the scenes on Dido's temple to Juno (*se
quoque principibus permixtum agnovit Achivis*). Recently Casali has also

---

[22] Quotation from Zetzel (1989) 273, continuing: "[Deiphobus'] account also contradicts
not only the Helen episode of Book 2, but the whole general sense of the final battle of
Troy;" he cites Norden on 6.494–547 and Austin on 518.

[23] See esp. the excellent Bleisch (1999) 208–9. In the year 2003 American soldier Jessica
Lynch similarly corrected heroic earlier versions of her capture and rescue in Iraq; see
her biography, Bragg (2003) 157–61.

[24] Cf. Reckford (1981) 96, Suzuki (1989) 94–102, esp. 102: Vergil's "contradictory portraits
encapsulate the doubleness of Helen – as did the two stories told about her in *Odyssey* 4;"
and Bleisch (1999) 209: "Palinurus' death, Deiphobus' death, Helen at the fall of Troy:
each is presented in conflicting versions, first from Aeneas' point of view, then from
another eyewitness' perspective. Vergil's dialogic narrative undermines the objective,
monologic authority of epos, as the single point of view of epic is refracted into multiple
perspectives." On the problematic "Helen passage" in Book 2, cf. Geymonat in Horsfall
(1995) 300, with further references, and more recently Murgia (2003). Several Greek
treatments of Helen are discussed in my Chapter 1.

argued that when Dido at *Aeneid* 4.596 mentions unspecified *facta impia*, she must be alluding to the betrayal story, and not to her own disloyalty to Sychaeus.[25]

Worthy of extended discussion here, and also related to our earlier discussion of inconsistency as a mark of deceptive prophecies, is "the thorny antiquarian question of Lavinia's descendants, which V[ergil] faces with elegant inconsistency."[26] Several passages suggest that Aeneas' Trojan son Ascanius will found Alba Longa, and be the ancestor of the Alban kings and the Julian *gens*.[27] When Anchises tells Aeneas about the son Lavinia will bear to him in old age (*quem tibi longaevo serum Lavinia coniunx*, 6.764), his words stress that Silvius and not Ascanius will be the ancestor of the Alban kings, naming him as *regem regumque parentem | unde genus Longa nostrum dominabitur Alba*, 765–6 ("king and father of kings, from whom our race will rule at Alba Longa") and stressing his Alban name Silvius (*Silvius, Albanum nomen, tua postuma proles*, 763).[28] We can say that Vergil is merely alluding to different versions, as an Alexandrian poet would, but the importance of the descent from Iulus to Julian ideology argues against such a bland reading, and the myth was already fraught with ideological struggle two generations before Vergil.[29] This also seems to be a genuine inconsistency and not the compromise version Norden claimed it was, such as we really do see in Dionysius of Halicarnassus *Ant. Rom.* 1.70. Stylistic features even suggest

---

[25] On *Aen.* 1.488, see Thomas (2001) 80, 109–10; on 4.596, Casali (1999), who also discusses 1.488, and Ahl (1989), who is extremely skeptical of the veracity of Aeneas as narrator in Book 2.

[26] Horsfall (2000) on 7.76.

[27] 1.267–71 and 288 *Iulius, a magno demissum nomen Iulo* (Jupiter to Venus), 8.628–9 *illic genus omne futurae | stirpis ab Ascanio* (Vulcan's shield, commissioned by Venus); 4.274–6 (Mercury to Aeneas) and (to some extent) 4.233–6, and even 6.789–90 *hic Caesar et omnis Iuli | progenies* (Anchises to Aeneas).

[28] This passage is extremely challenging: how can a man who is (currently? still?) *longaevus* (764) have a son who is *postumus* (763)? The literal meaning of *longaevus* says that Aeneas is still alive, but *postumus* (like the myth in Cato) says that he is dead. This question was debated in antiquity: see O'Hara (1990) 93 n. 12.

[29] The story that a son of Aeneas born in Italy, and not the Trojan Iulus, was the founder of Alba is thought to have had a political origin, as an attempt by an enemy of the Julius Caesar who was consul in 90 BCE to dismiss the "high-flying claims of the gens Iulia" to Trojan and divine origins (Ogilvie [1970] 43 on Livy 1.3.2, where Livy is unsure of whether Ascanius was born in Troy or Italy).

that we are meant to link some of the most problematic passages.[30] Vergil's inconsistency also fits patterns within his poem. The mythological problem is a conflict between a Trojan son of Aeneas and an Italian son, which is a kind of dispute central to the poem. We can say that in some of the Ascanius passages Venus as lover of all things Trojan is being deceived, since the knowledge of Aeneas' Italian, non-Trojan son is being kept from her, as I suggested in O'Hara (1990). If we reject the Silvius story entirely, and say that Anchises is simply misleading Aeneas, we could alternatively say, as Bleisch does, that Latinus is also being subtly deceived by his (also dead) father Faunus and told to acquire a son-in-law who will have no children.[31] Such deception, whether of Venus, Aeneas, or Latinus (the text allows us no certainty here), fits a pattern of deceptively optimistic prophecies designed to encourage Aeneas and others in the poem, in a way that can be related to the reader's encounter with the poem as well. Note too that Cato seems to have described at least a fear of struggle between Ascanius on the one hand and Lavinia and her son on the other: this is the reason Silvius is born or brought up in the woods that give him his name (*silvis*, 756): the two versions are at war in Vergil's text in a way that replicates the potential struggle between the two factions in the tradition. Finally, both versions may be alluded to in Jupiter's words at 4.232–6:

> Si nulla accendit tantarum gloria rerum,
> nec super ipse sua molitur laude laborem,
> Ascanione pater Romanas invidet arces?
> quid struit? aut qua spe inimica in gente moratur
> nec *prolem Ausoniam* et Lavinia respicit arva?

> If the glory of such important matters does not fire him,
> and he does not take on this toil to win praise for himself,
> does he as father begrudge Ascanius the Roman citadel?

---

[30] Cf. O'Hara (1990) 146–7 for references (including Norden), and for the polyptoton in both 6.765 *regem regumque parentem* and 9.642 *dis genite et geniture deos*, and on the resemblance between 1.271 *transferet, et **Longam** multa vi muniet **Albam*** and 6.766 *unde genus **Longa** nostrum dominabitur **Alba***.

[31] Bleisch (1996). This is a problem at the heart of the story Vergil has chosen for the *Aeneid*: for dynastic purposes, why must a man who already has a son give up two other loves (Creusa and Dido) and then fight a war to win a bride in Italy? Cf. too Clausen (2002) 131–4.

> What is his plan? Or with what expectation does he delay
>   among a hostile people
> And think not of *Ausonian offspring* and the Lavinian fields?

Literally these words fit the version in which *Romanae arces* are owed to Ascanius, but the carefully chosen wording of 236 also alludes, as Servius Auctus suggests, to Aeneas' *proles Ausonia* by his Italian wife Lavinia. *Lavinia . . . arva* literally refers to geography, but also suggests procreation and fertility, and in 6.763 Silvius is called *postuma proles*. Thus allusions to Silvius are not confined to Anchises' words in the underworld. We may also note that elite Romans of Vergil's day may have had a better ear than we for picking up allusions to struggles over inheritance and succession between children related by blood or marriage. And of course if we still believed as earlier ages did in Vergil's miraculous prescience we might even imagine him looking forward to the problem of Julio-Claudian imperial succession.

It may be timely to reflect briefly on what we have seen so far. There are clearly too many of these inconsistencies for all of them to be accidental, and they seem too thoroughly woven into the fabric of the poem. At the very least many of them suggest Hellenistic or Alexandrian learning about multiple versions of myth, as part of a literary tradition that goes back to Homer. But many of them also help to make certain specific thematic points, and to create a more general sense of doubt or uncertainty about what is going on in the poem, and about what kind of world we are reading about. With Alexandrian poetic technique one is often uncertain whether the poet is doing something like this just for playful, so-called "literary" reasons, or whether this (or any) literary playfulness serves a more serious purpose in terms of the themes or ideas of a poem. Recent work on Hellenistic poetry, as we have seen in Chapters One and Two, suggests that those poets' playfulness is indeed serious, and produces, as Goldhill (1986) puts it, "a deliberate fragmentation of any divinely inspired, proclamatory didactic status of the poet's voice into a multiplicity of citations, different levels of enunciation and conflicting or ambiguous attitudes," so that the poets to some extent embrace the potentially troublesome plural voices that we saw Plato worrying about in Chapter One. Gaisser (1995) made the link to Catullus 64, the *Peleus and Thetis*, which is now seen as "a work of competing perspectives whose authority is repeatedly called into question." In the *Aeneid* too the conflicting versions of myth are related to – and help produce – the sense of competing perspectives, plurality of voices, and conflicting or ambiguous attitudes, that so much recent scholarship has seen in the poem, though the question of whether or not these competing voices dominate the poem is one that different readers will answer in different ways.[32] The sense of indeterminacy or uncertainty produced by conflicting passages is perhaps nowhere as strong or as intriguing as in Vergil's underworld, to which we now turn.

Let Vergil be your guide

Vergil's depiction of Aeneas' descent to the underworld in Book 6 has long been known for its numerous inconsistencies of both detail and doctrine. Some problems of detail involve other passages within Book 6. The Sibyl tells Aeneas, for example, to pluck the golden bough, which will come easily and willingly into his hands (*volens facilisque*, 146), if the fates are calling him; otherwise neither brute strength nor even a sword will be able to tear it off. When Aeneas breaks off the golden bough, it is described not as *volens facilisque* but as delaying or hesitating (*cunctantem*, 211).[33] Did Theseus return from the underworld, as is implied by 6.122, or does he sit forever in Tartarus (6.617–18)?[34] This was one of the problems that Hyginus and Gellius said Vergil would have fixed if death had not taken him. But the problems in the underworld are too numerous to fix. The Eumenides, for example, are given several different locations.[35] The Sibyl tells Aeneas to draw his sword (6.260), then thirty lines later she stops him from using it, saying the shades are incorporeal (290–9; more on this below). Apuleius calls attention to and "corrects" two passages in *Aeneid* 6 that describe the underworld's rivers as both sluggish (323) and rough (627–8).[36] There are various judges in various parts of Vergil's underworld, but also a sense in which souls get to their proper place in the underworld without the help of judges, and at the same time some souls seem to be in the wrong place: Dido, for example, is among those who died for love (440–54), not among the suicides (434–9), and she

---

[32] Cf. e.g. Parry (1966), Lyne (1987), Conte (1986), Farrell (1990), Thomas (1990), (1993) = (1999) 206–28 (with emphasis on Callimachus as a model for ambiguity) and (2001), Fowler (1993), Perkell (1994), Bleisch (1999), Gale (2000). Cf. too the Ovidian scholarship cited in my Chapter 5 n. 28.

[33] Thomas (2001) 99–100, with further references.

[34] Cf. the Heracles of *Odyssey* 11.601–4, who both has a shade or at least an "eidolon" in the Land of the Dead and enjoys eternal life on Olympus.

[35] Cf. 280, 374–5, 555, 570–2, 605–7, with Weber (1983) 266 n. 11.

[36] Finkelpearl (1990) 340, citing Apuleius *AA* 6.13.4.

is accompanied by her husband Sychaeus, who did not die for love at all. Further, the catalogue of women who died for love includes both innocent victims like Procris, and notorious evil-doers like Eriphyle who one might think should be in Tartarus being punished. The whole issue of punishment in Tartarus – the narration of which is removed one level, because we are told not what Aeneas sees but what the Sibyl saw long ago – is fraught with confusion and problems, as Vergil presents versions of traditional underworld punishments that are so oddly out of step with the previous poetic tradition that many have wanted to posit problems with the text rather than deal with the complexity of the transmitted text.[37]

Much of what is said in the underworld, as we have seen earlier, is also in conflict with passages elsewhere in the poem. Notoriously, there are several striking discrepancies between the accounts of Palinurus' death presented by the narrator in 5.835–71 and by Palinurus himself in 6.337–83. In the first passage, the god Sleep causes Palinurus to fall into calm waters on the voyage from Sicily to Italy, the day before Aeneas gets to Cumae and enters the underworld. In the second, Palinurus says no god was involved, that he fell into stormy seas, and swam for three days before being killed onshore. The narrator also says in Book 6 that Palinurus fell while on the "Libyan voyage" (*Libyco . . . cursu*, 338). It is hard to know what to make of all of these problems, only some of which can be explained. Some discrepancies can be taken to be deliberate, "particularly those involving the perspectives of Aeneas and Palinurus," neither of whom knows what the god Sleep really did to Palinurus, so that "the course of destiny is experienced by human beings as chance contingency."[38] But this solution does not remove all of the problems. Some troublesome details in Book 6 serve to make Palinurus' story resemble that of Odysseus more: Palinurus clings to the rudder for three days, just as Odysseus clung to pieces of his ship for nine days before washing up on Calypso's island. We could say that the poet is tolerating an inconsistency

---

[37] See esp. Zetzel (1989).

[38] Quint (1993) 87, who also makes my next point about Palinurus and Odysseus; cf. too Zetzel (1989) 274–6 on the underworld's suggestions about the limitations of human knowledge. Thomas (2004) tentatively suggests that anthologized poems about men lost at sea, like those in the new Posidippus papyrus, may have contributed to the fractured nature of Palinurus' tale. On a separate aspect of the Palinurus scene: cf. Martindale (1993a) 45 on how Dante cleans up a perceived contradiction in 6.371, *desine fata deum flecti sperare precando*.

in order to make a local point (there are some other examples of this³⁹), but given the makeup of the Vergilian underworld, it might be better to speak of the poet welcoming rather than tolerating the inconsistency. The underworld contains far too many discrepancies with what is said elsewhere in the poem for them to have been accidental, or on Vergil's "List of Things to Fix After Trip to Greece." As Mackie notes, "it is difficult to see how Vergil could have created more gaping inconsistencies without actually intending to do so."⁴⁰ We have already mentioned the problems with Deiphobus' description of the last night of Troy, and with how Aeneas is told about the son he will have in old age, from whom will descend the kings of Alba Longa, in a passage which is in conflict in several ways with what is said elsewhere in the poem.⁴¹

That these difficulties are neither accidental nor trivial is also suggested by the way in which Vergil provides different answers to the most fundamental question about the underworld: what happens to human beings when we die? The different regions through which Aeneas passes in Vergil's underworld can be coerced retrospectively to fit into one extremely eclectic system, but it requires a great deal of work to do so; the impression that successive passages make on the reader is one of considerable inconsistency. Most readers feel that a "Homeric" or "mythological" picture of life after death (beginning at 6.268) yields to a "philosophical" or even an "Orphic-Pythagorean" view (which starts some time after Aeneas finds his father Anchises), but features of the two views are also intertwined throughout. We can see the problem as being a "conflict between 'static' and 'redemptive' views of the afterlife,"⁴² with the first suggesting that souls in the underworld reside permanently in

³⁹ Dyson (1996) looks at the use of *septima aetas* both at 1.753–6 and a year later at 5.626; in Book 5 "the inconsistency intentionally marks the phrase *septima aetas* in order to highlight the theme of sacrificial death" by alluding to *Geo.* 4.203–9, where "the seventh summer is the inevitable terminus of the individual bee's life, yet the hive continues forever . . ." Cf. too Nugent (1992) 280 n. 54 on "Ascanius' helmet here ([5.]673)" which "is difficult to reconcile with the wreath he was apparently wearing a hundred lines earlier (556). The problem, to my mind, merely emphasizes Vergil's desire to evoke the Homeric precedent [in Hector's removal of his helmet in *Iliad* 6] – despite some incongruity."
⁴⁰ Mackie (1988) 127–8.
⁴¹ Zetzel (1989) and Horsfall (1995) offer more detail than I can give here. See also Feldherr (1999) on the effect of generic tensions in the underworld, and Molviati-Toptsis (1995).
⁴² Horsfall (1995) 151; cf. Zetzel (1989) esp. 265–7, with references.

the state in which Aeneas encounters them (as they seem to in Homer, and as they seem to do when we first enter Vergil's underworld), and the second suggesting the purification and transmigration of souls – that souls are purified and go somewhere else, either back to new bodies on earth or perhaps, once they are perfect, back to join the heavenly fire from which they have come. It is possible to see the picture presented later in Aeneas' visit as correcting or rejecting or supplementing what comes earlier, and offering a contrast between incorrect mythological and correct philosophical views as in the opening of the *De Rerum Natura*, perhaps even with a suggestion of the historical movement from more "primitive" to more "philosophical" concepts.[43] But it is also possible, and arguably truer to the experience of reading Book 6, to see the poet as presenting a variety of incompatible beliefs, from different poetic, religious, and philosophical sources, and to admit that "the Virgilian underworld, therefore, embodies radically different and mutually incompatible accounts of the afterlife and the nature of the soul, and it is hard to see how they can be reconciled."[44]

What are we to make of the inconsistencies in Vergil's underworld? At the very least they help create a strong sense of uncertainty for the reader about exactly what is going on in Book 6, from the philosophical and religious eclecticism (comparable to Gale's view of the *Georgics*) to such simple details as whether Aeneas can use his sword on the shades. The detail of the sword need not be trivial: of those two nearby passages, Gordon Williams has argued, one suggests to us that we are dealing with a necromancy, a summoning of the spirits of the dead, whereas the other suggests a *katabasis*, a descent to the world of the dead.[45] Some readers may find in the underworld an untroubling catalogue of possible views of the afterlife, almost a *variorum* – this I think

---

[43] Cf. Solmsen (1972), Horsfall (1995) 152, Austin (1977) 221: "Virgil, through Anchises' exposition, has deliberately questioned, even perhaps rejected, the whole conception of the world of the dead through which Aeneas has been led by the Sybil;" and Zetzel (1989) 272: ". . . the anomalous versions of traditional legends tend to diminish the authority of the mythological underworld, and that authority is superseded by that of the moralizing versions of Orphic-Pythagorean eschatology." See also Hardie (1992) and (1993) 57–87 on how Vergilian notions of the underworld are further destabilized in *Aeneid* 7 and 12.

[44] Zetzel (1989) 267.

[45] Williams (1983) 50, faulting earlier suggestions that Vergil "mindlessly stitched together" the "*Odyssey* and a Golden Bough descent" or the *Odyssey* and "a *Descent of Herakles*;" cf. above in Chapter 1.

is the sense of Horsfall's brief but important discussion, where as often he focuses on the poetics, rather than the thematics, of examples of Alexandrian allusion to variants, and we cannot assume that this option was foreclosed for any reader. Others may be more inclined to consider "combinatorial" effects, to use a term Barchiesi has brought to bear on some disparate passages in Ovid's *Fasti*, which he suggests are best not read separately but in the light of their contradictions with one another.[46] Williams and others have argued that the whole underworld experience has a dream-like quality and seems "illusory or unreal,"[47] and of course Aeneas will exit the underworld through the gate usually used by false dreams, although Vergil will never tell us that Aeneas is dreaming or exactly what we should make of his exit through the ivory gate.[48] A persistently difficult question is whether the uncertainty, and any sense of falseness, extends to the whole underworld, including Anchises' speech about Aeneas' future descendants, which as we have seen has some deceptive aspects. Does the problem go "all the way down" (so to speak) in the underworld? This is a tough question. It is possible to assert that despite all the uncertainty, a sense of justice emerges from Vergil's picture of the underworld, a sense that virtue will be rewarded and crime punished. This is the central claim of Zetzel, but the claim is not hard to challenge: the climax of the Sibyl's description of Tartarus is the loud warning of one punished sinner that we should learn justice (*Phlegyasque miserrimus omnis | admonet et magna testatur voce per umbras: | "discite iustitiam moniti et non temnere divos*," "And most wretched Phlegyas warns all, and bears witness through the shades in a great voice: 'heed the warning, learn justice, and do not scorn the gods,'" 618–20). But Phlegyas is a curious choice to deliver this message: he is the father of the famous sinner Ixion, but his own crime is that when Apollo raped his daughter, he burned Apollo's temple; does he then proclaim *discite iustitiam* ("learn justice") or perhaps *discite 'iustitiam'* ("learn what 'justice' is")?[49]

[46] On Barchiesi (1994) see the start of my next chapter.
[47] Williams (1983) 47–58, cf. Zetzel (1989) 274–5, Mackie (1988) 138.
[48] I must insist, though, on my lack of admiration for evasive attempts to make the term *falsa insomnia* not have connotations of falseness, which are true neither to Vergil's Latin nor the Homeric model; see O'Hara (1990) 170–2 and (1996b) and Thomas (2001) 193–8, and cf. Chapter 3 at n. 47 on improperly excluding some meanings of words in order to tame inconsistencies.
[49] Cf. Thomas (2001) 31–2, who notes that many critics ignore the speaker here.

They might be giants

In the second half of the *Aeneid*, the question of the guilt, innocence, villainy, or heroism of Turnus and the Italians on one side and Aeneas and the Trojans on the other has been the focus of spirited debate. Most contributions to this debate, especially those that assert that Turnus and most of the Italians are villains who deserve whatever suffering comes to them in the poem, claim explicitly or implicitly to have done a better job than their opponents of assembling the clues or evidence Vergil gives us about the Trojans and Italians into a unified coherent picture of what the two groups are really like. Often this scholarship produces excellent observations about many aspects of the poem, but must ignore, distort, or implausibly explain away features of the poem that do not fit the view of the *Aeneid* it is promoting.[50] The same flaws sometimes mar attempts to defend Turnus and the Italians, or to stress negative aspects of the portrait of Aeneas and the Trojans. At times scholars on both sides of the debate resemble attorneys prosecuting or defending clients accused of crimes in the real world, rather than readers of a literary text or scholars trying to look impartially at data or evidence. The study of inconsistency in Roman epic and elsewhere in the *Aeneid*, I suggest, offers a new way of looking at these questions, which can account for all the evidence. From this new perspective we can see that a persistent and challenging inconsistency marks numerous aspects of the presentation of the Trojans and Italians in the second half of the poem. These include the question of whether the Italians were peaceful or warlike before the Trojans arrived; what associations the Trojans and Italians have with the myths of gigantomachy and titanomachy; and the myth of the Golden Age.

In the evocation of the Muse Erato at 7.37–45 the narrator calls the Trojans a "foreign army" (*advena exercitus*), and then describes the areas and peoples ruled by Latinus as peaceful, and as having been so for a long time (*rex arva Latinus et urbes | iam senior longa placidas in pace regebat*, 45–6). This description is soon directly contradicted. When Aeneas' men approach

---

[50] In this section I borrow much from O'Hara (1994), (1995) and (1996c). For other examples of reacting only to part of the evidence see the scholars discussed by Thomas (1998). On Vergil's Italy see Toll (1997), Zetzel (1997), Ando (2002), and forthcoming work by A. Barchiesi in the same series as this book. Horsfall (2000) 530 cites O'Hara (1994) as "uncomfortable with the 'invasionist' approach," which is true enough, but my paper also criticizes and even mocks some opponents of that approach for their one-sided descriptions of the text.

Latinus' city they see youths engaged in what must appear to the reader to be training for war (162–5). Inside the palace, they see images of Latinus' ancestors, earlier kings, and "those who have been wounded fighting wars for their homeland" (*Martiaque ob patriam pugnando vulnera passi*, 182). There are also weapons, armor, and captured war chariots and other spoils (183–6). This is a real inconsistency. There is no satisfying way to harmonize these passages. The provisional claim, for example, that these warlike people have enjoyed a recent period of long peace, will not hold up in the light of later passages, although it is a reasonable attempt to "concretize" (in Iser's terms) the details given so far.[51] In a poetic world closely imitating the real world, the peoples over whom Latinus ruled would either be peaceful peoples in long peace or they would not; to be at war and to be at peace may be complementary opposites, but one people generally does not experience these opposites at the same time. Horsfall, who knows both Vergil's sources and in particular *Aeneid* 7 as well as anyone, puts it succinctly: "Certainly, Virgil exhibits two opposed conceptions of the condition of primitive Italy; it seems likely that he found antecedents for both conceptions in his sources." More recently Horsfall has added that "the two conceptions are far too amply distributed for one or the other to have been eliminated in some grand final revision

---

[51] For Italy as peaceful cf. also 7.203–4 (Latinus): *Saturni gentem haud vinclo nec legibus aequam, | sponte sua veterisque dei se more tenentem*, 7.623 *ardet inexcita Ausonia atque immobilis ante* (which Servius feels needs to be explained away); the (not unqualified) suggestions of innocence in the tame deer in 7.475–539; 10.70–2 (Juno's perhaps biased words): *num puero summam belli, num credere muros, | Tyrrhenamque fidem aut gentis agitare quietas*?; 11.252–4 (Diomedes, less biased): *o fortunatae gentes, Saturnia regna, | antiqui Ausonii, quae vos fortuna quietos | sollicitat suadetque ignota lacessere bella*? For the Italians as fierce and warlike cf. the words of Jupiter: *populosque ferocis*, 1.263; Dido: *bello audacis populi vexatus et armis*, 4.615; and Anchises: *gens dura atque aspera cultu | debellanda tibi Latio est*, 5.730–1; the difficult question of Allecto's effect upon Turnus (see O'Hara [1990] 62–70, Mackie [1991] 59–61, Feeney [1991] 162–72, Thomas [1998] 285 and Horsfall [2000] 224–5, 237–8); Evander's constant war with the Latins (*hi bellum adsidue ducunt cum gente Latina*, 8.55); and the words and attitude of Numanus Remulus in 9.598–620 (e.g. *at patiens operum parvoque adsueta iuventus | aut rastris terram domat aut quatit oppida bello*, 607–8; see Thomas [1982a] 93–107, Horsfall [1971] 1108–16, and [1987], and Hardie [1994] ad loc. with my review in O'Hara [1995]). See now also Bleisch (2003), esp. 105, on the description of Latinus' palace in *Aen.* 7.152–93: "At one moment, Latinus' people are civilized, peaceful, Roman in all but name, but then a shift occurs, and Latium is again exotic, untamed, resistant to assimilation."

and both serve a clear purpose."[52] The inconsistency seems deliberate and functional. The narrator of the *Aeneid* states clearly that Latinus' peaceful people lived in peace for a long time before the arrival of the Trojans. He also clearly describes them as a warlike people with a strong martial tradition. Thus the popular opposing views that claim that Vergil "calls on us to weep for what to his mind made an earlier Italy fresh and true" or conversely that "the moral innocence of Italy was compromised before the Trojans ever set foot on its soil"[53] are both supported by the text, which allows the Trojans to be seen both as necessary civilizers and as invaders of a pastoral world, and the Italians to be seen both as innocent victims and as a fierce people in need of being civilized. The uncertainty over whether Italy is peaceful or warlike also mirrors that of the *Georgics* over whether the Italian farmer's life is idyllic or a life of grim toil, as well as the contradictions, discussed in earlier chapters, about whether Homer's Cyclopes are cruel savages or happy primitives, and whether primitive man lived a harsh or soft existence in Lucretius.

A similar inconsistency[54] marks the poem's allusions to the myth of Gigantomachy, many of which were first brought to our attention by Hardie's bold and learned demonstration that the *Aeneid* alludes often to the myths in which Zeus or Jupiter and the other gods, who represent the forces of order, fight for control of the universe against gigantic foes like the Titans or Giants, who represent disorder or even chaos. In the storm in Book 1, Hardie writes, Vergil "introduces an idea of cosmic order and of the forces that threaten it;" throughout the poem, we see "scenes which depict conflict, the attempt by the forces of Rome, of order, of civilization, to defeat the forces of barbarism and chaos: the Storm in book one, the battles against Cacus and the Egyptians in book eight, the war with the Italians in the last four books."[55] But the *Aeneid*'s gigantomachic imagery actually makes conflicting suggestions and pulls the reader in different directions.[56] Numerous passages indeed link Aeneas and the Trojans to Jupiter and the gods as they fight gigantic forces

---

[52] Horsfall (1981) 141–50 and (2000) on 7.183; cf. too Horsfall (1991a) ch. 6 "Incoerenze" and (2000) on 7.46. Cf. too Williams (1983) 40–2, and for references on "possible worlds" theory see my Chapter 1 n. 16.

[53] Quotations from Parry (1966) 110, Moorton (1989) 108, as discussed in O'Hara (1994).

[54] Argued in more detail in O'Hara (1994) and (1995).

[55] Hardie (1986) 100, 135.

[56] Some of this is acknowledged briefly in Hardie (1986) 155–6; see also Hardie (1993) 74–6.

of disorder, but in a considerable number of passages Turnus and the Italians fight Giant-like invaders who are threats to their civilization (cf. e.g. *ingentis . . . advenisse viros*, 7.166–7, and the description of Turnus' killing of the enormous Trojan brothers Pandarus and Bitias in Book 9); the association of Gigantomachy with the repelling of foreign invaders is no less prominent in literature and art than the struggle of order against disorder.[57] In 10.565–9 Aeneas, as he fights the Italians after the death of Pallas, is compared to the Hundred-hander Aegaeon:

> Aegaeon qualis, centum cui bracchia dicunt
> centenasque manus, quinquaginta oribus ignem
> pectoribusque arsisse, *Iovis cum fulmina contra*
> tot paribus streperet clipeis, tot stringeret ensis:
> sic toto Aeneas desaevit in aequore victor

> Like Aegaeon, who they say had a hundred arms
> and a hundred hands, and fire blazed from fifty mouths
> and chests, when *against the thunderbolts of Jupiter*
> he rattled that many identical shields, and drew that many swords:
> just so did Aeneas rage victorious over the whole field

Vergil follows an unusual variant: while in Hesiod the Hundred-handers help Zeus fight against the Titans, Vergil has him fighting on the side of the Titans against Jupiter (567), as in the *Titanomachia*.[58] When the first two-and-one-half lines compare Aeneas to Aegaeon, the reader is apt to think first of the more common myth of Aegaeon as the ally of Jupiter. Only with the second half of the third line comes the information that Aegaeon is fighting "against Jupiter's lightning:" *Iovis . . . fulmina contra*. Over the course of the few seconds it takes the reader to process the information presented in these lines, the Aegaeon simile embodies the contradictions and ambiguities of the poem's allusions to Gigantomachy, and of many aspects of the war in Italy, presenting Aeneas first apparently as the ally, but then in "reality" (for

---

[57] See O'Hara (1994) 219–20, where I mention the scenes of Gigantomachy on the metopes of the Parthenon, Pindar *Pyth.* 1, Callim. *Hymn to Delos* 172–5, the Great Altar at Pergamum, and the Gauls who invaded Italy.

[58] Hardie (1986) 155, whom I paraphrase closely; cf. Mack (1978) 115, O'Hara (1994) 218–19, Williams (1983) 179–80, Harrison (1991) 215, Horsfall (1995) 114, and on the problem of point of view or focalization more generally see Fowler (1990) = (2000a) 40–63.

now) as the enemy of Jupiter. Some would say that Aeneas is the enemy of Jupiter only as focalized through the Italians he is killing, but even the fact that the narrator seems to be taking the point of view of Aeneas' enemies for the moment seems significant, and a serious challenge to some simplistic ways of looking at right and wrong in the poem.

A number of passages in Book 12 associate Aeneas with Jupiter fighting a Gigantomachy, but one of them sends similarly conflicting signals. In 654–700 verbs suggesting lightning and thunder are used of Aeneas (*fulminat Aeneas*, 654; *intonat*, 700), associating him with the lightning Jupiter uses to fight the Giants, but then Aeneas is compared to three mountains in 701–3, which must associate him with the monstrous opponents of the gods in a Gigantomachy, no less than did the earlier comment that Pandarus and Bitias are "large as trees or mountains" (9.674). The result is that in some way, "the text is at war with itself."[59]

Mention of the Titanomachy points to another persistent ambivalence or inconsistency in allusions to Gigantomachic themes in the *Aeneid*. In much recent scholarship, references to Gigantomachy have obscured the distinctions between several stages of the myth, in which Zeus or Jupiter first drives out Cronos or Saturnus and the Titans, next fends off their attempt to regain power, and then later defeats attempts by forces like Typhoeus and the Giants to overthrow his rule. Vergil's allusions to Gigantomachy interact with his specific references to the myth of Jupiter's overthrow of Saturn, and the association of that overthrow with the end of the Golden Age. The frequent associations of Aeneas and the Trojans with Jupiter, for example, seem to suggest they are also to be linked with the end of the Golden Age.[60] In the *Georgics*, Jupiter brings about the change from the Golden Age to the present age of toil (1.121–46). In the *Aeneid*, Evander speaks of Saturnus being driven

---

[59] The phrase suggests Masters (1992) on Lucan (see my Chapter 6 below), but is also used of the *Aeneid* by Hardie (1990) 229. See too Hardie (1993) 22 ("from some angles Aeneas and Turnus are sharply distinguished, from others they merge into one figure . . ."), 58 (on Heaven and Hell: "Virgil's dualistic scheme already contains its own contradictions and tensions, of such a kind that final stability is never attained"), and 74 ("it is precisely the tendency of the *Aeneid* to install in the epic a partisanship that pits evil against good, yet at the same time radically to problematize that opposition"). On the instability of Gigantomachic imagery see also Feeney (1991) 297–9 on the depiction of Caesar in Lucan.

[60] A theme frequently discussed by Richard Thomas, e.g. (1982a) 100–3, (2001) 1–7, and (2004–5).

from heaven by Jupiter, then setting up a Golden Age in Italy (*aurea quae perhibent illo sub rege fuere | saecula: sic placida populos in pace regebat*, 8.324–5), described in terms that recall the narrator's own description of Latinus' rule at 7.45–6. Yet Vergil has Anchises in the underworld express hope for the future achievements of Augustus by saying that he will return the Saturnian Age to Italy (6.791–5).[61] If allusions to Gigantomachy sometimes make it unclear who is on Jupiter's side, allusions to the Golden Age make uncertain what it means to be on Jupiter's side. Jupiter's opponents can be thought of as invading barbarians, as barbarians standing in the way of progress, or as representatives of a Golden Age like that of Saturn. The possible associations of Aeneas and the Trojans with aspects of the myths of Jupiter, Saturn, Titanomachy, and Gigantomachy, then, are many and varied. On the one hand, we can see them as civilizing culture-heroes like Saturnus.[62] On the other hand, their arrival seems like that of earlier immigrants, whom Evander associates with change for the worse and decline.[63] Most significantly, any association of Aeneas and the Trojans with Saturnus' Golden Age flies in the face of the poem's frequent linking of the Trojan newcomers with Jupiter, who supplanted Saturn and put an end to the Golden Age. It is relentlessly difficult to come to grips with how the Gigantomachic imagery, itself ambiguous or indeterminate, interacts with the motif of the Golden or Saturnian Age. Which of the characters in the poem is associated with Jupiter and which with his opponents? In brief, who is Jupiter, and is being associated with Jupiter a good thing?[64]

---

[61] Thomas (2001) 1–7 however argues that this passage can be read to say that Augustus will end rather than re-found the Golden Age.

[62] Cf. Moorton (1989) 127–9, Thomas (1982a) 95–7, and on contradictions in the picture of the Golden Age in the *Eclogues*, *Georgics*, and *Aeneid* see Perkell (2002).

[63] Stressed by Thomas (1982a) 97.

[64] Cf. Feeney (1991) 221 on the association of Augustus with Jupiter in Ovid: "The comparison of man with god is subject to the same plasticity as any analogy, simile, or metaphor, for the boundaries of the analogy are malleable, and its applications cannot remain rigidly fixed. If Caesar, for example, is Saturn, and Augustus is Jupiter, then we must now be in the Iron, and not the Golden, Age." More generally on the instability of allusive connotations see Fowler (2000a) 120 and 174 on (*inter alia*) Bill Clinton and John F. Kennedy. My question, "who is Jupiter, and is being associated with Jupiter a good thing?" can be rephrased to apply to the shifting association of Turnus and Aeneas with Achilles. In some ways there is a clear plot in which first Turnus and then Aeneas is linked to Achilles, but for complications that could be discussed in the same way I

My analysis of the *Aeneid* has offered a flurry of examples, yet it might still be argued that the inconsistencies noted here do not dominate this long poem in quite the way they have dominated this chapter, and that one who re-reads the poem after absorbing this chapter still has the option of suppressing all thoughts of inconsistency to concretize the poem as a single-voiced poem in the supposedly traditional mode of epic. Certainly readers have enormous choice in terms of focus and foregrounding. Yet crucial aspects of the poem are touched by these inconsistencies. We have seen that significant discrepancies beset the poem's prophecies, including those most central to an uncomplicated Augustan reading of the poem. We have considered the *Georgics* "as a polyphonic text in which different 'voices' of the didactic tradition are brought together but not harmonized into a seamless whole." We have seen conflicting versions of myth sometimes called to mind by subtle allusion, and at other times more prominently displayed in the poem. We have noted how Vergil's underworld presents a vision of justice but also produces a strong sense of uncertainty for the reader. And we have described the ambivalent associations of Aeneas and the Trojans in the second half of the poem with giant-killers protecting order, invading giants, and both the enemies and allies of Jupiter, and thus with both the return and the end of the Golden Age. It seems difficult if not impossible now to "pay no attention to the man behind the curtain." As much as Hellenistic poetry or Ovid's version of epic, to which the next chapter will turn, the *Aeneid* seems to embody ambivalence, uncertainty, and a plurality of voices, not least through the strategic use of inconsistency. The poem seems genuinely ambivalent about the nature of Rome and about the historical process that has led to the culture and politics of Vergil's day. Whether the voices of doubt or regret are subordinate to, overwhelm, or are locked in an equal struggle with the more confident and certain Augustan voices is a question that different readers will answer in different ways.[65]

Of particular importance, I think, has been the realization of how much inconsistency besets the picture of Jupiter in the *Aeneid*. This chapter began with Jupiter and will now end with him, and one or two more inconsistencies

have treated Gigantomachy, see Van Nortwick (1980); cf. too Williams (1983) 87–93, 100–19, Hardie (1986) 150, Thomas (1998) 278–81.

[65] For important discussions see Perkell (1994) and (1997), Conte (1986), Martindale (1993a) and (1993b), Thomas (1990), (1993) and (2001), Gale (2000), Fowler (1990) = (2000a) 40–63, Horsfall (1995) 109–11 and 192–216, Hardie (1993), (1996) and (1998) 94–101, Carnes (2001).

(Jupiter will also be featured in the next chapter's treatment of Ovid's *Meta-morphoses*). I note again the centrality of faith in Jupiter to many modern readings of the poem; Schmidt has described his suspicion "that the belief in the morality of Jupiter and fate and in the moral justification of Aeneas as seen in the pro-Augustan reading of the *Aeneid* ultimately amounts to a fallacious moral and theological affirmation of historical factuality."[66] Earlier I discussed the passage at 1.263–6 in which Jupiter predicts to Venus that Aeneas will fight a great war and easily crush the peoples he finds in Italy. In the Council of the Gods that opens Book 10, Jupiter claims that he had forbidden war between the Italians and Trojans (*abnueram bello Italiam concurrere Teucris. | quae contra vetitum discordia?*, "I had forbidden Italy to clash in war with the Teucrians. What strife is this in defiance of my prohibition?" 8–9), even though he had predicted this war in speaking to Venus in Book 1. Servius reports attempts to "solve" the problem, some implausible (he predicted war with the *Rutulians* in Book 1, but at some point forbade war with *all* the Italians), some plausible (that Jupiter here in Book 10 is speaking rhetorically before Juno and the other gods). Hardie puts the problem this way:

> Coming from the god who should represent unswerving Fate, this unsettling inconsistency raises the possibility that the impressive-sounding and apparently impartial speech with which Jupiter concludes the Council of Gods . . . may in fact be as rhetorical as the splendidly impassioned speeches which Venus and Juno have just hurled at each other.[67]

I would note that after this deceptive rhetoric, and pronouncing himself impartial (*rex Iuppiter omnibus idem*, 112), in a war in which he is going to intervene in any number of ways, Jupiter nods to ratify the speech by swearing an oath by the river Styx (113–15). In *Aen.* 6.323–4, Vergil or the Sibyl calls the Styx, "the river by which the gods fear to swear falsely," and Juno says something similar in 12.816–17. You would think this would be the case, but apparently not for Jupiter. What kind of a world are we in, if Jupiter can swear falsely by the Styx? Can one be certain of anything in this poem?

There is no better question on which to turn to Ovid.

---

[66] Schmidt (2001) 168, who also discusses the flaws of "anti-Augustan" readings.

[67] Hardie (1998) 95–6, Lyne (1987) 78–81, Harrison (1991) 59–60, Thomas (2004–5) esp. 144–6.

CHAPTER
5
Inconsistency and authority in Ovid's *Metamorphoses*

Ovid wanted his readers to have a wrenching experience from his violations of decorum. He wanted the *Metamorphoses* to be disturbing, and regarded the violation of his readers' sensibilities as a valuable experience for them. Indeed, if there is a didactic purpose to the *Metamorphoses*, it is not so much in the inculcation of positive moral values as in the exposure of the audience to revealing – though sometimes unpleasant – experiences. Ovid makes his readers recognize the power of language to control and manipulate their responses, and exposes to them their susceptibility or willingness – or even craving – to be deceived by comforting and pleasant fictions.

Garth Tissol, *The Face of Nature*

Ovid's hexameter *Metamorphoses* follows an extensive body of work in elegy, and shares many features with both his own work in elegy and that of his Roman and Alexandrian predecessors, particularly Callimachus. These elegiac features include what is on some level a looser principle of organization like that of Callimachus' *Aetia*. Ovid's elegiac *Fasti*, on which he was working while writing the *Metamorphoses*, comes even closer to the Callimachean model, with disquisitions about the Roman calendar linked by the persona of the pseudo-scholar-poet interacting with his sources. Recent work on the *Fasti* stresses that poem's rich variety and multiplicity of voices, and the possibility of "combinatory" effects resulting from the juxtaposition of incongruities.[1]

---

[1] Barchiesi (1991) and (1994) "combinatory" (mentioned in the previous chapter's discussion of the Vergilian underworld), Newlands (1995), Hinds (1992), J. F. Miller (1991) and (1992), Hardie (1991). My epigraph to this chapter is from Tissol (1997) 124.

So too for the *Metamorphoses*, much recent work has focused on discontinuity, polyphony, and the poem's apparently "post-modern" features. Scholars have been more receptive to the idea of an inconsistent Ovid than that of an inconsistent Vergil, and part of what this chapter and book will show is that Ovid is not alone in the Roman epic tradition in making use of inconsistencies, and that his practice must be seen as in keeping with underappreciated aspects of earlier epic and other poetry.

To scan the scholarly literature on Ovid is also to see disagreement about whether to read the *Metamorphoses* as serious, playful, or seriously playful. Do so-called "literary" concerns dominate, as opposed to thematic or political issues? And if the poem has political concerns, what is its attitude toward questions of power, and toward the emperor Augustus? The problem of how to read inconsistent passages is at the heart of many of these questions, even though consideration of the poetic use of inconsistencies does not provide easy solutions. The poem seems perfectly polished (but for the existence in our manuscripts of some alternative lines which few would credit to the poet), even though Ovid, perhaps echoing what Hyginus said about the *Aeneid*, claims it lacks final revision, which he would have supplied if not for exile: *emendaturus, si licuisset, eram* (*Tristia* 1.7.40).[2] This chapter will begin with the proem to the *Metamorphoses*, and then discuss the philosophical cosmogony and its relationship to the poem's Olympian gods; later sections will move more quickly through some episodes that seem to combine variant versions, others that mix genres, passages marked by chronological problems, and aetiological variants. We shall end with Jupiter, and the end of the poem.

God and man in the proem

We begin with a neglected inconsistency in Ovid's proem, and with the gods, and with the kinds of questions of power and authority that will recur throughout the poem (1.1–4):[3]

---

[2] Lafaye (1904) 81–2 cites this passage to excuse some inconsistencies, although of course there is no real reason to think Ovid was unable to revise the poem in exile. On *Tristia* 1.7 see Hinds (1985) and (1999) 60, Masters (1992) 220, Connors (1994). For Hyginus see my Chapter 4 n. 1.

[3] My point here is discussed in more detail in O'Hara (2005a); annotation here will be limited.

in nova fert *animus* mutatas dicere formas
corpora: *di*, coeptis (nam vos mutastis et *illa*)
adspirate meis primaque ab origine mundi
ad mea perpetuum deducite tempora carmen.

My *mind* compels me to tell of shapes changed into new
bodies: *gods*, on my endeavors (for you have changed *them* too)
shed your inspiration, and from the very origin of the world
down to my own times do lead this eternal song.

Most Ovidians now agree that *Met.* 1.2 should end with the neuter *illa*, rather than the feminine *illas*, so that Ovid asks the gods for inspiration for his *coepta*, his "beginnings" or "new (poetic) endeavors," because "you gods have changed *them* too," i.e. the *coepta*, rather than the *formas* of line 1.[4] Thus "the words *nam vos mutastis et illa*, coming at the end of the second line, mark the point at which the meter reveals itself as hexameters rather than elegiacs,"[5] so this is the precise "Bob Dylan plugs in at Newport" moment of the poem, where Ovid becomes a writer of epic. Ovid had performed a similar trick at *Amores* 1.1.1–2, starting with a hexameter on weapons and war, before revealing lines 1–2 to be an elegiac couplet. In the *Metamorphoses*, an interesting, characteristically Ovidian complication is restored to the text of the proem when we read *illa*, a complication which looks both back towards a long tradition of epic and other musing about the role of the gods in human affairs, and forward to the complexly problematic notions of divinity and power that his own new poem will explore.

Ovid first attributes his move to epic to the impulses of his own mind (*fert animus*); he "declares that the primary force behind his poem is his own rational intelligence," and the phrase "suggests, above all, the poet's personal freedom in choosing to go where his inspiration leads him."[6] Ovid's language here will appeal to Lucan, who borrows the phrase *fert animus* near the start of his own Muse-less epic (*BC* 1.69).[7] But after Ovid begins by saying *fert*

---

[4] Kenney (1976) 46–53, Wheeler (1999) 16–17 (with further references, including to some who still prefer *illas*), Gildenhard and Zissos (2000) 77 n. 7.

[5] Tarrant (1982) 351 n. 35, cf. too Heyworth (1994) 75, Knox (1986) 9, Wheeler (1999) 16–17 (the last three all mentioning the connection to the *Amores*), and Gildenhard and Zissos (2000) 69.

[6] Anderson (1997) ad loc. ("declares"), Wheeler (1999) 8 with extensive references on the phrase.

[7] Cf. Wheeler (2002) with further references.

animus, his parenthetical declaration in line 2 – with the restored reading *illa* – attributes the change to the gods, for *vos mutastis et illa* must mean "you gods have changed my endeavors too." Lines 1–2a put Ovid and his own human freedom of choice at the center, but in the rest of line 2, Ovid asks for inspiration from the gods, and assigns them responsibility for his change in plans. The problem can be put in the form of the kind of comprehension question often used on standardized tests after students have read a passage of Latin: who changed Ovid's plans, his own heart or the immortal gods?

Different types of answer can be provided to this question, including some that see divine and personal motivation as complementary rather than contradictory. At the start of his "epic," Ovid alludes to "a famous dilemma" in the epic tradition, to cite the phrase used by Hardie of the question that Nisus asks Euryalus at *Aen.* 9.184–5, a passage that is part of the complex of ideas to which Ovid is alluding here.

> dine hunc ardorem mentibus addunt,
> Euryale, an sua cuique deus fit dira cupido?

> Do the gods add this ardor to our minds, Euryalus,
> or does each man's own dire desire become a god?

Nisus' question is to some extent Homeric: in the *Iliad*, divine and human motivation usually work in a complementary fashion, but several times in the *Odyssey*, and in at least one Iliadic passage, characters ask whether a god or his own bidding has caused someone to act.[8] But as Hardie notes, "Nisus' question wears the long history of post-Homeric speculation on the nature of the mind and of the traditional gods,"[9] for "the intervention of Homeric gods was later often allegorized in terms of a naturalistic psychology," for example, in discussions of the passage in *Iliad* 1.195–222, where Athena restrains Achilles. Apollonius seems to play with the convention in the *Argonautica*, making it difficult to know whether divine motivation or psychological factors are at issue: he "teasingly combines supernatural and human causation," and "the clammy atmosphere of uncertain confusion . . . is a major vehicle of the poem's central preoccupations."[10] Vergilian scholars have disagreed over whether the gods are to be seen as characters as real as Turnus and Aeneas, and so external influences who victimize the human characters, or as figurative

---

[8] Cf. *Od.* 4.712–13, 7.262–3, 9.337–9, 16.356–7, *Il.* 6.438–9.
[9] Hardie (1994) on *Aen.* 9.184–5.
[10] Quotations from Hardie ibid., Feeney (1991) 80–4, 89.

ways of describing the human characters' own inner qualities: "a good deal of the divine symbolism in the *Aeneid* revolves around [Nisus'] question – e.g. did Allecto drive Turnus to frenzy, or is his frenzy symbolized in Allecto?"[11] Ovid's entry into epic in *Metamorphoses* 1, then, is marked by allusion to this long-standing problem of epic interpretation.

Creation, philosophy, and the Olympians

Ovid's cosmogony differs from those of *Eclogue* 6 or *Argonautica* 1 (or of course *De Rerum Natura* 5) in that a god organizes chaos into an orderly cosmos,[12] a god described as "some god and better nature" (*deus et melior . . . natura*, 1.21), and then as "whatever god it was" (*quisquis fuit ille deorum*, 69). The creation of the cosmos over which this god presides is orderly, teleological, and on the whole rational, serious, even philosophical. This is "a well-designed, orderly universe" because of "the orderly disposal of its parts within the whole." This "higher nature . . . designs the cosmos as it must be designed to satisfy Reason's demands." "A divine creator, like the poet himself, produces a rational design of the world by separating the confused and discordant elements of chaos and fixing them in their proper places."[13] Ovid's account of this orderly creation is itself orderly and balanced, like that of the orderly worlds depicted by Vulcan on the doors of the Sun-god's palace in 2.1–30, and by Minerva in her depiction of the gods in the weaving contest at 6.53–128.[14]

The rational god of philosophy who presides over Ovid's creation, however, soon disappears from view, to be replaced not merely by the mythological Olympians, but by a particularly disorderly, unphilosophical, emotional, lustful version of the mythological gods.[15] The contrast between the world of the

---

[11] Williams (1973) on *Aen.* 9.184–5.

[12] As noted by Feeney (1991) 189–90, Wheeler (1995a); cf. Hardie (1991) 52–3. There is no creator in the brief cosmogony at Ovid *Ars* 2.467ff.

[13] Quotations from Brown (1987b) 216 and 215, McKim (1985) 100, Wheeler (1999) 30.

[14] Brown (1987b) 216; Wheeler (1995a): certain aspects of the creation liken it to the Homeric description of Achilles' shield, itself long the subject of cosmological interpretation, further suggesting a link between the orderly creation of a work of art and the ordering of the cosmos.

[15] The gods are mentioned in the proem (1.2 *di*), implied by the personifications of celestial beings "not yet" in place in 10–14, then casually introduced in 73 *astra tenent caeleste solum formaeque deorum*, and then more specifically in 113–14 *postquam Saturno*

cosmogony and the world in the hands of the Olympians is sharp and clear. After the description of the creation "the reader watches as the philosophical and ideological closure of the cosmogony is undone by passions, both mortal and divine, that confuse the elemental categories originally defined by the demiurge."[16] Jupiter himself "consistently works against the principles of order and harmony that sustain the Cosmos:" he brings on the flood, which violates boundaries, confuses categories, and returns things to a state like chaos (291–2).[17] In broader terms, the rationality of the cosmogony suggests a kind of philosophical optimism, which will quickly be contradicted. Human beings are presented as the crown of creation (76–7), as though "a divine intelligence directed the creation of natural order for the benefit of mankind," but soon Ovid will describe the decline from the Golden Age to the present Iron Age.[18] When Ovid speaks of "better nature" (21) or "a better world" (79), *melior* at first seems to be a blandly emphatic term for "good," but in retrospect must come to mean literally "better than" what comes later. An alternate creation for mankind says that we are born from the blood of the defeated giants, so we are "contemptuous of the gods, greedy for fierce slaughter, and violent" (161–2). Soon, in the Lycaon story, instead of being the crown of creation destined to rule over other creatures, mankind will become a problem in need of stamping out, a cancer to be removed (190–1).

What are we to make of this inconsistency? Several options are possible, and for Ovid I am not sure if we can tell which one is "right." This is an interpretive issue on which it is difficult to avoid reductive solutions, but I suggest that we can handle this problem in Ovid better if we keep in mind what other Roman poets do at the start of epics. Those who think the inconsistency is insignificant argue that Ovid is being "lax," "playful," or "literary." By "lax" I mean the claim that Ovid is "indifferent to the claims of consistency and unity,"[19] and mainly interested in producing good or enjoyable poetry, regardless of the content. Similarly one might claim that Ovid is merely being

tenebrosa in Tartara misso | sub Iove mundus erat, and 116 *Iuppiter antiqui contraxit tempora veris*.

[16] Wheeler (1999) 32.

[17] Rhorer (1980) 305. Soon the Sun-god's promise to Phaethon leads to more chaotic destruction and confusion. On the poet and the Creator-god see also below at n. 25.

[18] Wheeler (1999) 30.

[19] Little (1970) 360, on the relationship between the speech of Pythagoras in Book 15 and the rest of the poem. To be fair we should note that Little is reacting against an older, strict, and limiting notion of unity.

"playful," perhaps on the understanding that his earlier works would make readers expect him not to be serious in the *Metamorphoses*.[20] Ovid is certainly being playful, but the question is whether he is *merely* being playful, or whether his playfulness has a serious edge to it. A third way of playing down the problem would be to stress that Ovid's concerns, like those in some readings of Catullus 64 or many Hellenistic poems, are mainly or exclusively "literary." This has been a popular claim in recent decades, in part as a reaction to narrow scholarship that tried to pigeonhole the philosophical affiliations of Ovid's creation as a "key" to the whole poem. We now know that the cosmogony positions the poem both in the Callimachean-neoteric tradition, and also in the tradition of philosophical epic.[21] But we have probably gone too far in stressing purely literary concerns, while ignoring the thematic implications of "literary" choices. The reader who focuses on Ovid's skillful imitation and adaptation of earlier authors indeed has much to ponder and enjoy, and we cannot deny that some ancient readers must have reacted to this text in this way. We must always ask, however, what might be the thematic or interpretive or even political consequences of the mixing of genres, and combination of multiple models. Are readers expected, or even able, to put aside political or thematic or philosophical questions when "literary" themes are present? The question of whether the universe (or the Roman world) is orderly and run by a rational providence, or disorderly and under the control of irrational forces or beings, must have been a question of more than passing interest to many who read this text both in its Augustan political context, and in comparison with the complex picture of Jupiter in the *Aeneid* discussed in my previous chapter. It is inadequate to claim that Ovid is merely lax, ludic, or literary, for such claims unnecessarily narrow the potential range of responses to the opening of the poem.

---

[20] A reader of Vergil's *Eclogues* and *Georgics*, however, might just as well expect that even after *Arma virumque* and any number of Homeric-sounding lines, the poet would return to his traditional emphasis on pastoral and georgic themes. At what point could a reader of the *Aeneid* be certain that it was not going to offer an *Aetia*-like string of scenes such as we see in Tibullus 2.5?

The idea that Ovid is "merely" playful is easiest to trace in its recent opponents: Elliott (1985), Hinds (1987a) and at length Tissol (1997).

[21] Cf. Knox (1986) 12: "The cosmogony does not offer a coherent philosophical underpinning for the theme of metamorphosis. Rather, it is a statement of the literary affiliations of the poem;" Helze (1993); Myers (1994) 6–7 (who has only one foot in this camp; see below), Galinsky (1999) 7 "[T]he cosmogony (1.5–75) is poetic rather than philosophical;" he also speaks of (8) "The avoidance of emphasis on serious philosophy."

Critics who find the inconsistency significant in terms of content tend to say either that this is the type of inconsistency in which two views are contrasted, with one of them shown to be right and the other wrong, or that this is an ambivalent or ambiguous inconsistency in which two views are presented without making it clear which (if any) is right. Wheeler argues for the former reading, in which Ovid "invites his readers to share the assumptions of a popular philosophical view of the world that has gained normative status in Augustan Rome: namely, that a divine intelligence directed the creation of natural order for the benefit of mankind." These assumptions are then questioned by the destruction of order that follows; Ovid's strategy "is to win the reader's assent to a comforting picture of the [*Metamorphoses*] and then to reform it."[22] McKim suggests too that the shift from the rational-philosophical to the mythological

> serves to suggest . . . that the rational cosmos and its God never existed in the first place, being figments of philosophers' imaginations, and that the mythical cosmos of the poet's imagination, though according to the narrative it follows on the rational one, is the only one of the two which resembles or represents the world that does exist.[23]

If McKim is right, Ovid, in moving from philosophy to myth, is doing the reverse of what Lucretius did in going from myth to philosophy, and he also shares with Lucretius, Catullus 64, and Vergil the practice of beginning with a "comforting picture," which is then modified.[24] But it is also possible to reverse the hierarchy of the passages, to find in Ovid criticism of the power of figures like the Olympian gods, and sympathy for the original creator, who has much in common with the poet as artist – an equation that many scholars have found tempting.[25] Even if identifying the Creator-god with the

---

[22] Wheeler (1999) discusses this feature of the poem at length, as an introduction to such issues throughout the poem; I have quoted him as an epigraph to my Lucretius chapter. Tissol (1997, quoted as an epigraph to this chapter), Bernbeck (1967), and others have stressed Ovid's fondness for surprise and the defeat of expectations.

[23] McKim (1985) 102.

[24] See also Brown (1987b) on how the Creation in Book 1, the doors of the Palace of the Sun in Book 2, and the weaving of Minerva in Book 6 all depict a "well-designed, orderly universe" or a "theocentric, orderly world," and how this "view of things . . . is constantly called into question by the narrative of the poem."

[25] On the poet and Creator-god see Rhorer (1980), Fowler (1995) 13–14, Feeney (1991) 191.

poet raises problems later on, the first-time reader of the Creation episode – like the reader of Lucretius' proem or of Jupiter's speech to Venus in *Aeneid* 1 – cannot know what is coming later.

What is the relationship between the rational, orderly, idealized creation and the disorderly world ruled over by Jupiter? In part we need to ask whether either picture is meant to be normative, ideal, negative, or merely descriptive. Is creation *too* rigidly ordered, and the disorderly world preferable, or is order an ideal to which the world of Jupiter aspires but cannot reach? It is easy to fit many of the details of the early part of the poem into an approach that favors the world of the Creator-god: Jupiter seems to prefer a tightly organized hierarchy, but his actions and those of both other gods and mortals pull the world towards a kind of chaos. Is Ovid perhaps contrasting and comparing types of poetry or art, so that the "literary" approach returns but with more thematic bite? With the cosmogony Ovid makes a place for his new poem in the epic tradition of philosophical speculation, but then he turns away from philosophical toward other concerns. Is it that "Ovid hints that the idealizing formalistic tendency of art runs up against the Protean nature of reality" and then "intimates the possibility of a universal work which would bring to the forefront the infinite strangeness, particularity and flux of experience, as embodied in the less exalted figures of mythology," which would be "a work, in fact, like the *Metamorphoses*?"[26] Furthermore, what are the political implications in the Augustan context of a discussion of order and disorder? The possibility that many readers might be blandly indifferent to the question of whether the world is orderly or disorderly becomes more remote, I think, when we consider, as the poem seems to invite us to do, possible political interpretations of the creation and aftermath. Certainly the Creator-god's "exercise of divine control over discord can be read as prefiguring Augustus' own role in ending the civil wars and establishing a new order." Two Augustan divinities, Jupiter and Apollo, dominate the stories of the first book and a half, and these stories of an assassination attempt (Lycaon, discussed below), three rapes or attempted rapes (Daphne by Apollo, Io and Callisto by Jupiter), and a son's inability to handle his father's duties (Phaethon) easily lend themselves to political interpretations on various levels.[27]

[26] Brown (1987b) 220; cf. too Heyworth (1994) 72–6, Hardie (1993) 60–1.

[27] Quotation from Wheeler (1999) 31. Jupiter's palace is explicitly compared to the Palatine (175–6), and the gods' reaction to a reported assassination attempt is explicitly compared to Roman reaction to an attempt on the life of "Caesar" (199–205). The Apollo–Daphne

Perhaps Ovid endorses neither the view that the cosmos is orderly and under the control of a rational creator nor the contrary view that the universe is controlled only by irrational beings and forces. This would be to claim that the text is irresolvably ambiguous, or indeterminate, and that Ovid does not make clear whether the creator's orderly cosmos or the disorderly world of Jupiter is the one that does or should exist. We could combine this view with the claim that Ovid is not serious, or is mainly interested in literary matters, and so takes no position on philosophical matters. Others might claim that Ovid is seriously committed to the ambiguity or indeterminacy; that he finds whether the world is rational or irrational to be a serious question, but one that he can only explore, and not answer. Such a commitment to ambiguity or multiple explanations can certainly be seen in Ovid's claim that human beings were created either by the philosopher's god (78–9) or by the mythological figure of Prometheus (80–3). Such a reading would be consistent with Ovid's apparent fondness for what may be called ambiguity, paradox, indeterminacy, or in simpler terms offering at least two ways of looking at most issues.[28] The celebrated Arachne–Minerva episode in Book 6 dramatizes some of the same questions as the cosmogony, and we should try to resist identifying one or the other as the sole representative of Ovid's viewpoint:

> . . . if we adhere to one antithesis or the other we will fail to do what justice we can to the complexity of the poem's perspectives. Ovid's pendulum never rests in its oscillation between the poles of Minerva and Arachne, epic and neoteric canons: "As the creator of the poem, Ovid maintains a vision embracing both points of view."[29]

story ends with an aetion of Augustan practice (557–65). The Phaethon story, in which Phoebus Apollo turns over power to his underqualified son and brings back a kind of chaos, is at least open to a reading about concerns regarding imperial succession: cf. Schmitzer (1990) 89–107; Hinds (1987a) 28–9, and compare too what is said in my Chapter 4 about Silvius and Ascanius. In Suet. *Caligula* 11, Denis Feeney reminds me, Tiberius says that Caligula will be Phaethon.

[28] From a vast literature see Lafaye (1904) 219–20 (on the creation), Leach (1974) esp. 115–18, Hinds (1987b) 23–9, Feeney (1991) 192, 198, 230–1, Farrell (1992), Sharrock (1994), Barchiesi (1997), Tissol (1997) *passim* but esp. index s.v. paradox, Zissos and Gildenhard (1999) 167–70 (with further references), Wheeler (1995b) and (1999) esp. 27–30, 162–93, Gibson (1999) esp. 36–7. The Vergilian scholarship cited in Chapter 4 n. 32 is similar.

[29] Feeney (1991) 192, quoting Leach (1974) 104.

We can also see the poet as questioning both points of view; Myers argues that Ovid is "juxtaposing mythological and scientific ways of explaining things throughout his poem," and that he "wished to expose the difficulty of trying to make sense at all of his world through either of these traditional means."[30] Both philosophy and myth are exposed as inadequate or at least based on questionable claims of authority: Ovid seeks to "cast doubt . . . on the power of any poet to explain and perhaps even survive in a universe in which power is ultimately arbitrary and beyond the control of any poets or philosophers, since it rests in the hands of the powers in the heavens and on the Palatine." This reading is attractive, though it is easy to imagine some readers not yet being persuaded. We need to look, of course, at more of the poem.

Variants combined: Phaethon, Ino, and Lycaon

Many attempt to excuse Ovid's numerous discordant or inconsistent passages because of the scale of his poetic task, or by claiming that he was simply indifferent to questions of consistency. But we often see signs that Ovid wishes to flaunt rather than hide his incongruous details, for he furnishes many of them with cross-references that invite the reader to focus on the problem; to paraphrase Seneca *Contr.* 2.2.12 and apply it to different phenomena, Ovid was not ignorant of, but cherished, some of his inconsistencies. Some of these occur in the three episodes discussed in this section, which exhibit different kinds of inconsistencies, one temporal, one involving goals and motivation, and one in a quoted narrative that is arguably deceptive. Each episode seems to suggest that more than one version of a story has been combined into a complicated and not fully harmonious whole.

The Phaethon narrative is one of several in Book 2 that present chronological problems; the others will be discussed in more detail below, but the Phaethon story belongs here because it gives the impression that variants are being combined. After Phaethon's fall, his mother traverses the whole world (2.335), then his sisters grieve for four months (*luna quater iunctis inplerat cornibus orbem*, 344), and then his uncle Cycnus becomes a swan. Then, with a casual "meanwhile" (*interea*, 381) Ovid seems to return to the immediate aftermath of the fall, with the Sun ending his work-stoppage (cf. 330–1, 394–7), and gaining control of his horses, which are "still mindless and

[30] Myers (1994) 57, 136.

terrified" (398), as though Phaethon's ride had concluded recently, and not over four months earlier. Ovid has either leapt back in time without telling us, or has combined "competing variants" of the story, so that "narrative 'reality' seems to be torn."[31]

The tale of Juno's revenge on Ino in 4.416–562 was the focus of one of the first studies to point with approval rather than censure to Ovid's fondness for incongruous or incompatible details.[32] In his picture of the Furies in the underworld, for example, some details stress their fearsome aspect, but others defuse any fear, like the domestic notion of them combing their hair-like snakes. The same is true of the overall structure and development of the tale. The beginning of the episode says that Juno's goal is to afflict Ino with a Bacchic frenzy (420–31), but when her agent Tisiphone goes after Ino and her husband Athamas, the madness of Athamas is what is stressed (512–19). After Athamas has killed one child and Ino grabs the other and runs off madly (*male sana*), Ovid suddenly becomes a less than omniscient narrator, uncertain whether she has been maddened by Tisiphone's poison, or is simply moved by maternal pain, as any mother would be at the murder of a child by her husband (***seu** dolor hoc fecit **seu** sparsum causa venenum*, 520).[33] Alternatives introduced by *seu . . . seu* are a familiar Ovidian technique, but for Ino to be moved only by maternal *dolor* would contradict the notion that she has been poisoned by Tisiphone. Two incompatible versions seem present in the text: one in which Ino is maddened by the Fury and so leaps off the cliff with her child, another in which Ino flees in madness because her husband has killed one child and is trying to kill another.[34] The issue is to some extent whether humans are controlled by divine forces, as at the start of the poem (and of my chapter).

---

[31] Zissos and Gildenhard (1999) 39–42, to whom this paragraph is much indebted; the "competing variants" of which they speak are apparent rather than extant: the text gives the impression that variants have been combined.

[32] Cf. esp. Bernbeck (1967) 14, 16.   [33] For the text of 520 see Kenney (1978) 252.

[34] Another small allusion to variants in the Ino story: Kenney (1980) 178, in a discussion of how Apuleius "exploited contradictions" (178) in the literary tradition about Venus, notes that Ovid's Venus addresses her "uncle" Neptune, the brother of her father Jupiter (4.531–2), but alludes to the tradition that she was born from the foam from the severed genitals of Ouranos/Saturn (4.536–78): "Far from showing himself indifferent to the contradiction (Bömer ad loc.), Ovid wittily exploits it by, in effect, allowing the goddess to correct the more genteel version of her nativity." As Kenney notes, Apuleius refers to Caelus/Ouranos as Venus' father in *AA* 6.6.4, but if Mercury is her brother in 6.7.2, then Jupiter is her father.

The Lycaon story is both the first metamorphosis of an individual in the poem, and also the first of many stories told by an internal narrator, in this case Jupiter, whose reliability as a speaker we saw put in doubt in the previous chapter's discussion of the *Aeneid*. As the first quoted narrative in the poem, the Lycaon episode may well have something to teach us about how to read quoted narratives.[35] What it teaches us may be to be skeptical of story-tellers, even divine ones, especially when their stories involve inconsistencies, which can function, as we have seen in earlier chapters, as a part of the characterization of a speaker.[36] Some inconsistencies undercut the justice of Jupiter's claim that mankind needs to be destroyed. Jupiter says that he visited earth in disguise (213), but that when he came to Arcadia he revealed himself to be a god (220). He claims that mankind must be destroyed utterly (188), but everyone except Lycaon worshiped him piously (220–1). When he destroys Lycaon's house, Lycaon escapes and becomes a wolf, but his household gods are destroyed (230–1); Jupiter's claim that they deserved their fate is unsupported.[37]

On its own terms, then, discrepancies in Jupiter's story undercut his claim to justice (perhaps like some of his statements in the *Aeneid*), but further inconsistencies cast doubt on whether Jupiter is even reporting the facts correctly. What exactly did Lycaon do to make Jupiter want to punish him – and all mankind? The claim that he made an attempt on Jupiter's life (197–8) is given serious Augustan political relevance by the simile citing an attempt on the life of Caesar (199–205). Jupiter's story breaks down, however, when he describes what Lycaon did, for he makes two charges. The first is that while Jupiter slept Lycaon "prepared" to kill him in a surprise attack (*nocte gravem somno necopina perdere morte | me parat: haec illi placet experientia veri*; "at night as I lay heavy with sleep he prepared to surprise and kill me; he had decided on this as a test of the truth," 224–5). The second is that

---

[35] Cf. Winkler (1985) 27–37 on the first quoted narrative in Apuleius' *Golden Ass*; and on Ovid here Rosati (2002) 274.

[36] In Ovid's story of Cephalus and Procris (*Met.* 7.661–865), traces of variant versions may be read as indications that Cephalus is not telling the whole truth about how his wife died: see Otis (1970) 176–80, Mack (1988) 131–4, Ahl (1989) 17–21, and Rosati (2002) 303 n. 73, who notes that 687–8 may be an interpolation, as Tarrant (1995) has argued.

[37] The oddity was enough, Wheeler (1999) 179 notes, to make scholars want to emend *penates* to *ministros*, or dismiss the word *penates* as a content-free metonymy; cf. too Anderson (1997) 97 n. 6.

Lycaon served cooked human flesh to Jupiter (226–9), at which point Jupiter used his lightning. Is this a credible story? Did Lycaon form a plan to kill Jupiter while he slept, but never get a chance to implement it, because during dinner he served human flesh and brought on his wrath? Or did he make an unsuccessful attempt to kill Jupiter while he slept, and then serve human flesh to the curiously patient divinity the next day? Careful consideration of the whole passage may suggest the first alternative, that Lycaon "never actually attempts to kill Jupiter in his sleep; Jupiter says he only *prepared* to do so (1.225, *parat*)."[38] But this is to ignore how the text must unfold to the reader (or audience of gods) encountering the text or story in a linear fashion. When we first read *nocte gravem somno necopina perdere morte | me parat*, it is natural to assume that the object of the verb is indeed asleep, and that Lycaon is on the verge of killing him, not merely that he has jotted it down on his to-do list. Only when we read on to discover the second part of Jupiter's charge might we realize that the plans were more distant than that. Indeed some scholars think that the attempt to kill Jupiter came on the first night, and the meal the next day: we could say that this is wrong, or that they are responding to certain signals in the text, and that others are responding to other signals, in the attempt to fashion a harmonious narrative, to "concretize" the text in a way that makes sense. It is exceedingly generous to Jupiter, however, to construct this harmonious narrative: we might just as easily suggest that Jupiter has combined two incompatible stories, one of Lycaon making an attempt on his life, and one of Lycaon serving him human flesh to eat. An audience might well assume that one or both of the stories is in fact false. "When subjected to close analysis this story does not make very good sense," so Ovid is "representing Jupiter as a clumsy and biased narrator of Lycaon's crime and punishment."[39] In fact we have no credible explanation of what Lycaon has done or why the human race needs to be destroyed. Such is the potential for narrative inconsistencies to create a portrait of an unreliable narrator.

Jupiter figures in two major stories in Book 1, the story of Lycaon, which he tells himself, and the story of Io, which is told by the main narrator. At one point in the Io story, after Jupiter has turned Io into a cow, he must explain the

[38] Wheeler (1999) 179, Anderson (1997) 96, Rosati (2002) 274 and 301; contrast Due (1974) 106 and Lee (1953) 90, who suggest that the meal came the day after the assassination attempt.

[39] Due (1974) 106, Wheeler (1999) 171.

cow to Juno. He lies (*mentitur*, 615).[40] If he lies about Io, should we believe his story of Lycaon?

Genre and inconsistency: Medea, Meleager, Polyphemus

Ovid often engages in extensive simultaneous adaptation of varied sources; his borrowings are characterized by literary comprehensiveness, the use of mythological variants, and the mixing or juxtaposition of material from different genres. We turn here to three examples of comprehensive generic mixing that produces interesting and problematic inconsistencies, as Ovid thinks through interesting aspects of the literary or mythological tradition. Each has recently been the subject of intelligent scholarly comment, which I recontextualize here.

Ovid's typically comprehensive treatment of the Medea tradition in Book 7 includes both a sympathetic portrait of the inexperienced virgin who falls in love with Jason, and several almost comic scenes featuring the formidable witch using magic for murder without remorse.[41] Newlands' fresh approach to the problem of Ovid's dissonant portrait sees the discontinuities as part of a deliberate strategy in which "Ovid invites reflection on the difficulties and dangers involved in the rewriting of myth." Ovid explores the contradictions in the Medea myth in his treatment of the other myths about women that surround his story of Medea (Procne and Philomela, Scylla, Procris, and Orithyia), and

> offers us not one figure but refracted images that vary according to the different perspectives from which the reader is invited to survey them . . . Rejecting organic form in favor of a certain degree of thematic fragmentation and dislocation, Ovid offers us not one canonical Medea but many perspectives on the central idea of the powerful woman.

In Book 8, Ovid's tale of Meleager, Atalanta, and the Caledonian boar hunt similarly yokes together elements from different genres, combining epic or

---

[40] For this famous lover's lie see Maltby (2002) on Tib. 1.4.23–4.

[41] Newlands (1997); cf. Larmour (1990), and on Medea in Apollonius cf. Hunter (1987) and for *Heroides* 12, Hinds (1993), who argues that "the confusion about the Argonauts' route" in that poem should be seen "as a piece of learned contamination rather than as an inept mistake." On character cf. Chapter 1 after n. 21 on Aristotle's comments on Iphigenia. To some extent Vergil's Dido may also be a model for Medea's transformation here.

classical elements with the erotic, which has associations for this story both with Euripides and with Hellenistic poetry.[42] The added erotic element is the way Meleager falls in love with Atalanta at first sight (324–8) and tries to share the spoils with her (426–7), leading to the dispute in which he kills his uncles and incurs his mother's wrath. Here we almost literally have a "clashing" of genres, as epic figures object to Meleager's non-epic behavior (*captus amore*, 435), and violence erupts.[43] When Meleager is dying in a subsequent scene, however, he calls upon various family members, in a way that resembles the list of suppliants at *Iliad* 9, and Ovid produces a choice bit of inconsistent detail: "with a groan he calls upon his aged father and his brothers, and his loyal sisters and the **partner of his bed** . . ." (*grandaevumque patrem fratresque piasque sorores | cum gemitu **sociamque tori** vocat ore supremo . . .*, 520–1). Some have taken *sociam tori* here as a reference to Atalanta, but the pair hardly has had time to become bedmates, and *socia tori* is an epic way of saying "wife," not "new girlfriend."[44] It is more natural to think of the wife Cleopatra who plays such an important role in *Iliad* 9, whom Homer calls παράκοιτις, "bedmate." Commentators either say that "Atalanta is forgotten" or note that the *socia tori* is Cleopatra without mentioning Atalanta. I suggest that Ovid, in combining the love story of Meleager and Atalanta with the version from *Iliad* 9, includes an epic detail in conflict with the erotic aspects of the story, as an acknowledgment that he knows what he is doing in mixing genres.

Ovid's long portrait of the Cyclops in *Met.* 13 and 14 plays with the various genres in which Polyphemus had figured earlier, especially *Odyssey* 9, Theocritus 11, and *Aeneid* 3, as well as the adaptation of Theocritus 11 in

---

[42] Epic or classical elements from *Iliad* 9, and presumably from lost works of Sophocles and others; erotic and/or Hellenistic features from Euripides, Nicander, Accius, and Apollonius (whose Jason excluded Atalanta from the Argonautic expedition "because he feared terrible conflicts for the sake of eros" *Arg.* 1.769–73); see the excellent observation of Segal [1999] 225). On sources see Hollis (1970) 66–9, Segal (1999), and Keith (1999) 223–30; it may seem as though Ovid has added the element of Meleager's love for Atalanta, but Euripides "here (as elsewhere) anticipates Alexandrian motifs" (Segal [1999] 313 n. 36). Cf. also Edmunds (1997) 425–8 on variation in the Meleager story even in the time of Homer.

[43] Segal (1999) 313: "their reproach to Atalanta is the voice of the male-centered epic tradition protesting the intrusion of Alexandrian eroticism."

[44] Cf. Ov. *Am.* 3.6.82 *socii iura dedisse tori*; though see James (2003) 48–9 for the way that elegists play, often with pointed ambiguity, on similar terms for married and unmarried relationships.

Eclogue 2. The Cyclops is thus a creature of epic and pastoral both Greek and Roman, and already the subject of much intertextual work and generic mixing by Theocritus and Vergil.[45] In Ovid's treatment in *Met.* 13 Farrell sees aspects not only of elegiac, pastoral, and epic, but also elegy in all its aspects: erotic, erotodidactic, and plaintive.[46] The crossing or blending of these genres does not produce factual inconsistencies or implausibilities, but Galatea's tale of the Cyclops does work with incongruity and surprise, and perhaps even "deception," as Tissol puts it. The Cyclops, as he sings of his love for Galatea, plays first an elegiac or pastoral role in which his potential for epic violence seems to have been suppressed (*caedis amor feritasque sitisque inmensa cruoris | cessant, et tutae veniuntque abeuntque carinae*, 13.768–9, "his love of slaughter, fierceness, and huge thirst for blood ceased, and ships came and went safely"). But then he sheds the pastoral role and brutally kills Galatea's lover Acis (described in epic fashion as the "Symaethian hero," 878), as "Ovid suddenly introduces stark and gruesome violence at the end" of the story.[47] As with Medea, the incongruity is inherent in the tradition about Polyphemus, and Ovid's treatment draws attention to it rather than suppressing it. A well-known iconographic treatment, the Polyphemus–Galatea landscape from the Villa Boscotrecase, similarly involves the spectator "in the integration of incongruous scenes," for "its images juxtapose two events from the history of Polyphemus as literature has shaped it – one is his pastoral courtship of Galatea, the dramatic situation of Theocritus' eleventh idyll, the other his vengeful stoning of the departing ship of Odysseus, an incident drawn from an epic context."[48] Ovid's story can be said to involve a Bakhtinian "dialogue of genres" in which, from a formal point of view, the episode "draw[s] upon a variety of constituent genres without belonging to any of them, but rather to quite a different genre defined only by its ability to subsume these other forms."[49] The dialogue is a precarious one, however, in keeping with larger trends in the poem, and with the poem's "contrasts between a pluralistic, anti-authoritarian stance[,] and an aggressive, domineering, and, as it were, monologic force" in the poem. In terms of my chapter's concerns, these two types of stances or forces recall the

[45] And perhaps even in Homer, who adds what might seem to be non-epic or even mock-epic touches to his portrayal in *Od.* 9.446–61, and in Philoxenus' lost dithyramb.
[46] Farrell (1992). For related thoughts on Cyclopean intertextuality see Hinds (1998) 111–16, Thomas (1996) 240 = (1999) 26–63, and O'Hara (2001) 379 n. 28.
[47] Tissol (1997) 108–24: 109.   [48] Leach (1988) 339, cited by Tissol (1997) 108–9.
[49] Farrell (1992) 267, from whose next page I quote in my next sentence.

problem of the well-ordered cosmogony and its aftermath as discussed above. Although there is no specific inconsistency here, the move from pastoral and elegiac song to epic violence parallels Medea's move from innocent virgin to murderous witch, and also – to speak in larger terms – the move from the orderly world of the creation to the disorderly world over which Jupiter rules.

As time goes by

Wheeler and others have now convincingly demonstrated that Ovid deliberately creates and then flaunts or calls attention to chronological problems; we have used Wheeler's term "flaunts" above in Chapter Two's discussion of Catullus 64.[50] Rejecting "the bland conclusion that temporal order does not matter in the *Metamorphoses*," Wheeler shows that through such anachronisms Ovid "challenges and reshapes the audience's understanding of time;" the problems serve to "deauthorize any single version of mythological history by opening up alternative possibilities and force the audience to reevaluate its understanding of the poem's narrative."[51] We have mentioned problems in the Phaethon story. In the Callisto story later in *Met.* 2 there are "strong indications that the poet's erratic chronology is a deliberate and self-conscious effect," as Ovid "underscores the chronological contradiction in his narrative," both by providing an aetion for why the Triones never set in the sea (2.528–30) after already mentioning this prohibition earlier (2.171–2), and by thrice calling Callisto the daughter of Lycaon (485, 496, and 526), even though the tradition offered several other choices, and Lycaon's daughter should have died in the flood.[52] Ovid's references to Atlas include the Titan already holding up heaven in the Phaethon story (2.296–7), the king of Hesperia guarding the golden apples until he is petrified by Perseus (4.632, 657–62), Atlas as mountain already in a story told by Perseus (4.772–3, a tale which

---

[50] Earlier scholars had attributed such problems to the unfinished state of the poem, Ovid's carelessness, or the difficulty of handling mythological material; cf. Lafaye (1904) 81–2, Solodow (1988) 29, Granobs (1997) 38–9; Mack (1988) 109–11 instead describes how Ovid "seems to go out of his way to break up continuity."

[51] Wheeler (1999) 121, 128; my debt to Wheeler (1999) 125–39 on chronological problems will be clear; see also Kenney (1986) xxviii–xxix, Zissos and Gildenhard (1999), Feeney (1999), and Rosati (2002) 280–1.

[52] Zissos and Gildenhard (1999) 32, 41; on the effect here cf. also Wheeler (1999) 128–30.

"casts doubt upon Perseus's reliability as a storyteller," or perhaps even suggests "the primary narrator's own unreliability"[53]), a brief reference to the story about Hercules and the apples that Ovid skips by having Perseus petrify Atlas (9.198), and a final ambiguous reference in the speech of Pythagoras (15.149). Wheeler argues that

> The contradictory treatment of Atlas suggests the arbitrariness of the events themselves. Stories are shaped to effect a particular response on a given occasion. Ovid expects these discrepancies to be noticed; they are not to be dismissed as the product of a miscellany of unrelated stories. Nor is the narrator simply displaying his *doctrina* by juxtaposing different mythological traditions about Atlas; rather, he expects his audience to remember and to notice the different constructions of "reality" depending upon who is the narrator. At the level of communication between narrator and narratorial audience, this conflict leads to ambiguity and doubt about what is believable and what is not, which version is authoritative and which is not.[54]

Elsewhere Hercules "dies and is deified in Book 9 (134–272), but Ovid brings him back into the main narrative 1,400 lines later, in connection with Laomedon's Troy (11.212–215)." The Argo is called the first ship (6.721 and 8.302), but we see seafaring both before the flood (1.293ff.) and in the story of Tereus almost immediately before the first mention of the Argo (6.444ff.). In the Calydonian boar hunt, "Ovid introduces Peleus as the father of great Achilles (8.309, *magnique creator Achillis*)," but Peleus' rape of Thetis comes later, in Book 11. Wheeler suggests that

> Ovid deliberately violates his earlier chronological scheme . . . In seeking to create the illusion of chronological continuity, Ovid simultaneously violates the chronological framework that he earlier intimated and makes mythological time circle back on itself. This and other chronological contradictions are not casual. They challenge the participants of the performance to revise their notions about the poem's chronology, to redefine the character of time itself, and to reconsider the purposes to which time is put.

---

[53] Wheeler (1999) 132, 133; note especially that Wheeler's discussion (135) of Atlas as an "ideologically loaded figure" in "the Augustan context" adds special interest to the chronological problems here; see also Rosati (2002) 280–1.

[54] Wheeler (1999) 134.

Chronological incongruities mark the historical period as well; in *Met.* 15, Ovid plays with the tradition that King Numa was a student of Pythagoras, even though it was well known at Rome that this was chronologically impossible.[55] Ovid distances himself from the error here somewhat (cf. *ferunt*, "they say" in 480), but the effect is that he "reminds the audience that it has been listening to a story, not an event that actually occurred."[56]

Origins original and otherwise

The problems with Ovid's references to Atlas can be described either as chronological problems (when did Atlas begin to hold up the heavens?), or as variant aetiologies (how did Atlas come to support the heavens?). Recent work has stressed the way in which major portions of the *Metamorphoses* present themselves as aetiological poetry explaining the origins of things, explaining how things got to be the way they are in the poem's "now." We have seen cases in which Ovid presents more than one explanation for something, most notably the creation of man, and most oddly the two possible reasons for why Ino and her child jumped off a cliff and became sea deities. In terms of both style and content these passages resemble the multiple explanations of cultural practices and especially natural phenomena common in aetiological and didactic poetry.[57] At the same time, appreciation of Ovid's interest in aetiology has gone hand in hand with the claim that like many of the Alexandrians,[58] Ovid undercuts his position as a writer able to give authoritative explanations by calling attention to the fictive, arbitrary, and contingent nature of poetic authority. Multiple explanations of phenomena can be a sign of honest scientific uncertainty, as they often are in Lucretius; we have also seen inconsistency reflecting uncertainty or ambivalence when Lucretius talks about early mankind and when Vergil describes the early Italians. But multiple explanations, like chronological impossibilities, can also serve to

---

[55] Wheeler (1999) 127, Feeney (1999) 22–4, Myers (1994) 136–7, Barchiesi (2001) 63 and 71.

[56] Wheeler (1999) 128.

[57] Myers (1994) 140, 153–4 and *passim*, Tissol (1997) 191. On Ovid's fondness for multiple etymologies, see O'Hara (1996c), and for his "variant aetiologies," esp. in the *Fasti*, see the scholars cited there at 266 n. 33.

[58] Cf. Goldhill (1986), Depew (1993), Haslam (1993), Lüddecke (1998), as well as my Chapters 1 (the final section on Alexandrian poets) and 2 (on Catullus 64). Cf. too the review of O'Hara (1996a) by Bleisch (1998).

undercut the authority of a speaker describing the world through an aetiological approach, especially when the manner of presentation pushes the reader towards skepticism or doubt. Skepticism or doubt is encouraged particularly when aetiology incorporates irreconcilable mythological variants, so that multiple, mutually exclusive explanations are offered for the same phenomenon. Here Ovid's comprehensiveness, seen above in his fondness for including all types of stories about Medea or Polyphemus or Meleager, becomes an inclusiveness that welcomes all variants of a particular story. These variants would be perfectly at home in a scholarly catalogue of admittedly literary constructs, but make a different impression when presented as part of a poetic world that keeps teasing the reader with the pretense of making sense as a consistent whole.[59]

Several examples may be briefly mentioned. Ovid gives a full version of how Aeolus' daughter Alcyone became the bird called alcyone or kingfisher (11.410–748), but also alludes briefly to the rare version in which it is Sciron's daughter who becomes the kingfisher (7.401). Anius tells how his daughters became doves (13.644–74); Ovid also alludes briefly to the story of how Semiramis became a dove (4.47). More prominently, three men named Cycnus are turned into swans: Cycnus son of Sthenelus in 2.377–80, the son of Hyrie and Apollo in 7.371–80, and the invulnerable son of Neptune in 12.64–145. Myers suggests that these "three different versions in the poem of Cycnus' transformation . . . stand as a sort of leitmotif for Ovid's treatment of this mythical material for which no 'true' version ever was considered to exist."[60] These variants are one reason for thinking that Ovid "ultimately is more interested in drawing attention to the narrative strategies traditionally employed to create authentication and verisimilitude than in maintaining his own authority." A literal-minded reader could perhaps counter that none of

---

[59] Tarrant (1995) 106 shows that Ovid sometimes "calls attention to a detail or to an entire version of a story that he has rejected by incorporating it into his own narrative," often in the form of a rejection of the alternate version, as at 10.60–1, when he says that Eurydice has nothing to complain about despite the complaints in Verg. *Geo.* 4.494–8, or in the stories of Pygmalion in *Met.* 10 or Byblis in *Met.* 9; Tarrant promises a "larger discussion of 'untold stories.'" My earlier chapters have cited this practice in Homer (as described by Herodotus 2.116), Pindar, tragedians, the Alexandrians and Vergil. At *Met.* 13.145 Odysseus denies the variant paternity story that Ajax has mentioned in 13.26; Ovid makes use of both variants, but without (here) disturbing anyone's sense of reality. In a similar way Theseus can be both the reputed son of the mortal Aegeus (8.174, 405, 560) and the son of Neptune (9.1).

[60] Myers (1994) 158.

these is actually presented in Ovid's text as being the origin of a bird that did not exist before. Lafaye suggested that each legend pleased Ovid and so he treated it, and that the long interval between treatments suggests we are not meant to compare or worry about them – they would "demand inattention," in Scodel's terms.[61] This view, however, ignores the way in which Ovid calls attention to the multiple swan metamorphoses at one point by saying that in 12.580–2 Neptune grieves that his son Cycnus has been turned into the "Phaethontid bird," i.e. into a swan just like the relative of Phaethon in Book 2.

Ovid's two stories of the hyacinth flower are linked in a similar way. When both Hyacinthus, the doomed beloved of Apollo, and the blood of the suicidal hero Ajax turn into the hyacinth flower, Ovid provides explicit cross-references. Hyacinthus dies in Book 10, and a flower grows, and the apparent letters AI on the flower are said to spell out Apollo's cry of woe as he laments Hyacinthus. But Apollo at this time also predicts Ajax's death: "that time will come, when the bravest hero will add himself to this flower and be read on the same leaf" (*tempus et illud erit, quo se fortissimus heros | addat in hunc florem folioque legatur eodem*, 10.207–8). In Book 13, Ajax's blood causes the hyacinth to grow – the hyacinth that was born from the wound of the "Oebalian" Hyacinth (*Oebalio . . . de vulnere*, 396) – and the letters inscribed in the plant are now ambiguous, referring both to Apollo's lament for Hyacinth and to the name Ajax: *littera communis mediis pueroque viroque | inscripta est foliis, haec nominis, illa querelae* ("letters common to the boy and the man – to the name of the latter and the lament for the former – are written on the inner leaves," 13.397–8). It is hard to say with confidence what is being said in these passages. The commentators' suggestion that *se . . . addat in hunc florem* in 10.207–8 is equivalent to "be changed into the same flower" tames Ovid too much; Ajax literally will "add himself to this flower," so that he "is read on the same leaf." Something odd is going on here, so odd that Hill endorses a nineteenth-century suggestion to excise 207–8.[62] This cross-reference resembles the details we have seen earlier, which call attention to, rather than "demand inattention" for, Ovid's inconsistencies.

---

[61] Lafaye (1904) 70–5, 81 (with many of the examples I cite); for Scodel see Chapter 1.

[62] Cf. Haupt, Ewald, von Albrecht (1966), Bömer (1980), Hill (1999); and on Hyacinthus cf. now Janan (1988). The appearance in Verg. *Ecl.* 3.106–7 of the inscribed hyacinth as the likely solution to a riddle means that it may have been a well-known topic of scholarly debate; cf. Clausen (1994) ad loc.

The problem of the "pseudo-scientific"

We must step back now and consider the effect of this kind of writing. It seems clear that as in his proem, cosmology, genre-mixing and chronology, Ovid works to create and then call attention to these problems in his aetiological passages. Does this kind of flaunting of multiple aetiology undercut the authority of any aetion? Or are we moderns misreading, and underestimating the ancient ability to think of multiple explanations or aetia (or etymologies) as being both or all true? Even in the case of the swan, however, for which I have mentioned a method of explaining away the problem, we have brought up a difficult question: how many of Ovid's metamorphoses actually do offer aetiological explanations of what we see today? Only those when he explicitly says "this story explains how such-and-such came to be" or "and this is why even now . . ."? Or is this true of some or all of the others as well? To examine the question adds to the uncertainty: is Lycaon the first wolf? How can he run with the (other?) wolves later (after surviving the flood, of course), in 2.495? Are these really aetia? When someone turns into an animal or a plant, is that really the origin of the plant? Or does the person turn into an animal or plant that already existed? Do we need to be told by the text? If this question is one that we should not worry about, is it not features of the text described above that have led to the questions?

What we are dealing with, at its heart, is the problem of the "pseudo-scientific," to cite a term used several times by Myers in her discussions of the interplay of the philosophic and scientific with the poetic and the mythological in the *Metamorphoses*. At one point she argues that "The aetiological focus of Ovid's mythological stories actively engages with and challenges the claims of Lucretius' cosmological epic to explain the world."[63] But she also observes that "in both the *Argonautica* and the *Metamorphoses* we can see aetiology creating an ironic contrast between the authoritative 'scientific' voice of the aetiological narrator and the fantastic mythical material of his poetry." She shows that

> The pseudo-scientific handling of myth which aetiology represents pro-
> vided Callimachus and Apollonius with a voice of scholarly authority and
> the credentials of the traditional cosmological poet. Ovid understood this,
> and in his own *Metamorphoses* and *Fasti* he combines aetiological and

[63] Myers (1994) 54–5. The notion of "pseudo-statements" goes back to Richards (1970, repr. of 1926); cf. Fish (1980) 54–7, Martindale (2005) 184–5, with further references.

"scientific" approaches in his own exploration of the creation of narrative credibility and of the "vatic" voice.

We have mentioned already Myers' ultimate conclusion that Ovid seeks to "cast doubt . . . on the power of any poet to explain and perhaps even survive in a universe in which power is ultimately arbitrary and beyond the control of any poets or philosophers . . ." The difficult challenge that such a reading proposes is to pinpoint the level at which Ovid's presentation stops being "pseudo-." Is Ovid at the start of the poem a cosmologist or a pseudo-cosmologist? This is not the most difficult question. When he implies that his poem can explain the way things are, is he being a pseudo-aetiologist? The questions get harder as we move along. Myers would reject "a purely ludic or programmatic reading of this poem" because it "ignores the multiplicity of meanings and the deep psychological insights that Ovid's mythical stories convey."[64] But how do we know Ovid is not also being a pseudo-psychologist, pseudo-conveyor of thematic meaning, pseudo-protestor against violence or rape or suffering? I began the chapter by noting that scholars and readers have been receptive to the idea of an inconsistent *Metamorphoses*, but I am not sure that we have fully confronted all the ramifications of this idea. If Ovid undercuts his own poetic authority, as well as that of Lucretius or Vergil, the position of the critic becomes extremely difficult. It is hard for even Myers to escape this problem: in her "Epilogue" she argues that Ovid expresses confidence about his own claim to immortality in the last line of the poem (*siquid habent veri vatum praesagia, vivam*, "if the predictions of the prophet-priests are true at all, I shall live," 15.879), even though she has argued throughout the book that the poem continually calls into question poetry's truth claims – and I would add that the truth claims of prophecy are often on very shaky grounds.[65] I raise this point not to criticize Myers, to whom this chapter has been much

---

[64] Myers (1994) 25.

[65] As one reviewer noted: Wheeler (1995c). Some perspective on this problem may be gained by considering similar difficulties that dog analogous claims in a 1993 study of Horace's *Satires*. Zetzel (1980) had called attention to inconsistencies within Horace's first book of *Satires*, and to "the contradictory structures of the book, its creation of a unified sense of disorder, of a speaker who is consistent only in his lack of logic and consistency." Freudenburg (1993) developed these ideas further, but perhaps without fully confronting the way that his ideas about Horace's inconsistencies complicate assessment of the programmatic message also delivered by that same speaker, as some reviewers have noted: cf. Lowrie (1993): "How do we understand the literary criticism through the mask, what are the limits to the parodied persona?"

indebted, but to stress the elusiveness and difficulty of this poet and poem: "Ovid refuses to be pinned down, to yield to interpretive stability, although his readers may crave it."[66]

The poet and the anger of Jupiter

I have mentioned the last line of the *Metamorphoses*, and will end here with consideration of the poem's last 135 lines, which means that this chapter, like the previous one, will end with brief words about Jupiter. Before Ovid's nine-line epilogue, the last episode of the poem describes the death and deification of Julius Caesar (745–870), as Ovid "recreates the atmospherics of the Lycaon story" from Book 1, in which an attempted assassination of Jupiter was linked to plots against Caesar, as we saw above.[67] The episode ends with the words first of Jupiter, then of the narrator. We hear first a prophecy from Jupiter to Venus (807–42) that complements the speech of Jupiter to Venus in *Aeneid* 1 discussed in my last chapter. Then we hear the narrator's own words about Augustus, which include an explicit comparison linking Augustus to Jupiter, as two sons greater than their fathers (858–60):

> sic et Saturnus minor est Iove: Iuppiter arces
> temperat aetherias et mundi regna triformis,
> terra sub Augusto est; pater est et rector uterque.

> So too Saturn is less great than Jove: Jupiter controls
> the heavenly citadels and the kingdoms of the tri-part world,
> the land is under Augustus; each is a father and a ruler.

The link is strengthened in the prayer that follows, which asks the gods and especially Jupiter to delay the day on which Augustus will leave behind the earth and take his place in the heavens (861–70).

These words about Jupiter and Augustus are then followed by the start of Ovid's epilogue, in which he claims that his poetry will outlast any threats (871–2):

> Iamque opus exegi, quod nec Iovis ira nec ignis
> nec poterit ferrum nec edax abolere vetustas.

> Now I have completed a work, which neither the anger of Jove
> Nor fire nor the sword nor devouring time will be able to destroy.

---

[66] Tissol (2002) 310.   [67] White (2002) 14.

Suddenly now the "anger of Jupiter" is a danger to the poet's work, just as it had been a danger to the world Jupiter drenched with flood in the story of Lycaon. We cannot know whether this is a passage written or re-written after Ovid was exiled by Augustus,[68] or fortuitously written in such a way as to take on a special resonance after the exile, a resonance Ovid himself encourages with his insistence in *Tristia* 1.1 and 1.7 that we read the *Metamorphoses* in the light of his banishment.[69] But the change in attitude towards Jupiter and by implication Augustus, at least of the surface meaning of the lines, when we move from 858–70 to 871–2, is indeed a "shock;" this is a striking and challenging inconsistency.[70] Some have attempted to dismiss the problem: Galinsky criticizes "the case for the identification of Jupiter with Augustus in 15.871," arguing that although the link between Jupiter and Augustus is clear in 857–60 and in other Augustan texts, "in line 866, however," when Ovid prays to Jupiter to delay Augustus' apotheosis, "Ovid discontinues this analogy."[71] This reading seems to have won few adherents, but this type of reading, in which it is granted that a poet may "discontinue" an analogy at will and expect each of his readers to snap smartly into line, is still common. But the instability of "the comparison of man with god" is one that is not easily dismissed,[72] as we saw in the last chapter's discussion of the association of Aeneas with Jupiter. Here in Ovid, as there in the *Aeneid*, we see the reminder that Jupiter ended the Saturnian Age. And the remarkable words in Jupiter's speech about the deification of Julius by the Senate can be read as sincere praise by Ovid, as sardonic reference to fraudulent piety in the service of politics, or as a neutral description of the changes that have taken place in Roman conceptions of divinity in the Augustan age, open to being read in different ways.[73] On the other hand, it is probably illegitimate to seize upon *Iovis ira* as the key to Ovid's "true" feelings, and dismiss the several passages in which the poem seems explicitly to align itself with Augustan ideology. Ovid presents numerous reasons for doubting or at least not worshiping the Olympian gods who seem to be in control of the world of the poem, but Wheeler has shown how Ovid also repeatedly and with great emphasis dramatizes the dire dangers of disbelief in or resistance to the gods,

---

[68] Kovacs (1987).   [69] Wheeler (1999) 194–5, Hinds (1985) and (1999).

[70] For "shock" see Segal (1969) 290–2.   [71] Galinsky (1975) 254.

[72] Cf. Feeney (1991) 221 on Ovid, Fowler (2000a) 120 and 174 on the slipperiness of intertextual associations for leaders; see above, Chapter 4 n. 64.

[73] See Feeney (1991) 210–24, Barchiesi (1997), Hardie (1997b), Wheeler (1999) 194–5.

so that the poem may at once be said to be both subversive and curiously anti-subversive.[74] Neither the position that Ovid is an Augustan loyalist, nor the contrary view that Ovid's poem is thoroughly anti-Augustan, can be defended with great confidence. We should not underestimate the difficulty of pinning down the politics of the *Metamorphoses*, or of the *Aeneid*, or, as we move now to a brief concluding chapter, of Lucan's *Bellum Civile*.

[74] See esp. Wheeler (1999) 162–93, "The Danger of Disbelief."

Postscript: Lucan's *Bellum Civile* and the inconsistent Roman epic

Thirty-five years ago Froma Zeitlin's study of Petronius' *Satyricon* argued that "Petronius sees the world as irrational, confused, and illusory," and that the incongruities of his novel are "integral emblems of a world-view that expresses a consistent vision of disintegration." When she wanted to find another ancient author to whom her Petronius could be compared, Zeitlin had to reach back five centuries to name Euripides and his "chaotic contemporary world."[1] Today, and especially I hope after the last five chapters, we can see that changes in the way that scholars approach Greek and especially Latin poetry have meant that it is not so hard to find authors who see the world as "irrational, confused, and illusory."[2] Within Petronius' own period, of course, such a description fits many scholars' view of the Neronian poet Lucan, especially among those who have stressed the "fractured" or disunified aspects of the *Bellum Civile*.[3]

What these pages will briefly suggest is that Lucan's epic has much in common not only with Petronius' novel, but also with the work of the Roman epic poets who preceded him, and so the question of whether and to what purpose Lucan might be "fractured" or disunified must be approached in the context of their practice. Lucan's epic, for all its revolutionary novelty,

---

[1] Zeitlin (1971) 633 = (1999) 3; (1971) 676–80 = (1999) 42–6.

[2] Again I note, as I did in my Introduction, that a larger study than mine could have included more on the traditions and influence of non-epic Roman poetry regarding inconsistency.

[3] Henderson (1998, originally 1988), Masters (1992) and (1994), Feeney (1991), Hinds (1987b) and (1998); more detailed citations below.

stands in a tradition which features Catullus 64 (with its professed admiration for the heroic age and numerous hints that such admiration is misplaced), Lucretius' *De Rerum Natura* (which plays with inconsistency, and often looks at issues at least temporarily through the eyes of a resisting reader), Vergil's *Aeneid* (which at times blurs sympathies in its version of a civil war, and puts a variety of voices before the reader), and Ovid's *Metamorphoses* (which offers multiple theories about whether the world is orderly or disorderly, and a shifting amalgam of genres, time-frames, and claims for origins). Even Vergil's *Georgics* (whose opening speculation on Augustus' future apotheosis is one model for Lucan's encomium of Nero) is a poem often "at war with itself," to cite again the suggestive formulation of Masters and Henderson on Lucan that my Chapter Four also applied to Vergil. To look beyond Lucan in the epic tradition for a moment: Zissos (1999) has shown that Valerius Flaccus' *Argonautica* alludes or refers to details of the Argonautic myth not consistent with his own version of the story – often the version Apollonius had followed. The influence of Ovid on Lucan in this respect has not been neglected; the *Metamorphoses* have long been cited as precedent for Lucan's tendency for episodic, loosely unified structure.[4] But Lucan's inconsistency has never been fully contextualized.

This concluding chapter on Lucan is short, both for considerations of space, and because of my conviction that those who have read the preceding chapters and know the text of Lucan should be able to write this chapter themselves, so that extended arguments about Lucan would largely reprise what I have said earlier about Vergil and Ovid. The chapter will look at Lucan to some extent, but will also look back at earlier chapters to pull together some of what we have learned about inconsistencies in Roman epic.

Poet and princeps again

As in earlier chapters, we begin at the start of the epic, but this time, we will not get very far into the poem. Lucan's *Bellum Civile* opens by announcing that its theme is to be civil war; thirty-three lines into the poem comes an encomium of the emperor Nero (1.33–66). Lucan says that the civil wars were worth it, if there was no other way for Nero to come: *quod si non aliam venturo fata Neroni | invenere viam* ... (33–4). Romans "have no complaints, O gods;

---

[4] Quint (1993) 140, citing Williams (1978) 248ff. For Ovid's influence on Lucan more generally see the extensive references in Wheeler (2002).

the unspeakable crimes themselves are an acceptable bargain for this," *iam nihil, o superi, querimur; scelera ipsa nefasque | hac mercede placent . . .* (37–8). In 45–62, he speculates on the site of Nero's future apotheosis, and where his reign (*regnum*) should be: *ubi regnum ponere mundi* (52). In 63–6 he says that Nero is sufficient inspiration for his Roman song: *tu satis ad vires Romana in carmina dandas* (66).

Scholars have long noted that this praise of Nero is in conflict with the praise given later in the poem to Brutus the assassin of Julius Caesar, and with the condemnation of slavish acquiescence to tyrannical one-man rule (*regnum*), in such passages as 7.442–7, where Lucan says *sors ultima nostra est, | quos servire pudet* (444), "our fate is the worst, for we are ashamed to be slaves," and 7.638–46, where he complains, *quid meruere nepotes | in regnum nasci*? 642–3, "what have their descendants done to deserve to be born into *regnum*?"

What are we to make of this discrepancy, which Fantham has called "the biggest dilemma in considering the *De Bello Civili*?"[5] For Lucan, we can again, as in the treatment in Chapter Three of the start of the *De Rerum Natura*, adapt the terminology of Homeric criticism: it has been possible to pursue Separatist or Unitarian solutions to this problem, to give us two options. Option One is to separate Book 1 from Book 7, and therefore account for the inconsistency, because of the story in the biographical tradition that Lucan published only three books of the poem before falling out of favor with Nero, and then dying at the age of twenty-five. The encomium thus would predate Lucan's hostility to Nero, and his death made him unable to fix the inconsistency (like Vergil, or Lucretius, and perhaps Catullus and the exiled Ovid). Lucan's epic is the most clearly incomplete of all the poems studied in this book (although there is an attractive argument that the present ending works, whether deliberate or not[6]), and so this explanation may be right. But this explanation is neither necessary nor satisfying, and it even seems possible that the biographical tradition about three books, which as Masters points out bears a curious similarity to the story in the life of Vergil

---

[5] Fantham (1992) 13. Cf. Ahl (1976) 17–61, esp. 47–9, Hinds (1987b) 4–31, esp. 28–31 and (1998) 86–8, Johnson (1987) 121–2, Masters (1992) 136–7, Dewar (1994), Rudich (1997) 113–17.

[6] Henderson (1998) 170–1, Masters (1992) 216–59, Connors (1994), Sklenár (2003) 148 n. 66. Cf. (again, as in Chapter 4) Ahl and Roisman (1996) 16 on the "escape hatch for the critic of the *Aeneid* or the *Pharsalia*" created by the death of Vergil and Lucan with the poems "left unrevised."

about *his* reading three books publicly, was invented partly to account for the inconsistency.[7]

Option Two, the Unitarian view, is to explain away the problem, by following the scholia in seeing irony in the encomium, and sneakily clever insults of the squinting, fat, balding Nero. In lines 55, *obliquo sidere* can be taken as a reference to Nero's squinty eyes, then the references to *onus* and *pondera* in 57 as jokes about Nero's ample girth, and the mention of a clear, cloudless sky (58–9) as a reference to his losing his hair. We can also perhaps see an uncomplimentary allusion to Phaethon's disastrous chariot ride in the reference to climbing into the chariot of Apollo (48) and the assurance that the world would not need to fear any "wandering flame" (*igne vago*, 50) if Nero were to take over the reins.[8] Thus we are able to "Republicanize" the encomium to Nero, and remove the inconsistency, just as some scholars have wanted to "Epicureanize" Lucretius' "Hymn to Venus."

Some of the scholiasts' suggestions are tempting, but not quite all, and Dewar (1994) has argued that Nero probably was not as squinty and fat as the scholia claim. The problem also remains that this supposed irony is easily missed by first-time readers, as even some proponents of the irony theory admit, and so we still have a poem that begins with an encomium of Nero, then later denounces tyranny and the principate.

That Lucan's prologue is either deliberately or at least functionally inconsistent with other parts of the poem was argued a while ago in two unpublished dissertations, one by Kepple, who says that "Lucan intended the 'encomium' to be read as a statement of the ideology he wrote the *Bellum Civile* to attack" (this is a very stable and intentionalist view of inconsistency), and one by Barton, who posited a more radical and indeterminate inconsistency in both Seneca and Lucan.[9] More recently Hinds (1998) suggests, in words that resemble Zeitlin's claims about Petronius, that the inconsistency of the praise of Nero with what comes later in the poem can be read productively: "The world of Lucanian epic is a world in which failures of aesthetic and moral consistency are inevitable; and that is precisely Lucan's point." Both Hinds and to an extent Dewar note that regardless of Lucan's intention and goals when he originally wrote 1.33–66, it is possible that either deliberately

---

[7] Masters (1992) 220–1.

[8] For Phaethon see Hinds (1987b) 28–31 (with specific links between Lucan's allusion to Phaethon and Ovid's version of the Phaethon myth in *Met.* 1–2), Dewar (1994) 211.

[9] Kepple (1980) – I have seen only the summary in Kepple (1981); Barton (1984).

or through naturally following his goals in other parts of the poem he offers a "recantation" (Dewar) or "recontextualization" (Hinds) of the encomium to Nero.[10] In the simplest terms: if you write an encomium of the current emperor in your first book, and then write a denunciation of your age's enslavement to the principate in a later book, and then go to bed that night with the two parts of your poem in conflict like this, you have chosen to produce an inconsistent poem.

The broader picture: Hinds' 1998 discussion, which revisits a passage he had discussed in 1987, comes in the wake of work on Lucan by Henderson and Masters and Feeney and others, which has offered *largely* convincing arguments in support of the view that Lucan is often deliberately inconsistent elsewhere in the poem. Masters shows that the clash between Lucan's professed sympathy for the Republican cause and his apparent attraction towards his poem's exciting villains Erictho and Caesar (which is much stronger, I would suggest, than the grudging admiration for the "villain" found in many Roman works) produces a disunified work with a "fractured" narrative voice. "In spite of the fact that L[ucan]'s violence, his perversity, his savage manipulation of the epic genre marks him clearly as a 'Caesarian' type of poet . . . none the less we must take seriously [his] claim to be a Pompeian. . ." The result is that in this poem about Roman civil war, "Lucan is at war with himself." Feeney demonstrates the "uncertainty" of the poem's "confrontation between the Stoic dispensation and a non-teleological randomness," in which the "ignorant narrator," like the characters in the poem, cannot "understand whether the catastrophe of the poem is the will of the gods or simply haphazard accident." Earlier Johnson had anticipated some of these ideas to some extent, but credited Lucan's inconsistency to his youthful if serendipitous lack of "control."[11]

These scholars have presented extremely attractive insights into Lucan, but with perhaps insufficient reflection on the extent to which this way of reading Latin poetry represents a break with earlier methods, and perhaps

---

[10] Hinds (1998) 88 n. 76 (he continues: "The best commentary on the praise of Nero may be the very denunciation of Caesarism later in the poem which has seemed to many to be so irreconcilable with it [7.454–9]"), Dewar (1994) 210; on first and subsequent readings see also Feeney (1991) 298 and my Chapter 3 n. 16.

[11] Masters (1992) 214–15 (see my review, O'Hara [1993a]), Feeney (1991) 278–81, Johnson (1987) 3; related to this work, but hostile to it, are Rudich (1997), which attributes the poem's "numerous inconsistencies" to Lucan's (and the age's) "rhetoricized mentality," and Narducci (1999) 71 (commenting on his own earlier work).

inadequate arguments about why older views should be abandoned.[12] Given scholarly reaction to their work, I would say that they are at the same time both right and not fully convincing. Consideration of two books resistant to this trend in scholarship on Lucan will provide an opportunity to review some issues that have come up repeatedly in this book, in ways that I hope will reinforce both that trend in work on Lucan, and what I have done in my earlier chapters.

All the king's horses

Two 1997 books, by Matthew Leigh and Shadi Bartsch, strive valiantly to resolve the ambiguity in Lucan's attitude toward Caesar and Nero and the principate, and restore a dependably Republican poet; I have heard these attempts to put Lucan "back together again" referred to as the "Republic Strikes Back" approach.

Part of Leigh's method is to examine passages where scholars have said the surface commitment to Republicanism is undercut by features of the text that make Caesar's side seem sympathetic, or attractive to the poet.[13] Leigh finds in these passages "traces" of another view (cf. e.g. 56), which undercuts the "superficial" (54) pro-Caesarian aspects which had allegedly undercut the pro-Republican surface of the text. These traces reveal to the discerning (Republican) reader the flaws of Caesarism, so that the subversive readings of Henderson and Masters are themselves subverted, and the surface Republicanism is restored. This is a brilliant argument, in some ways, because it takes one of the tools of deconstructive or post-structuralist readings – finding the "traces" of another meaning – and uses it against a deconstructive or indeterminate reading. But the argument is ultimately unsuccessful, in part because one cannot use the enemy's tools without becoming like the enemy, without admitting that the enemy's methods and way of looking at the world are partly right. When an attractive argument has been made that a surface or primary meaning of a text is challenged or undercut by a subversive subtext, the counterargument that the subversive subtext itself contains "traces" of the primary or surface meaning is interesting, but it does not serve to re-establish the stable reliability of the surface meaning. This counterargument does show

---

[12] Cf. the scorn of some European scholars for "post-modern" or deconstructionist approaches to Lucan: Rudich (1997) 107–8; Narducci (1999).

[13] O'Hara (1999) is a review of Leigh (1997); I do not repeat much of what I said there.

the weaknesses of both smug insistence on the subtext, and also comfortable reliance on the surface meaning. It may also destabilize notions of primary and secondary meaning. But it cannot be used to bring us back to a pristine view of the surface meaning as the only legitimate meaning.

Leigh argues that readers are invited to share the Caesarian viewpoint at times, but only with complete confidence (on the part of Lucan, as well as Leigh) that readers will be led inevitably to realization of the weaknesses and ultimate unsuitability of that viewpoint, and will find it disturbing, disgusting, unsatisfactory. The method bears some similarity to that attributed to Lucretius, who we saw in Chapter Three is now thought by many to look first at some issues through the eyes of a traditional Roman reader, before trying to move the reader towards his Epicurean views. But Leigh's confidence that all Roman readers would respond in exactly the way his Lucan wants them to seems misplaced, both on literary and on historical grounds. As earlier chapters have argued, an author cannot expect every member of an audience to respond in exactly the same way to subtle clues and direction.[14] And historically, if there were not a good number of Romans who would react favorably or at least with ambivalent admiration to the depiction of naked power and its exploitation, then Roman history would have been rather different.

Leigh does dramatize what it means to make a choice when reading. At times his book presents itself as an attempt to imagine what a "Republican reading" of the text would be like (e.g. 63, "the stance of an unreconciled Republican malcontent"), but more often he proceeds as though that Republican reading were the only possible, correct meaning; in a sense, like many of us today, he is caught between methodologies, using both traditional and newer ways of constructing arguments. Many of the arguments presented in my preceding five chapters involve making choices when reading, and I hope I have acknowledged that, even when I outline differing responses, I have been making choices. But this book has argued for making choices *while*, and not *before*, reading.

Bartsch's book on Lucan is also both brilliant and ultimately unconvincing. The first half of her study both summarizes and adds ammunition to the readings of Masters and Henderson, which suggest that Lucan's text is at war with itself. But then the second half suggests that even though the

---

[14] Cf. too Hinds (1998) 46: "the ideal of the reader who sees exactly the same cues within the topos as the author, and constructs them in the same order and in the same way, will always in the final analysis be unattainable."

poem has also firmly established the flaws of Pompey and the futility of the Republican cause, still the narrator and the poet and the poem eventually come down firmly on the side of Pompey and the Republican cause. Her solution leans heavily on the biographical tradition that Lucan was a leader of the conspiracy against Nero, and on Rorty's idea of the modern moral ironist, which leads her to make Lucan a kind of political ironist: "Where Rorty suggests the coexistence of ethical commitment and ethical ironism as the unlikely bedmates of the modern intellectual, Lucan instead seems to enact the coexistence of political cynicism and despair with political commitment and fervor even in the face of the deadlock of upper-class myths of power lost" (102). If I could put that in simpler terms, it would be that the pro-Pompeian position of the narrator is simultaneously both undercut and recommended, but that the recommendation outweighs the undercutting, so that Pompeian Republicanism is being firmly recommended. Like Leigh's argument, this is admirably nimble, but ultimately very hard to accept. To mention Petronius one more time: the year before Bartsch's and Leigh's books appeared, Conte's study of Petronius argued that the position of Encolpius, the narrator of the *Satyricon*, is consistently undercut by the "hidden author" so that he appears to be a fool caught up in delusional views about how his life relates to that of mythic or literary models (Conte 1996). Conte's argument can be resisted somewhat, so that Encolpius remains at least partly attractive or enviable, but surely he is not being held up as a model whom the reader is urged fervently to emulate. The views of the "hidden author" of the *Bellum Civile* are even more elusive than are those of the author of the *Satyricon*; the choice to remain an adherent of Pompey or Cato despite how they are portrayed in the poem may be one that the text *allows*, but it is not something the text demands.

Ultimately I would say that so far the case for Lucan being fractured is looking pretty good, and the attempts to put him back together again have not worked. One key is that no one, to my knowledge, has successfully refuted Masters' metapoetic argument that the poet or speaker seems attracted to Caesar's accomplishments in part because they are like his own. Leigh and more recently Sklenár have made valiant attempts to stress the negative aspects of every mention of Caesar.[15] But they have not successfully refuted

---

[15] The claim of Sklenár (2003) that Lucan is a complete nihilist with no political position seems to me not actually to be a necessary conclusion to his book's fine close readings of numerous passages in the poem.

the claim that the revolutionary accomplishments of Caesar in politics can easily be seen as analogous to those of the iconoclastic poet who produced the *Bellum Civile*. This potential identification between poet and "villain" is similar to the problem discussed briefly in Chapter One, as Plato worried about the effects of poetic depictions of lesser or wicked men – in fact about the identification between rhapsode and character. This identification also dovetails well with the depiction of a flawed or at least unappealing Cato (a somewhat subjective judgment, to be sure) and especially of a flawed Pompey. It seems clear that different readers or even readers of different sections of the poem can feel drawn to Caesar, Pompey, Cato, or perhaps to none of them.

Appeals continue to be made to biography, and to Tacitus' claim that Lucan was virtually a standard-bearer for the conspiracy against Nero. But like many appeals to biography, this one involves cheating: we decide what we think the poem should be saying, then pretend that the poem says it. My book has been about trying to avoid such "cheating;" not "cheating" is discussed in Chapters Two and Three and is an implicit goal of Four and Five (see too more explicitly O'Hara 2005). I have been trying to react to all (or as many as possible) of a work's signals rather than choosing to highlight aspects of a poem that fit one reading and suppressing those that offer conflicting voices.[16] To make Lucan a Republican and a Pompeian, and his poem a Republican poem with Pompey and then Cato as the heroes to be emulated, is to simplify a complex poem on the basis of exiguous biographical evidence. Indeed the poem's attraction to Caesar can even be made compatible with opposition to Nero: Caesar in this poem is a monster, but also an effective revolutionary, who successfully takes arms against a corrupt system and overthrows it. Partial admiration for Caesar is in no way incompatible with taking up arms against the corrupt regime of Nero, even to the extent of knowing that the conspiracy against Nero, like Pompey's opposition to Caesar, if successful would only lead to a different ruler being in charge. We can change one word from *BC* 1.670 to make it fit Lucan's own age: *cum domino mors ista venit* ("along with that death would come a master"). Nero's assassination, the conspirators must have known, would surely lead to the rule of a new emperor.

---

[16] To be sure, I can be accused, as the end of the Vergil chapter acknowledges, of choosing to highlight those aspects of each poem that make it seem inconsistent or indeterminate. But I do not think I have imagined or invented them.

Inconsistency and Roman epic

The suggestions of Masters, Henderson, Hinds and Feeney look more convincing, both because of the failure of these intelligent and energetic attempts to combat them, and in the light of what other Greek and especially Roman poets do with inconsistencies in their poems and especially their epics. And indeed recent scholarship on Lucan resonates with much of what we have seen earlier in this book. Hinds' claim that "failures of aesthetic and moral consistency are inevitable" in the Lucanian world resembles the views not only of Zeitlin, but of scholars discussed in earlier chapters. Homeric scholars speak of "representational inconsistency as a reflection of ideological uncertainty" (Nagler) or "an indeterminacy of both narrative form and character representation" (Katz).[17] This chapter has mentioned Zeitlin's comparison of the "chaotic contemporary world[s]" reflected in Euripides and Petronius. In Goldhill's view, Hellenistic poetry "develops a multiplicity of points of view . . . with no authoritative viewpoint" in part as "a demonstration of the variegated nature of reality as perceived by the Hellenistic poets." Gaisser views Catullus 64 "as a work of competing perspectives whose authority is repeatedly called into question," and we have seen that the games the poet is playing with the narrator and the reader are even more complex than Gaisser showed. Lucan's narrator remains fully committed to the Republican cause, despite the flaws which the poem (and poet) display so clearly – just as the narrator of Catullus 64 remains devoted to the heroic age even as the poem demonstrates the flaws of that world.

Lucretius most often seems to aim at presenting an unambiguous message, but on matters not central to Epicurean doctrine, such as the early history of man, conflicting juxtaposed passages "disclose the poet's explicitly ambivalent conception of the earth's (and humankind's) original state" (Farrell). And Lucretius' epic begins, like Lucan's, with a proem that takes a position quite different from that which will appear later in the epic: Lucretius' "Hymn to Venus" and Lucan's "Praise of Nero," for all their dissimilarities, play similar roles in their poems.

The inconsistencies in Vergil and Ovid are more extensive and arguably more often exploited for thematic purposes, and serve I think to establish

---

[17] Nagler (1990) 231, Katz (1991) 192, both discussed in Chapter 1. The quotations on the next few pages, all discussed in earlier chapters, are from Goldhill (1986) 32–3, Gaisser (1995) 579, Farrell (1994) 88, Wheeler (1999) 33, Feeney (1991) 280.

some degree of inconsistency as the norm for Roman epic. Vergil's most explicitly hopeful and Augustan passages come in the prophecies made by Jupiter and others, but prophecy in the poem is often cast in doubt by inconsistency between prediction and outcome, and the recipient of a prophecy is at times likened to the reader of this ambiguous poem. Allusion to mythological variants at times suggests an alternate version of events, but at other times puts incompatible versions in the same poem. The Vergilian underworld suggests different and incompatible ways of looking at crucial philosophical questions. The depiction of the war in Italy can be read as the triumph of the good Trojans and their allies over Italians opposed to Jupiter's plan, but the varied associations of Trojans and Italians with giants fighting against Jupiter, and of Jupiter as the agent or opponent of the Golden Age, provide as ambivalent a portrait of this (almost civil) war as Lucan offers in the *Bellum Civile*. Near the start of the *Aeneid* comes Jupiter's prophecy to Venus, which some readers have thought "makes possible a correct understanding of the poem from the beginning," but in the *Aeneid* (and as Gale has shown, in the *Georgics*), as in Lucan, the start of a poem is not a reliable indication of the whole poem.

The importance of Ovid's influence on Lucan is well known; it extends to the tradition of using inconsistencies in Roman epic. Like Lucretius, Ovid begins his poem by taking a philosophical position that will quickly be modified. "How does one know on a first reading," Wheeler rightly asks of Ovid's cosmogony, "that Ovid is *not* committed to the orthodox view that he is presenting? Part of his strategy . . . is to win the reader's assent to a comforting picture of the work and then to reform it." Similarly Lucan's depiction (in Feeney's words) of the "confrontation between the Stoic dispensation and a non-teleological randomness," and uncertainty over "whether the catastrophe of the poem is the will of the gods or simply haphazard accident" mirrors and at times even echoes (*fert animus* in *Met.* 1.1 and *BC* 1.67) Ovid's uncertainty over what kind of gods are in charge in his world. The problem of which side to take in Lucan also involves a more extreme problem than the one discussed earlier in our treatment of Ovid's *Metamorphoses*, namely whether the shifting generic and philosophical affiliations of Ovid's poem do not complicate thematic interpretation even more than scholars have acknowledged. Bartsch's idea that the position of the narrator of the *Bellum Civile* is both untenable, and being recommended, strongly resembles (except for her confidence that this conflict is clearly resolved) Wheeler's demonstration, cited at the end of my Ovid chapter, that the *Metamorphoses* shows both that gods are unworthy of respect, and that it is dangerous not to respect them: the poem problematizes both belief and non-belief.

Contrary to Bakhtin's neat formulation in which the novel is polyphonic and epic monologic, mentioned briefly in my introduction, we have seen ample indication that Roman epic regularly features conflicting passages, voices, versions, chronologies, sympathies, ideas, and themes. Readers or scholars may still want to attribute some of these inconsistencies to failures on the part of either the poet or the transmission of his text, but there is no justification for giving priority to this kind of response. At the same time, assuming that every inconsistency in every poem is being used in some brilliantly clever thematic way is also unwarranted. To read better we need to look carefully at the details of each poem, with an open mind about what effects are being produced by each feature. Often, these poets did use inconsistency to characterize speakers or narrators, make thematic suggestions, dramatize problems or conflicts, produce ambiguity or indeterminacy, raise questions about power and authority, and represent the varied complexity of the world. A Homeric scholar quoted in a footnote in my chapter on Greek material claimed that positing deliberate incoherence or contradiction "ought to be the last resort of the serious unitarian critic." Not any more.

Bibliography

Ahl, F. (1976) *Lucan: An Introduction.* Ithaca.

    (1989) "Homer, Vergil, and Complex Narrative Structures in Latin Epic: An Essay," *ICS* 14: 1–31.

    (1991) *Sophocles' Oedipus: Evidence and Self-Conviction.* Ithaca.

Ahl, F. and H. M. Roisman (1996) *The Odyssey Re-Formed.* Ithaca.

Alter, R. (1981) *The Art of Biblical Narrative.* New York.

Anderson, W. S. (1960) "Discontinuity in Lucretian Symbolism," *TAPA* 91: 1–29.

    (1989) "Lycaon: Ovid's Deceptive Paradigm in *Metamorphoses* 1," *ICS* 14: 91–101.

    (1993) "Form Changed: Ovid's *Metamorphoses*," in A. J. Boyle (ed.), *Roman Epic*, 108–24. London and New York.

    (1997) *Ovid's Metamorphoses, Books 1–5.* Norman, Oklahoma.

Ando, C. (2002) "Vergil's Italy: Ethnography and Politics in First-century Rome," in D. S. Levene and D. Nelis (eds.), *Clio and the Poets*, 123–42. Leiden.

Armstrong, D. (1993) "The Addressees of the *Ars poetica*: Herculaneum, the Pisones and Epicurean Protreptic," *MD* 31: 185–230.

Ashline, W. L. (1995) "The Problem of Impossible Fictions," *Style* (DeKalb, Ill.) 29: 215–34.

Asmis, E. (1982) "Lucretius' Venus and Stoic Zeus," *Hermes* 110: 458–70.

Austin, R. G. (1964) *P. Vergili Maronis Aeneidos Liber Secundus.* Oxford.

    (1977) *P. Vergili Maronis Aeneidos Liber Sextus.* Oxford.

Bailey, C. (ed.) (1947) *T. Lucreti Cari De Rerum Natura Libri Sex.* Oxford.

Barchiesi, A. (1991) "Discordant Muses," *PCPS* 37: 1–21.

    (1993) "Future Reflexive: Two Modes of Allusion and Ovid's Heroides," *HSCP* 95: 333–65; repr. in Barchiesi (2001), 105–27.

    (1994) *Il poeta e il principe: Ovidio e il discorso augusteo.* Rome; trans. as *The Poet and the Prince: Ovid and Augustan Discourse.* Berkeley (1997).

    (1997) "Endgames: Ovid's *Metamorphoses* 15 and *Fasti* 6," in D. Roberts, F. Dunn and D. Fowler (eds.), *Classical Closure: Reading the End in Greek and Latin Literature*, 181–208. Princeton.

    (1999) "Venus' Masterplot: Ovid and the *Homeric Hymns*," in Hardie, Barchiesi, and Hinds (1999), 112–26.

(2001) *Speaking Volumes: Narrative and Intertext in Ovid and Other Latin Poets*. Translated by M. Fox and S. Marchesi. London.

Barton, C. (1984) "Vis mortua: Irreconcilable Patterns of Thought in the Works of Seneca and Lucan." Dissertation Berkeley.

Bartsch, S. (1997) *Ideology in Cold Blood: A Reading of Lucan's* Civil War. Cambridge, Mass.

Bate, J. (1998) *The Genius of Shakespeare*. New York and Oxford.

Batstone, W. (1993) "Logic, Rhetoric, and Poesis," *Helios* 20.2: 143–72.

(1997) "Virgilian Didaxis: Value and Meaning in the *Georgics*," in Martindale (1997), 125–44.

Bennett, W. (1993) *The Book of Virtues: a Treasury of Great Moral Stories*. New York.

Bernbeck, E. (1967) *Beobachtungen zur Darstellungsart in Ovids Metamorphosen*. Munich.

Bing, P. (1988) *The Well-Read Muse: Present and Past in Callimachus and the Hellenistic Poets*. Göttingen.

Bleisch, P. R. (1996) "On Choosing a Spouse: *Aeneid* 7.378–84 and Callimachus' *Epigram* 1," *AJP* 117.3: 453–72.

(1998) Review of O'Hara (1996a). *AJP* 119: 300–3.

(1999) "The Empty Tomb at Rhoeteum: Deiphobus and the Problem of the Past in *Aeneid* 6.494–547," *CA* 18.2: 187–226.

(2003) "The *Regia* of Picus: Ekphrasis, Italian Identity, and Artistic Definition in *Aeneid* 7.152–93," in P. Thibodeau and H. Haskell (eds.), *Being There Together: Essays in Honor of Michael C. J. Putnam on the Occasion of His Seventieth Birthday*, 88–109. Afton, Minnesota.

Blondell, R. (2002) *The Play of Character in Plato's Dialogues*. Cambridge.

Blusch, J. (1989) "Vielfach und Einheit: Bemerkungen zur Komposition von Catull c. 64," *Antike und Abendland* 35: 116–30.

Bömer, F. (1980) *P. Ovidius Naso, Metamorphosen: Kommentar. Buch X–XI*. Heidelberg.

Bornmann, F. (1968) *Callimachus, Hymnus in Dianam*. Firenze.

Bragg, R. (2003) *I Am a Soldier, Too: The Jessica Lynch Story*. New York.

Bramble, J. (1970) "Structure and Ambiguity in Catullus 64," *PCPS* 16: 22–41.

Braund, D. (1993) "Writing a Roman Argonautica: the Historical Dynamic," *Hermathena* 154: 11–18.

Brown, P. M. (1988) *Lucretius: De Rerum Natura I*. Bristol.

Brown, R. D. (1987a) *Lucretius on Love and Sex. A Commentary on De rerum natura IV, 1030–1287 with prolegomena, text, and transl.* Leiden.

(1987b) "The Palace of the Sun in Ovid's *Metamorphoses*," in M. Whitby, P. Hardie, M. Whitby (eds.), *Homo viator: Classical Essays for John Bramble*, 211–20. Bristol.

Büchner, K. (1955) "P. Vergilius Maro," *RE* 8A: 1021–1486.

Burkert, W. (1979) "Kynaithos, Polycrates, and the Homeric Hymn to Apollo," in G. Bowersock, W. Burkert, M. Putnam (eds.), *Arktouros: Hellenic Studies Presented to Bernard M. W. Knox*, 53–62. Berlin and New York.

Cameron, A. (1995) *Callimachus and his Critics*. Princeton.

Campbell, G. (1999) Review of Sedley (1998). *BMCR* 1999.10.29. http://ccat.sas.upenn.edu/bmcr/1999/1999-10-29.html.

(2003) *Lucretius on Creation and Evolution: A Commentary on De Rerum Natura Book Five, Lines 772–1104.* Oxford.

Carnes, J. S. (2001) "Degenerate Neoptolemus: Praise Poetry and the Novelization of the *Aeneid*," in Peter I. Barta (ed.), *Carnivalizing Difference: Bakhtin and the Other*, 99–117. London and New York.

Carson, A. (1992) "How Not to Read a Poem: Unmixing Simonides from Protagoras," *CP* 87: 11–30.

Casali, S. (1999) "*Facta Impia* (Virgil, *Aeneid* 4.596–9)," *CQ* 49: 203–11.

Clare, R. J. (1996) "Catullus 64 and the *Argonautica* of Apollonius of Rhodes: Allusion and Exemplarity," *PCPS* 42: 60–88.

(2002) *The Path of the Argo: Language, Imagery and Narrative in the Argonautica of Apollonius Rhodius.* Cambridge.

Clausen, W. V. (1994) *A Commentary on Virgil, Eclogues.* Oxford.

(2002) *Vergil's Aeneid. Decorum, Allusion and Ideology.* Munich and Leipzig.

Clay, D. (1983) *Lucretius and Epicurus.* Ithaca.

(1998) "The Theory of the Literary Persona in Antiquity," *MD* 40: 9–40.

Clay, J. S. (1983) *The Wrath of Athena: Gods and Men in the Odyssey.* Princeton.

(1989) *The Politics of Olympus: Form and Meaning in the Major Homeric Hymns.* Princeton.

Cole, T. (1998) "Venus and Mars (*De Rerum Natura* 1.31–40)," in P. Knox and C. Foss (eds.), *Style and Tradition: Studies in Honor of Wendell Clausen.* Beiträge zur Altertumskunde, Bd. 92, 3–15. Stuttgart.

Colum, P. (1921) *The Golden Fleece: And the Heroes Who Lived Before Achilles.* New York.

Conington, J. (1963) *The Works of Virgil with a Commentary.* Rev. by Henry Nettleship. Hildesheim. Reprint of 1883–84 London edition.

Connors, C. (1994) "Famous Last Words: Authorship and Death in the *Satyricon* and Neronian Rome," in J. Elsner and J. Masters (eds.), *Reflections of Nero: Culture, History, & Representation*, 225–35. Chapel Hill and London.

Conte, G. B. (1986) *The Rhetoric of Imitation: Genre and Poetic Memory in Virgil and Other Latin Poets.* Ithaca and London.

(1991) *Generi e Lettori: Lucrezio, L'elegia d'amore, l'enciclopedia di Plinio.* Milan.

(1994) "Instructions for a Sublime Reader: Form of the Text and Form of the Addressee in Lucretius' *De rerum natura*," chap. 1 in *Genres and Readers: Lucretius, Love Elegy, Pliny's Encyclopedia.* Baltimore.

(1996) *The Hidden Author: an Interpretation of Petronius' Satyricon.* Berkeley.

Costa, C. D. N. (1984) *Lucretius: De Rerum Natura V.* Oxford.

Courtney, E. (1987) "Quotation, Interpolation, Transposition," *Hermathena* 143: 7–18.

(1990) "Moral Judgement in Catullus 64," *GB* 17: 113–22.

(2001) "The Proem of Lucretius," *MH* 58.4: 201–11.

Cramer, R. (1998) *Vergils Weltsicht: Optimismus und Pessimismus in Vergils Georgica.* Berlin.

Dalzell, A. (1982) "Lucretius," in E. J. Kenney and W. V. Clausen (eds.), *The Cambridge History of Classical Literature.* Vol. II: *Latin Literature*, 207–29. Cambridge.

de Jong, Irene J. F. (2001) *A Narratological Commentary on the Odyssey*. Cambridge and New York.

De Lacy, P. H. (1957) "Process and Value: An Epicurean Dilemma," *TAPA* 88: 114–26.

DeBrohun, J. (1999) "Ariadne and the Whirlwind of Fate: Figures of Confusion in Catullus 64.149–57," *CP* 94.4: 419–30.

Depew, M. (1993) "Mimesis and Aetiology in Callimachus' Hymns," in M. A. Harder, R. F. Regtuit, G. C. Wakker (eds.), *Callimachus: Hellenistica Groningana* I, 57–77. Groningen.

Deufert, M. (1996) *Pseudo-Lukrezisches im Lukrez: die unechten Verse in Lukrezens "De rerum natura."* Berlin and New York.

Dewar, M. (1994) "Laying It On with A Trowel: The Proem to Lucan and Related Texts," *CQ* 44.1: 199–211.

Dolezel, L. (1998) *Heterocosmica: Fiction and Possible Worlds*. Baltimore and London.

Due, O. (1974) *Changing Forms*. Copenhagen.

Dyson, J. T. (1996) "*Septima Aestas*: The Puzzle of *Aen.* 1.755–6 and 5.626," *CW* 90.1: 41–3.

(2001) *King of the Wood: The Sacrificial Victor in Virgil's Aeneid*. Norman, Oklahoma.

Eco, U. (1984) *The Role of the Reader*. Bloomington and London.

Edmunds, L. (1997) "Myth in Homer," in B. Powell and I. Morris (eds.), *New Companion to Homer*, 415–41. Leiden.

(2001) *Intertextuality and the Reading of Roman Poetry*. Baltimore.

Edwards, M. J. (1993) "*Aeternus lepos*: Venus, Lucretius, and the Fear of Death," *G&R* 40: 68–78.

Elder, J. P. (1954) "Lucretius 1.1–149," *TAPA* 85: 88–120.

Elliott, A. G. (1985) "Ovid and the Critics: Seneca, Quintilian, and 'Seriousness'," *Helios* 12: 9–20.

Erler, M. (1997) "Physics and Therapy," in K. A. Algra, M. H. Koenen, P. H. Schrijvers (eds.), *Lucretius and his Intellectual Background*, 79–92. Amsterdam.

Ernout, A. (1957) *Recueil de textes latins archaïques*. Paris.

Everdell, W. R. (1997) *The First Moderns: Profiles in the Origins of Twentieth-Century Thought*. Chicago and London.

Fantham, E. (1992) *Lucan: De Bello Civili Book II*. Cambridge.

Fantuzzi, M. and R. Hunter (2004) *Tradition and Innovation in Hellenistic Poetry*. Cambridge.

Farrell, J. (1990) "What *Aeneid* in Whose Nineties?" *Vergilius* 36: 74–80.

(1991) *Vergil's Georgics and the Traditions of Ancient Epic: The Art of Allusion in Literary History*. Oxford.

(1992) "Dialogue of Genres in Ovid's 'Lovesong of Polyphemus' (*Metamorphoses* 13.719–897)," *AJP* 113: 235–68.

(1994) "The Structure of Lucretius' 'Anthropology' (*DRN* 5.771–1457)," *MD* 33: 81–95.

Feeney, D. C. (1991) *The Gods in Epic: Poets and Critics of the Classical Tradition*. Oxford.

(1998) *Literature and Religion at Rome: Cultures, Contexts, and Beliefs*. Cambridge.

(1999) "*Mea Tempora*: Patterning of Time in the *Metamorphoses*," in Hardie, Barchiesi, and Hinds (1999), 13–30.

Feldherr, A. (1999) "Putting Dido on the Map: Genre and Geography in Vergil's Underworld," *Arethusa* 32: 85–122.

Felson-Rubin, N. (1996) "Regarding Penelope," in S. L. Schein (ed.), *Reading the Odyssey: Selected Interpretive Essays*, 163–83. Princeton.

Ferrari, G. R. F. (1987) *Listening to the Cicadas: a Study of Plato's Phaedrus*. Cambridge and New York.

(1989) "Plato and Poetry," in Kennedy (1989), 92–148.

(2000) Review of G. A. Press (ed.), *Who Speaks for Plato? Studies in Platonic Anonymity* (Lanham, MD 2000). *BMCR* 2000.11.10. http://ccat.sas.upenn.edu/bmcr/2000/2000-11-10.html.

Finkelpearl, E. (1990) "Psyche, Aeneas, and an Ass: Apuleius *Metamorphoses* 6.10–21," *TAPA* 120: 333–47.

Fish, S. E. (1980) "Literature in the Reader: Affective Stylistics," in Fish, *Is There a Text in This Class? The Authority of Interpretive Communities*, 21–67. Cambridge, Mass., and London.

Fitzgerald, W. (1995) *Catullan Provocations: Lyric Poetry and the Drama of Position*. Berkeley.

Ford, A. (1991) "Unity in Greek Criticism and Poetry," *Arion* 1.3: 125–54.

Fowler, D. P. (1988) Review of Ross (1987). *G&R* 35: 93–5.

(1989a) "Lucretius and Politics," in M. Griffin and J. Barnes (eds.), *Philosophia Togata: Essays on Philosophy and Roman Society*, 120–50. Oxford.

(1989b) Review of Thomas (1988). *G&R* 36: 235–6.

(1990) "Deviant Focalisation in Virgil's *Aeneid*," *PCPS* 36: 42–63 = Fowler (2000a), 40–63.

(1991) Review of Segal (1990) and A. Schiesaro, *Simulacrum et imago: gli argomenti analogici nel De Rerum Natura* (Pisa 1990). *G&R* 39: 237–9.

(1993) "Response to P. R. Hardie 'Tales of Unity and Division in Latin Epic'," in J. Molyneux (ed.), *Literary Responses to Civil Discord*, 73–6. Nottingham.

(1995) "From Epos to Cosmos: Lucretius, Ovid, and the Poetics of Segmentation," in D. C. Innes, H. Hine, and C. Pelling (eds.) *Ethics and Rhetoric: Essays for Donald Russell on his 75th Birthday*, 1–18. Oxford.

(2000a) *Roman Constructions. Readings in Postmodern Latin*. Oxford.

(2000b) "Philosophy and Literature in Lucretian Intertextuality," in Fowler (2000a), 138–55.

(2000c) "On the Shoulders of Giants: Intertextuality and Classical Studies," in Fowler (2000a), 115–37 = *MD* 39 (1997), 13–34.

Freudenburg, K. (1993) *The Walking Muse: Horace on the Theory of Satire*. Princeton.

Friedlander, P. (1939) "The Epicurean Theology of Lucretius' First Proem (Lucr. 1.44–49)," *TAPA* 70: 368–79.

Frischer, B. (1991) *Shifting Paradigms: New Approaches to Horace's Ars poetica*. Atlanta.

Furley, D. J. (1966) "Lucretius and the Stoics," *BICS* 13: 13–33.

Fusillo, M. (1985) *Il tempo delle argonautiche: un'analisi del racconto in Apollonio Rodio*. Rome.

Gaisser, J. H. (1995) "Threads in the Labyrinth: Competing Views and Voices in Catullus 64," *AJP* 116: 579–616.

Gale, M. R. (1994a) *Myth and Poetry in Lucretius*. Cambridge.

    (1994b) "Lucretius 4.1–25 and the Proems of the *De Rerum Natura*," *PCPS* 40: 1–17.

    (2000) *Virgil on the Nature of Things. The Georgics, Lucretius and the Didactic Tradition.* Cambridge.

Galinsky, G. K. (1975) *Ovid's Metamorphoses: An Introduction to the Basic Aspects.* Berkeley and Los Angeles.

    (1999) "Ovid's Poetology in the *Metamorphoses*," in *Ovid. Werk und Wirkung. Festgabe für Michael von Albrecht zum 65. Geburtstag*, 305–14. Frankfurt.

Gantz, T. (1993) *Early Greek Myth: a Guide to Literary and Artistic Sources.* Baltimore and London.

Gibson, B. (1999) "Ovid on Reading: Reading Ovid. Reception in Ovid *Tristia 11*," *JRS* 89: 19–37.

Gilchrist, K. (n.d.), "Paradox in the Mythological Chronology of Apollonius Rhodius." Unpublished manuscript.

Gildenhard, I. and A. Zissos (2000) "Inspirational Fictions: Autobiography and Generic Reflexivity in Ovid's Proems," *G&R* 47: 67–79.

Givens, B. (1996) *Roman Soldiers Don't Wear Watches: 501 Film Flubs – Memorable Movie Mistakes.* Secaucus, NJ.

Godwin J. (1995) *Catullus, Poems 61–68*. Warminster.

Goldberg, S. M. (1995) *Epic in Republican Rome.* New York and Oxford.

Goldhill, S. (1986) "Framing and Polyphony: Readings in Hellenistic Poetry," *PCPS* 32: 25–52.

Görler, W. (1985) "Eneide: La Lingua," *Enciclopedia Virgiliana* 2: 262–78. Rome.

Gotoff, H. C. (1984) "The Transformation of Mezentius," *TAPA* 114: 191–218.

Gottschalk, H. B. (1999) Review of Deufert (1996). *Mnem.* ser. 4 vol. 52: 748–55.

Gow, A. S. F. (1942) "The Twenty-Second *Idyll* of Theocritus," *CR* 56: 11–18.

    (1950) *Theocritus: Edited with a Translation and Commentary.* Cambridge.

Granobs, R. (1997) *Studien zur Darstellung römischer Geschichte in Ovids "Metamorphosen."* Frankfurt am Main.

Gransden, K. W. (1991) *Virgil: Aeneid Book XI.* Cambridge.

Green, P. M. (1997) *The Argonautika by Apollonios Rhodios. Translated, with introduction, commentary, and glossary.* Berkeley.

Griffin, A. H. F. (1989) "Virgil's Unfinished *Aeneid*," *Pegasus* 32: 3–10.

Griffith, M. (1990) "Contest and Contradiction in Early Greek Poetry," in M. Griffith and D. Mastronarde (eds.), *Cabinet of the Muses: Essays in Classical and Comparative Literature in Honor of Thomas G. Rosenmeyer*, 185–205. Atlanta.

Griffiths, F. T. (1980) "The Structure and Style of the 'Short Epics' of Catullus and Virgil," in *Studies in Latin Literature and Roman History* 2: Collection Latomus 168: 123–37.

Günther, H.-C. (1996) *Überlegungen zur Entstehung von Vergils Aeneis.* Hypomnemata Heft 113. Göttingen.

Halleran, M. R. (1997) "It's Not What You Say: Unspoken Allusions in Greek Tragedy?" *MD* 39: 151–63.

Halliwell, S. (1987) *Aristotle's Poetics.* Chapel Hill.

    (1989) "Aristotle's Poetics," in Kennedy (1989), 149–83.

    (1991) Review of Heath (1989). *JHS* 111: 230–1.

Halperin, D. (1992) "Plato and the Erotics of Narrativity," in Selden and Hexter (1992), 95–126.

Hardie, P. R. (1986) *Virgil's Aeneid: Cosmos and Imperium*. Oxford.

(1988) "Lucretius and the Delusions of Narcissus," *MD* 20–1: 71–89.

(1990) "Ovid's Theban History: The First 'Anti-*Aeneid*'?," *CQ* 40: 224–35.

(1991) "The Janus Episode in Ovid's *Fasti*," *MD* 26: 47–64.

(1992) "Augustan Poets and the Mutability of Rome," in A. Powell (ed.), *Roman Poetry and Propaganda in the Age of Augustus*, 59–82. London.

(1993) *The Epic Successors of Virgil: A Study in the Dynamics of a Tradition*. Cambridge.

(1994) *Virgil: Aeneid Book IX*. Cambridge.

(1995) "The Speech of Pythagoras in Ovid, *Metamorphoses* 15: Empedoclean Epos," *CQ* 45: 204–14.

(1996) "Virgil: A Paradoxical Poet?" *PLLS* 9: 103–21.

(1997a) "Closure in Latin Epic," in D. Roberts, F. Dunn and D. Fowler (eds.), *Classical Closure: Reading the End in Greek and Latin Literature*, 139–62. Princeton.

(1997b) "Questions of Authority: the Invention of Tradition in Ovid *Metamorphoses*, 15," in T. Habinek and A. Schiesaro (eds.), *The Roman Cultural Revolution*, 182–98. Cambridge.

(1998) *Virgil*. Greece & Rome. New Surveys in the Classics, no. 28. Oxford.

(1999) Review of Günther (1996). *CR* 49.1:49–50.

Hardie, P., A. Barchiesi, and S. Hinds (eds.) (1999) *Ovidian Transformations: Essays on the Metamorphoses and its Reception*. Cambridge Philological Society Suppl. Vol. 23. Cambridge.

Harrison, S. J. (ed.) (1990) *Oxford Readings in Vergil's Aeneid*. Oxford.

(1991) *Vergil: Aeneid 10. With Introduction, Translation, and Commentary*. Oxford.

Harrison, S. J. and S. J. Heyworth (1998) "Notes on the Text and Interpretation of Catullus," *PCPS* 44: 85–109.

Haslam, M. W. (1993) "Callimachus' Hymns," in M. A. Harder et al. (eds.), *Callimachus: Hellenistica Groningana* 1, 111–25. Groningen.

Haupt, M. (1966) *P. Ovidius Naso: Metamorphosen*. Revised by R. Ewald and M. von Albrecht. Zürich and Dublin.

Heath, M. (1989) *Unity in Greek Poetics*. Oxford.

Heiden, B. (1989) *Tragic Rhetoric: An Interpretation of Sophocles' "Trachiniae."* Bern, Frankfurt am Main, New York, Paris.

Helzle, M. (1993) "Ovid's Cosmogony: *Metamorphoses* 1.5–88 and the Traditions of Ancient Poetry," *PLLS* 7: 123–34.

Henderson, J. G. W. (1998) "Lucan: The Word at War," in *Fighting for Rome: Poets and Caesars, History and Civil War*, 165–211. New York and Cambridge. Revised from *Ramus* 16 (1987), 122–64.

Hexter, R. (1989–90) "What Was the Trojan Horse Made Of?: Interpreting Vergil's *Aeneid*," *YJC* 3: 109–31.

(1992) "Sidonian Dido," in Selden and Hexter (1992), 332–84.

(1994) "Commentary, Reading, Writing," One Hundred Twenty-Sixth Annual Meeting of the American Philological Association: Abstract (Worcester, MA), 278.

Heyworth, S. (1994) "Some Allusions to Callimachus in Latin Poetry," *MD* 33: 51–79.

Hill, D. E. (1999) *Ovid, Metamorphoses IX–XII*. Warminster.

Hinds, S. E. (1985) "Booking the Return Trip: Ovid and *Tristia* 1," *PCPS* 211, n.s. 31: 13–32.

(1987a) *The Metamorphosis of Persephone: Ovid and the Self-Conscious Muse*. Cambridge.

(1987b) "Generalising About Ovid," *Ramus* 16: 4–31.

(1992) "*Arma* in Ovid's *Fasti*: Part 2: Genre, Romulean Rome and Augustan Ideology," *Arethusa* 25: 113–53.

(1993) "Medea in Ovid: Scenes from the Life of an Intertextual Heroine," *MD* 30: 9–47.

(1998) *Allusion and Intertext: Dynamics of Appropriation in Roman Poetry*. Cambridge.

(1999) "After Exile: Time and Teleology from *Metamorphoses* to *Ibis*," in Hardie, Barchiesi, and Hinds (1999), 48–67.

Hofmann, J. B. (1965) *Lateinische Syntax und Stilistik*. Revised by A. Szantyr. 3rd edn. Munich.

Hollis, A. S. (1970) *Ovid: Metamorphoses, Book VIII*. Oxford.

(1990) *Callimachus: Hecale*. Oxford.

Hopkinson, N. (1984) "Callimachus' Hymn to Zeus," *CQ* 34: 139–48.

Horsfall, N. M. (1971) "Numanus Remulus, Ethnography and Propaganda in Aen. IX, 598f," *Latomus* 30: 1108–16.

(1981) "Virgil and the Conquest of Chaos," *Antichthon* 15:141–50 = Harrison (1990), 466–77.

(1987) "Numano Remulo," *Enciclopedia Virgiliana* Vol. III: 778–9. Rome.

(1991a) *Virgilio: l'epopea in alambicco*. Naples.

(1991b) "Virgil, Parthenius, and the Art of Mythological Reference," *Vergilius* 37: 31–6.

(1995) *A Companion to the Study of Virgil*. Leiden and New York.

(1997) Review of Günther (1996). *RFIC* 125: 468–72.

(2000) *Virgil, Aeneid 7: A Commentary*. Mnemosyne Suppl. 198. Leiden.

(2003) *Virgil, Aeneid 11: A Commentary*. Leiden.

(2006) *Virgil, Aeneid 3: A Commentary*. Leiden.

Hunter, R. (1987) "Medea's Flight: the Fourth Book of the Argonautica," *CQ* 37: 129–39.

(1989) *Apollonius of Rhodes, Argonautica Book III*. Cambridge.

(1991) "'Breast is Best': Catullus 64.18," *CQ* n.s. 41: 254–5.

(1993) *The Argonautica of Apollonius: Literary Studies*. New York and Cambridge.

(1996) *Theocritus and the Archaeology of Greek Poetry*. New York and Cambridge.

Hutchinson, G. O. (1988) *Hellenistic Poetry*. Oxford.

(2001) "The Date of *De Rerum Natura*," *CQ* 51: 150–62.

Jackson, S. (1997) "Argo: the First Ship?," *RhM* 140: 249–57.

James, S. L. (2003) *Learned Girls and Male Persuasion: Gender and Reading in Roman Love Elegy*. Berkeley.

Janan, M. (1988) "The Book of Good Love. Design versus Desire in *Metamorphoses* 10," *Ramus* 17: 110–37.

(1994) *"When the Lamp is Shattered:" Desire and Narrative in Catullus*. Carbondale, Ill.

Janko, R. (1998) "The Homeric Poems as Oral Dictated Texts," *CQ* 48: 1–13.

(2000) *Philodemus. On Poems: Book 1*. New York and Oxford.

Jenkyns, R. (1982) "Catullus and the Idea of a Masterpiece," in *Three Classical Poets: Sappho, Catullus, and Juvenal*, 85–150. Cambridge, MA.

Johnson, W. R. (1976) *Darkness Visible: A Study of Vergil's Aeneid*. Berkeley, Los Angeles and London.

(1987) *Momentary Monsters: Lucan and His Heroes*. Ithaca, N.Y.

(2000) *Lucretius and the Modern World*. London.

Katz, M. A. (1991) *Penelope's Renown: Meaning and Indeterminacy in the "Odyssey."* Princeton.

Keith, A. M. (1999) "Versions of Epic Masculinity in Ovid's *Metamorphoses*," in Hardie, Barchiesi and Hinds (1999), 214–39.

(2000) *Engendering Rome: Women in Latin Epic*. Cambridge.

Kennedy, G. (ed.) (1989) *The Cambridge History of Literary Criticism*. Vol. I. *Classical Criticism*. Cambridge.

Kenney, E. J. (1976) "Ovidius Prooemians," *PCPS* 22: 46–53.

(1978) Review of F. Bömer, *P. Ovidius Naso, Metamorphosen: Kommentar. Buch IV–V*. *CR* n.s. 28: 251–3.

(1980) "Psyche and her Mysterious Husband," in D. A. Russell (ed.), *Antonine Literature*, 175–98. Oxford.

(1986) *Introduction and Notes to Ovid, Metamorphoses*, trans. A. D. Melville. Oxford.

Kepple, L. (1980) "The Textual and Thematic Contexts of Lucan's 'Praise of Nero' in the Bellum Civile." Dissertation Harvard.

(1981) Summary of Kepple (1980). *HCSP* 85: 383–5.

Kinsey, T. E. (1965) "Irony and Structure in Catullus 64," *Latomus* 24: 911–31.

Kleve, K. (1966) "Lukrez und Venus (*De Rerum Natura* 1.1–49)," *SO* 41: 86–94.

Klingner, F. (1964) "Catulls Peleus-Epos," in *Studien zur Griechischen und Römischen Literatur*, 156–224. Zurich.

Knox, P. E. (1986) *Ovid's Metamorphoses and the Traditions of Augustan Poetry*. Cambridge.

Konstan, D. (1977) *Catullus' Indictment of Rome*. Amsterdam.

Kovacs, D. (1987) "Ovid, *Metamorphoses* 1.2," *CQ* 37: 458–65.

Lafaye, G. (1904) *Les métamorphoses d'Ovide et leurs modèles grecs*. Paris; Repr. Hildesheim, 1971.

Laird, A. (1999) *Powers of Expression, Expressions of Power: Speech Presentation and Latin Literature*. Oxford and New York.

Lamberton, R. (1991) Review of Heath (1989). *Ancient Philosophy* 11: 465–73.

Larmour, D. H. J. (1990) "Tragic Contaminatio in Ovid's *Metamorphoses*: Procne and Medea, Philomela and Iphigeneia (6.424–674), Scylla and Phaedra (8.19–51)," *ICS* 15: 131–41.

Laursen, S. (1992) "Theocritus' Hymn to the Dioscuri. Unity and Intention," *C&M* 43: 71–92.

Leach, E. (1974) "Ekphrasis and the Theme of Artistic Failure in Ovid's *Metamorphoses*," *Ramus* 3: 102–42.

(1988) *The Rhetoric of Space: Literary and Artistic Representations of Landscape in Republican and Augustan Rome*. Princeton.

Lee, A. G. (1953) *Ovid: Metamorphoses Book I*. Cambridge.

Leigh, M. (1997) *Lucan: Spectacle and Engagement*. New York and Oxford.

Little, D. (1970) "The Speech of Pythagoras in *Metamorphoses* xv and the Structure of the *Metamorphoses*," *Hermes* 98: 340–60.

Lloyd-Jones, H. (1972) "Tycho von Wilamowitz-Moellendorff on the Dramatic Technique of Sophocles," *CQ* 22: 214–28.

Long, A. A. (1997) "Lucretius on Nature and the Epicurean Self," in K. A. Algra, M. H. Koenen, P. H. Schrijvers (eds.), *Lucretius and his Intellectual Background*, 125–39. Amsterdam.

Lord, A. B. (1960) *The Singer of Tales*. New York.

Lowrie, M. (1993) Review of Freudenburg (1993). *BMCR* 4.3.5. http://ccat.sas.upenn.edu/ bmcr/1993/04.03.05.html.

Lucas, D. W. (1968) *Aristotle: Poetics*. Oxford.

Lüddecke, K. (1998) "Contextualizing the Voice in Callimachus' Hymn to Zeus," *MD* 41: 9–33.

Lyne, R. O. A. M. (1978) *Ciris: A Poem Attributed to Vergil*. Cambridge.

(1983) "Vergil and the Politics of War," *CQ* 33: 188–203 = Harrison (1990), 316–38.

(1987) *Further Voices in Vergil's "Aeneid."* Oxford.

Mack, S. (1978) *Patterns of Time in Vergil*. Hamden, Connecticut.

(1988) *Ovid*. New Haven.

Mackie, C. J. (1988) *The Characterisation of Aeneas*. Edinburgh.

(1991) "Nox erat . . .: Sleep and Visions in the *Aeneid*," *G&R* 38: 59–61.

Maltby, R. (2002) *Tibullus: Elegies: Text, Introduction and Commentary*. Leeds.

Martin, R. P. (1989) *The Language of Heroes: Speech and Performance in the Iliad*. Ithaca.

Martindale, C. (1993a) *Redeeming the Text: Latin Poetry and the Hermeneutics of Reception*. Cambridge.

(1993b) "Descent into Hell: Reading Ambiguity, or Virgil and the Critics," *PVS* 21: 111–50.

(ed.) (1997) *The Cambridge Companion to Virgil*. Cambridge.

(2005) *Latin Poetry and the Judgement of Taste: an Essay in Aesthetics*. Oxford.

Masters, J. M. (1992) *Poetry and Civil War in Lucan's "Bellum Civile."* Cambridge.

(1994) "Deceiving the Reader: the Political Mission of Lucan Bellum Civile 7," in J. Elsner and J. Masters (eds.), *Reflections of Nero: Culture, History, and Representation*, 151–77. Chapel Hill.

May, C. (1995) "A Postmodern Challenge to Reference-World Construction: Gilbert Sorrentino's *Mulligan Stew*," *Style* (DeKalb, Ill.) 29: 235–61.

Mayer, R. G. (1988) "*Aeneid* 8.573 and Callimachus' *Hymn to Zeus*," *CQ* 38: 260–1.

(2003) "Persona Problems. The Literary Persona in Antiquity Revisited," *MD* 50: 55–80.

McHale, B. (1987) *Postmodernist Fiction*. London.

McKim, R. (1985) "Myth Against Philosophy in Ovid's Account of Creation," *CJ* 80: 97–108.

Miles, G. B. (1980) *Virgil's "Georgics:" A New Interpretation*. Berkeley, Los Angeles, and London.

Miller, A. M. (1986) *From Delos to Delphi: a Literary Study of the Homeric Hymn to Apollo*. Leiden.

Miller, J. F. (1991) *Ovid's Elegiac Festivals: Studies in the "Fasti."* Frankfurt am Main.

(1992) "The *Fasti* and Hellenistic Didactic: Ovid's Variant Aetiologies," *Arethusa* 25: 11–31.

Miller, P. A. (1994) *Lyric Texts and Lyric Consciousness: the Birth of a Genre from Archaic Greece to Augustan Rome*. London and New York.

(2004) *Subjecting Verses: Latin Love Elegy and the Emergence of the Real*. Princeton.

Minyard, J. D. (1985) *Lucretius and the Late Republic. Mnemosyne Supplement* 90. Leiden.

Mitsis, P. (1993) "Committing Philosophy on the Reader: Didactic Coercion and Reader Autonomy in *De Rerum Natura*," *MD* 31: 111–28.

Molviati-Toptsis, U. (1995) "*Sed Falsa ad Caelum Mittunt Insomnia Manes* (*Aeneid* 6.896)," *AJP* 116: 639–52.

Moorton, R. (1989) "The Innocence of Italy in Vergil's *Aeneid*," *AJP* 110: 105–30.

Morrison, J. (1992) *Homeric Misdirection: False Predictions in the "Iliad."* Ann Arbor.

Morwood, J. (1999) "Catullus 64, Medea, and the François Vase," *G&R* 46: 221–31.

Müller, G. A. (2003) *Formen und Funktionen der Vergilzitate und -anspielungen bei Augustin von Hippo*. Paderborn.

Murgia, C. (1987) "Dido's Puns," *CP* 82: 50–9.

(2003) "The Date of the Helen Episode," *HSCP* 101: 405–26.

Murray, P. (1997) *Plato on Poetry*. Cambridge.

Myers, K. S. (1994) *Ovid's Causes: Cosmogony and Aetiology in the "Metamorphoses."* Ann Arbor.

Mynors, R. A. B. (1990) *Virgil: Georgics: Edited with a Commentary*. Oxford.

Nagler, M. (1990) "Ethical Anxiety and Artistic Inconsistency: The Case of Oral Epic," in M. Griffith and D. Mastronarde (eds.), *Cabinet of the Muses: Essays in Classical and Comparative literature in Honor of Thomas G. Rosenmeyer*, 225–39. Atlanta.

Nagy, G. (1979) *The Best of the Achaeans: Concepts of the Hero in Archaic Greek Poetry*. Baltimore.

(1990) *Pindar's Homer: The Lyric Possession of an Epic Past*. Baltimore and London.

(1992) "Mythological Exemplum in Homer," in Selden and Hexter (1992), 311–31.

(1996) *Poetry as Performance: Homer and Beyond*. Cambridge.

Narducci, E. (1999) "Deconstructing Lucan, ovvero Le nozze (coi fichi secchi) di Ermete Trismegisto e di Filologia," in L. Nicastri and P. Esposito (eds.), *Interpretare Lucano. Miscellanea di studi*, 37–81. Naples = *Maia* 51 (1999), 349–87.

Nelis, D. (2001) *Vergil's Aeneid and the Argonautica of Apollonius Rhodius*. Leeds.

Newlands, C. (1995) *Playing with Time: Ovid and the Fasti*. Ithaca, N.Y.

(1997) "The Metamorphosis of Ovid's Medea," in J. Clauss and S. Johnston (eds.), *Medea: Essays on Medea in Myth, Literature, Philosophy and Art*, 178–208. Princeton.

Newman, J. K. (1990) *Roman Catullus and the Modification of the Alexandrian Sensibility*. Hildesheim.

Nishimura-Jensen, J. (2000) "Unstable Geographies: The Moving Landscape in Apollonius' *Argonautica* and Callimachus' *Hymn to Delos*," *TAPA* 130: 287–317.

Norden, E. (1981) *P. Vergilius Maro Aeneis Buch VI*. 7th edn. Stuttgart. Only light corrections from 2nd edn. of 1916.

Norwood, F. (1954) "The Tripartite Eschatology of *Aeneid* 6," *CP* 49:15–26.

Nugent, S. G. (1992) "Vergil's Voice of the Women in *Aeneid* v," *Arethusa* 25: 255–92.

Nünlist, R. (2003) "The Homeric Scholia on Focalization," *Mnemosyne* 56.1: 61–71.

Nussbaum, M. (1994) *The Therapy of Desire: Theory and Practice in Hellenistic Ethics.* Princeton.

O'Connell, M. (1977) "Pictorialism and Meaning in Catullus 64," *Latomus* 36: 746–56.

O'Hara, J. (1990) *Death and the Optimistic Prophecy in Vergil's "Aeneid."* Princeton.

(1993a) "Dido as 'Interpreting Character' in *Aeneid* 4.56–66," *Arethusa* 26: 99–114.

(1993b) Review of Feeney (1991). *Vergilius* 39: 87–96.

(1994) "They Might Be Giants: Inconsistency and Indeterminacy in Vergil's War in Italy," in H. Roisman and J. Roisman (eds.), *Studies in Roman Epic, Colby Quarterly* 30: 206–26.

(1995) Review of Hardie (1994). *BMCR* 95.07.11. http://ccat.sas.upenn.edu/bmcr/1995/95.07.11.html.

(1996a) *True Names: Vergil and the Alexandrian Tradition of Etymological Wordplay.* Ann Arbor.

(1996b) "An Unconvincing Argument about Aeneas and the Gates of Sleep," *Phoenix* 50: 331–4.

(1996c) "Vergil's Best Reader? Ovidian Commentary on Vergilian Etymological Wordplay," *CJ* 91: 255–76.

(1996d) Review of Ahl and Roisman (1996). *BMCR* 95.07.11. http://ccat.sas.upenn.edu/bmcr/1996/96.11.08.html.

(1997) "Virgil's Style," in Martindale (1997), 241–58.

(1999) Review of Leigh (1997). *CJ* 94.2: 200–3.

(2001) "Callimachean Influence on Vergilian Etymological Wordplay," *CJ* 96: 369–400.

(2005a) "'Some God . . . or his Own Heart:' Two Kinds of Epic Motivation in the Proem to Ovid's *Metamorphoses*," *CJ* 100.2: 149–61.

(2005b) "Trying not to Cheat: Responses to Inconsistencies in Roman Epic," *TAPA* 135: 15–33.

Obbink, D. (ed.) (1995) *Philodemus and Poetry: Poetic Theory and Practice in Lucretius, Philodemus, and Horace.* Oxford.

(1996) *Philodemus on Piety: Critical Text with Commentary Part 1.* Oxford.

Ogilvie, R. M. (1970) *A Commentary on Livy Books 1–5.* Oxford.

Oliensis, E. (1998) *Horace and the Rhetoric of Authority.* Cambridge.

Olson, S. D. (1991) Review of Katz (1991). *BMCR* 02.06.13. http://ccat.sas.upenn.edu/bmcr/1991/02.06.13.html.

Otis, B. (1970) *Ovid as an Epic Poet.* Cambridge, 2nd edition.

Parker, H. (1984) *Flawed Texts and Verbal Icons: Literary Authority in American Fiction.* Evanston, Ill.

Parry, A. (1966) "The Two Voices of Vergil's *Aeneid*," in S. Commager (ed.), *Virgil: A Collection of Critical Essays*, 107–23. Englewood Cliffs.

Pasquali, G. (1920) "Il carme 64 di Catullo," *SIFC* 1: 1–23.

Patin, M. (1868) "L'Anti-Lucrèce chez Lucrèce," in *Études sur la poésie latine I*, 117–37. Paris.

Perkell, C. (1989) *The Poet's Truth: A Study of the Poet in Virgil's "Georgics."* Berkeley and Los Angeles.

(1992) Review of Farrell (1991). *CP* 87: 269–74.

(1994) "Ambiguity and Irony: the Last Resort?," *Helios* 21: 63–74.

(1997) "The Lament of Juturna: Pathos and Interpretation in the *Aeneid*," *TAPA* 127: 257–86.

(2002) "The Golden Age and Its Contradictions in the Poetry of Vergil," *Vergilius* 48: 3–39.

Pratt, L. H. (1993) *Lying and Poetry from Homer to Pindar: Falsehood and Deception in Archaic Greek Poetics*. Ann Arbor.

Quinn, K. (1970) *Catullus: The Poems*. London.

Quint, D. (1993) *Epic and Empire: Politics and Generic Form from Virgil to Milton*. Princeton.

Rabinowitz, N. S. (1993) *Anxiety Veiled: Euripides and the Traffic in Women*. Ithaca.

Reckford, K. J. (1981) "Helen in *Aeneid* 2 and 6," *Arethusa* 14: 85–99.

(1995) "Recognizing Venus I: Aeneas Meets his Mother," *Arion* 3.2–3: 1–42.

Rhorer, C. C. (1980) "Ideology, Tripartition and Ovid's *Metamorphoses* (1.5–451)," *Arethusa* 13: 299–313.

Richards, I. A. (1970) *Poetries and Sciences; a Reissue of Science and Poetry (1926, 1935) with Commentary*. New York.

Rosati, G. (2002) "Narrative Techniques and Narrative Structures in the *Metamorphoses*," in B. W. Boyd (ed.), *Brill's Companion to Ovid*, 271–304. Leiden.

Rosenmeyer, P. A. (1997) "Her Master's Voice: Sappho's Dialogue with Homer," *MD* 39: 123–49.

Ross, D. O., Jr. (1975) *Backgrounds to Augustan Poetry: Gallus, Elegy and Rome*. Cambridge.

(1987) *Virgil's Elements: Physics and Poetry in the "Georgics."* Princeton.

Rudich, V. (1997) *Dissidence and Literature under Nero: The Price of Rhetoricization*. New York.

Schenkeveld, D. M. (1992) "Unity and Variety in Ancient Criticism, Some Observations on a Recent Study," *Mnemosyne* 45: 1–8.

Schmidt, E. A. (2001) "The Meaning of Vergil's *Aeneid*: American and German Approaches," *CW* 94: 145–71.

Schmitzer, U. (1990) *Zeitgeschichte in Ovids Metamorphosen: Mythologische Dichtung unter politischem Anspruch*. Stuttgart.

Scodel, R. (1977) "Apollo's Perfidy: *Iliad* V 59–63," *HSCP* 81: 55–7.

(1986) "Literary Interpretation in Plato's *Protagoras*," *AncPhil* 6: 25–37.

(1997) "Pseudo-Intimacy and the Prior Knowledge of the Homeric Audience," *Arethusa* 30.2: 201–20.

(1998) "The Removal of the Arms, the Recognition with Laertes, and Narrative Tension in the *Odyssey*," *CP* 93.1: 1–17.

(1999) *Credible Impossibilities: Conventions and Strategies of Verisimilitude in Homer and Greek Tragedy*. Stuttgart.

Sedley, D. N. (1998) *Lucretius and the Transformation of Greek Wisdom*. Cambridge.

Segal, C. (1969) "Myth and Philosophy in the *Metamorphoses*: Ovid's Augustanism and the Augustan Conclusion of Book XV," *AJP* 90: 257–92.

(1990) *Lucretius on Death and Anxiety: Poetry and Philosophy in De Rerum Natura*. Princeton.

(1999) "Ovid's Meleager and the Greeks: Trials of Gender and Genre," *HSCP* 99: 301–40.

Selden, D. L. (1992) "*Caveat lector*: Catullus and the Rhetoric of Performance," in Selden and Hexter (1992), 461–512.

  (1998) "Alibis," *CA* 17.2: 290–419.

Selden, D. L. and R. Hexter (eds.) (1992) *Innovations of Antiquity*. New York and London.

Sens, A. (1992) "Theocritus, Homer, and the Dioscuri: Idyll 22.137–223," *TAPA* 122: 335–50.

  (1997) *Theocritus, Dioscuri (Idyll 22): Introduction, Text, and Commentary*. Göttingen.

Sharrock, A. (1994) *Seduction and Repetition in Ovid's Ars Amatoria 2*. Oxford.

  (2000) "Intratextuality: Texts, Parts, and (W)holes in Theory," in Sharrock and H. Morales (eds.), *Intratextuality: Greek and Roman Textual Relations*, 1–39. Oxford.

Shumate, N. (1996) *Crisis and Conversion in Apuleius' Metamorphoses*. Ann Arbor.

Skinner, M. (1989) "Ut decuit cinaediorem: Power, Gender, and Urbanity in Catullus 10," *Helios* 16: 7–23.

  (1994) "Remembrance of a Guest: Theseus in Callimachus' *Hecale* and Catullus 64," *LCM* 19: 147–8.

Sklenár, R. (2003) *The Taste for Nothingness. A Study of "Virtus" and Related Themes in Lucan's "Bellum civile."* Ann Arbor.

Smith, M. F. (ed.) (1982) *Lucretius. De rerum natura*. Cambridge, Mass.

Solmsen, F. (1972) "The World of the Dead in Book 6 of the *Aeneid*," *CP* 67: 31–41 = Harrison (1990), 208–23.

Solodow, J. B. (1988) *The World of Ovid's "Metamorphoses."* Chapel Hill.

Squillante Saccone, M. (1987) "Discordanze," *Enciclopedia Virgiliana* Vol. ii: 95–7. Roma.

Stern, J. (1978) "Theocritus' Epithalamium of Helen," *RBPh* 56: 29–37.

Sternberg, M. (1985) *The Poetics of Biblical Narrative: Ideological Literature and the Drama of Reading*. Bloomington.

Summers, K. (1995) "Lucretius and the Epicurean Tradition of Piety," *CP* 90.1: 32–57.

Sutherland, J. (1996) *Is Heathcliff a Murderer? Great Puzzles in Nineteenth-Century Literature*. Oxford.

  (1997) *Can Jane Eyre Be Happy? More Puzzles in Classic Fiction*. Oxford.

  (1998) *Where was Rebecca Shot? Curiosities, Puzzles, and Conundrums in Modern Fiction*. London.

Suzuki, M. (1989) *Metamorphoses of Helen. Authority, Difference and the Epic*. Ithaca, N.Y.

Syndikus, H. P. (1984) *Catull: eine Interpretation*. Darmstadt.

Tarrant, R. J. (1982) "Review Article. Editing Ovid's *Metamorphoses*: Problems and Possibilities," *CP* 77: 342–60.

  (1995) "The Silence of Cephalus: Text and Narrative Technique in Ovid, *Metamorphoses* 7.685ff.," *TAPA* 125: 99–111.

Taylor, P. (1995) "*The Green Berets*: Film in Context," *History Today* 45.3: 21–5.

Theodorakopoulos, E. (2000) "Catullus 64: Footprints in the Labyrinth," in A. Sharrock and H. Morales (eds.), *Intratextuality: Greek and Roman Textual Relations*, 115–41. Oxford.

Thomas, R. F. (1982a) *Lands and Peoples in Roman Poetry: The Ethnographic Tradition*. Cambridge.

(1982b) "Catullus and the Polemics of Poetic Reference," *AJP* 103: 144–54 = Thomas (1999), 12–32.

(1985) "From Recusatio to Commitment: The Evolution of the Vergilian Programme," *PLLS* 5: 61–73 = Thomas (1999), 101–13.

(1988) *Virgil: Georgics*. Cambridge.

(1990) "Ideology, Influence, and Future Studies in the *Georgics*," *Vergilius* 36: 64–70.

(1993) "Callimachus back in Rome," in M. A. Harder, R. F. Regtuit, G. C. Wakker (eds.), *Callimachus: Hellenistica Groningana* 1, 197–215. Groningen = Thomas (1999), 206–28.

(1996) "Genre Through Intertextuality: Theocritus to Virgil and Propertius" in M. A. Harder, R. F. Regtuit, and G. C. Wakker (eds.), *Theocritus: Hellenistica Groningana* II, 227–44. Groningen = Thomas (1999), 246–66.

(1998) "The Isolation of Turnus. *Aeneid* Book 12," in H.-P. Stahl (ed.), *Vergil's "Aeneid:" Augustan Epic and Political Context*, 271–302. London.

(1999) *Reading Virgil and His Texts: Studies in Intertextuality*. Ann Arbor.

(2001) *Virgil and the Augustan Reception*. Cambridge.

(2004) "'Drownded in the Tide:' The Nauagika and Some 'Problems' in Augustan Poetry," in B. Acosta-Hughes, E. Kosmetatou, M. Baumbach (eds.), *Labored in Papyrus Leaves: Perspectives on an Epigram Collection Attributed to Posidippus (P. Mil. Vogl. VIII 309)*, 259–75. Cambridge, Mass.

(2004–5) "Torn between Jupiter and Saturn: Ideology, Rhetoric and Culture Wars in the *Aeneid*," *CJ* 100.2: 121–47.

Thomson, D. F. S. (1997) *Catullus. Edited with a Textual and Interpretative Commentary*. Toronto.

Timpanaro, S. (1976) *The Freudian Slip: Psychoanalysis and Textual Criticism*. London.

Tissol, G. (1997) *The Face of Nature: Wit, Narrative, and Cosmic Origins in Ovid's Metamorphoses*. Princeton.

(2002) "The House of Fame: Roman History and Augustan Politics in *Metamorphoses* 1–15," in B. W. Boyd (ed.), *Brill's Companion to Ovid*, 305–35. Leiden.

Todorov, T. (1977) *The Poetics of Prose*, trans. R. Howard. Ithaca.

Toll, K. (1997) "Making Roman-ness and the *Aeneid*," *CA* 16.1: 34–56.

Townend, G. B. (1983) "The Unstated Climax of Catullus 64," *G&R* 30: 21–30.

Traube, E. G. (1992) *Dreaming Identities: Class, Gender, and Generation in 1980s Hollywood Movies*. Boulder, Col.

Tsagarakis, O. (1979) "Oral Composition, Type-scenes, and Narrative Inconsistencies in Homer," *GB* 8: 23–48.

Uhrmeister, V. and P. Bing (1994) "The Unity of Callimachus' Hymn to Artemis," *JHS* 114: 19–34.

Van Nortwick, T. (1980) "Aeneas, Turnus, and Achilles," *TAPA* 110: 303–14.

Van Sickle, J. (1987) "The Elogia of the Cornelii Scipiones and the Origins of Epigram at Rome," *AJP* 108: 41–55.

Waldock, A. J. A. (1966) *Sophocles the Dramatist*. Cambridge.

Weber, C. (1969) "The Diction of Death in Latin Epic," *Agon* 3: 45–68.

(1983) "Two Chronological Contradictions in Catullus," *TAPA* 113: 263–71.

Wheeler, S. M. (1995a) "*Imago mundi*: Another View of the Creation in Ovid's *Metamorphoses*," *AJP* 116: 95–121.

(1995b) "Ovid's use of Lucretius in *Metamorphoses* 1.67–8," *CQ* 45: 200–3.

(1995c) Review of Myers (1994). *BMCR* 95.03.31. http://ccat.sas.upenn.edu/bmcr/1995/95.03.31.html.

(1999) *A Discourse of Wonders: Audience and Performance in Ovid's Metamorphoses*. Philadelphia.

(2002) "Lucan's Reception of Ovid's *Metamorphoses*," *Arethusa* 35: 361–80.

White, P. (1993) *Promised Verse. Poets in the Society of Augustan Rome*. Cambridge, Mass.

(2002) "Ovid and the Augustan Milieu," in B. W. Boyd (ed.), *Brill's Companion to Ovid*, 1–25. Leiden.

Wilkinson, L. P. (1982) *Virgil: The Georgics*. New York.

Williams, G. W. (1968) *Tradition and Originality in Roman Poetry*. Oxford.

(1978) *Change and Decline: Roman Literature in the Early Empire*. Berkeley, Los Angeles and London.

(1983) *Technique and Ideas in the "Aeneid."* New Haven and London.

Williams, R. D. (1973) *The Aeneid of Virgil: Books 7–12*. London.

Wilson, J. B. (2000) *Sense and Nonsense in Homer: a Consideration of the Inconsistencies and Incoherences in the Texts of the Iliad and the Odyssey*. Oxford.

Winkler, J. (1985) *Auctor & Actor: A Narratological Reading of Apuleius's "The Golden Ass."* Berkeley and Los Angeles.

Wiseman, T. P. (1974) *Cinna the Poet, and Other Roman Essays*. Leicester.

Zeitlin, F. I. (1999) "Petronius as Paradox: Anarchy and Artistic Integrity," in S. J. Harrison (ed.), *Oxford Readings in the Roman Novel*, 1–49. Oxford = *TAPA* 102 (1971), 631–84.

Zetzel, J. E. G. (1980) "Horace's *Liber Sermonum*: The Structure of Ambiguity," *Arethusa* 13: 59–77.

(1983) "Catullus, Ennius, and the Poetics of Allusion," *ICS* 8: 251–66.

(1989) "ROMANE, MEMENTO: Justice and Judgement in *Aeneid* 6," *TAPA* 119: 263–84.

(1997) "Rome and Its Traditions," in Martindale (1997), 188–203.

Zissos, A. (1999) "Allusion and Narrative Possibility in the *Argonautica* of Valerius Flaccus," *CP* 94: 289–301.

Zissos, A. and I. Gildenhard (1999) "Problems of Time in *Metamorphoses* 2," in Hardie, Barchiesi, and Hinds (1999), 31–47.

Zwierlein, O. (1999) *Die Ovid- und Vergil-Revision in tiberischer Zeit*. Band I: *Prolegomena*. Berlin and New York.

Index of passages discussed

Aeschylus
  Agamemnon 247: 18
    414–15: 16–18
    617–80: 18, 56
    fr. 284 Mette = 350 Nauck or
      Radt: 49, 54
Antiphanes
  fr. 189 K–A: 29
Apollonius of Rhodes
  Argonautica 1.1: 36, 42, 45
    1.547–52: 32
    1.609–835: 31
    3.375–6: 31
    3.997–1108: 39
    3.1071–4: 31
    4.316–22: 32
    4.784–967: 31
Apuleius
  Golden Ass 1.1: 33
    6.6–7: 115
Aristotle
  Metaphysics IV (Γ) 1005b 18–34: 20
  Poetics: 21–2
    15.9, 1454a31: 16
Athenaeus
  Deipnosophistae 5.178d: 11
Augustine
  Sermo 105, 7, 10: 16
Aulus Gellius
  Noctes Atticae 10.16.11: 56, 77, 91

Callimachus
  Aetia fr. 1 Pf.: 25
    fr. 732 Pf.: 48
  Hymn to Artemis: 26, 28
  Hymn to Zeus: 28–9, 42, 44
  Hecale frs. 232–4 Pf. = 3–8 H.: 39
Catullus
  1.6: 40
  11: 46
  64: 33–54
    1–54: 34–41
    22–3: 42, 45
    25: 47
    51: 44
    111: 39
    217: 39
    218–19: 42, 44
    299–302: 53
    306: 48
    322: 48, 49
    323–83: 47–54
    348: 49
    362: 51–3
    362–74: 49, 75
    372: 17, 49, 51, 53
  68: 43, 46
  95.1–2: 43
Cicero
  Ad Quintum fratrem 2.9.3: 68
  Pro Arch. : 43, 46

159

Dionysius of Halicarnassus
  Ant. Rom. 1.70: 88

Euripides
  Andromache 865: 40
  Trojan Women: 17

Herodotus
  2.116: 15, 85
Hesiod
  Theogony 526–616: 15
  Works and Days 167–73: 15
Homer
  Iliad 1.195–222: 107
    1.590–94: 15
    6.265: 11
    9.182–200: 12
    9.190: 45
    9.590: 112, 119
    17.588: 11
    18.54: 50
    18.395–407: 15
    20.290–352: 13
    21.237: 14
    24.62–3: 49, 54
    24.534–42: 51
  Odyssey 4.235–89: 13, 18, 29, 87
    4.351: 14
    8.73: 42, 45
    9.106–7: 11
    9.275: 11
    11.134–7: 81
    12.66–72: 31
  Homeric Hymn to Apollo: 15–16, 26
Horace
  Ars Poetica 1–23: 22

Lucan
  Bellum Civile 1.33–66: 132–5
    1.67: 141
    1.69: 106
    7.442–7: 133, 135
    7.638–46: 133, 136–7

Lucretius
  De Rerum Natura 1.1–51: 57–64, 76, 83, 94
    1.926–50: 70
    2.646–51: 60
    3.830: 5
    4.1–53: 70–4
    4.1058–1287: 73
    5.155: 67
    5.509–770: 74
    5.771–1010: 74–6

Ovid
  Amores 1.1.1–2: 106
  Metamorphoses 1.1: 141
    1.1–4: 105–8
    1.5–162: 108–14
    1.78–83: 113
    1.161–2: 109, 118
    1.163–252: 109–12, 116–18, 128
    1.291–2: 109, 116
    1.615: 110, 118
    2.1–30: 108, 115
    2.171–2: 121
    2.296–7: 121
    2.333–400: 108, 114–15
    2.377–80: 124
    2.485–530: 121
    2.495: 126
    4.47: 124
    4.416–562: 108, 115
    4.531–78: 115
    4.632–62: 121
    4.772–3: 121
    6.53–128: 108, 113, 115, 119
    6.721: 122
    7.1–424: 111, 118
    7.371–80: 124
    7.401: 124
    7.661–865: 116
    8.270–528: 111, 118–19
    8.302: 122
    8.309: 122
    9.134–272: 122
    9.198: 122

10.207–8: 125
11.212–15: 122
11.410–748: 124
12.580–2: 125
12.64–145: 124
13.396–8: 125
13.644–74: 124
13.750–896: 120–1
15.149: 122
15.480: 123
15.745–872: 128–9
15.879: 127
Tristia 1.1: 129
1.7.40: 5, 129

Philodemus
  On Poems 1.83 : 42
Pindar
  Olympian 1: 15, 42
  Pythian 2: 15
  Pythian 3: 51
Plato
  Phaedrus 264c: 20
  Protagoras 339–48: 18
  Republic 2 and 3: 6, 19
Polignac
  Antilucretius 5.35–6: 59
Porphyrius
  Quaest. Hom. p. 100, 4 Schrader:
      11

Sappho
  fr. 16: 29
Seneca
  Contr. 2.2.12: 114
Sophocles
  Electra: 17
  Oedipus Tyrannus: 17
  Philoctetes 570–97: 17

Theocritus
  Idyll 18: 29–30, 48
  Idyll 22: 27
Tibullus
  1.5: 42, 45

Vergil
  Aeneid 1.256–96: 79–82, 103, 128
    1.267–71: 88
    1.288: 88
    1.488: 87
    1.753–6: 93
    2.257–9: 86
    2.550–7: 86
    2.566–88: 87
    2.780–4: 82
    3.104: 85
    3.254–7: 82
    3.388–93: 82
    4.232–6: 88, 89
    4.274–6: 88
    4.420–3: 85
    4.596: 88
    4.620: 82
    4.625: 36
    5.626: 93
    5.673: 93
    5.810–11: 13
    5.835–71: 92
    6.122: 91
    6.146: 91
    6.211: 91
    6.260: 91
    6.268–899: 91–5
    6.290–9: 91
    6.323: 91
    6.323–4: 103
    6.337–83: 92
    6.371: 55
    6.434–54: 91
    6.494–534: 87, 93
    6.595–607: 92
    6.617–18: 91
    6.618–20: 95
    6.627–8: 91
    6.718: 85
    6.763–6: 81, 88–90, 93
    6.789–90: 88
    6.791–5: 101
    6.893–99: 95
    7.37–46: 96

Vergil (*cont.*)

7.45–6: 101
7.122–7: 82
7.162–5: 97
7.166–7: 99
7.182–6: 97
8.40–8: 82
8.324–5: 101
8.628–9: 88
9.184–5: 107
9.674: 100
10.1–117: 103
10.565–9: 99
11.16: 85

12.15: 87
12.189–94: 80
12.654–700: 100
12.816–17: 103
12.834–7: 79
Georgics 1.118–258: 84
1.121–2: 83
1.121–46: 100
2.149–54: 83
2.173: 83
2.323–45: 83
2.458–60: 83
2.490–4: 68, 84
3.242–83: 64, 83, 84

General index

Achilles 12, 22, 49, 101
Aeneas 13
  as narrator 86
  as traitor 87
  compared to hundred-hander 77,
    99
  to have son in old age 77, 81, 93
aesthetic or literary response to
    inconsistencies 41–2, 47, 90, 105,
    110, 112, 113, 118, 119
aetiology 4, 123–7, 131
Ajax 12, 125
Alcyone 124
Alexandrian or Hellenistic poets 2, 6, 8,
    14, 24–32, 34, 38, 78, 85, 90, 95, 102,
    104, 111, 119, 123, 140
Antiphanes 29
Apollonius of Rhodes 24, 30–2, 107, 108,
    114–15, 126, 132
Argo 3, 32, 34–41, 51, 54, 122
Aristotle 2, 8, 16, 20–2, 23, 24–5
Ascanius 77, 80, 88–90
Atlas 121–2, 123
Augustine 16
Augustus 77, 80, 101, 105, 109, 112, 116,
    119, 128–30, 132, 141

Bakhtin, Mikhail 6, 120, 142
Bennett, William 33, 47
Borges, Jorge Luis 14

Caesar, Julius 64, 80, 109, 116, 128–9,
    133, 134, 135, 136–7
Callimachus 2, 16, 24, 25, 26, 28–9, 39,
    104, 110, 118, 126
Cato the Elder 89
Catullus 1, 3, 6, 18, 30, 32, 33–54, 56, 64,
    75, 78, 85, 90, 111, 118–19, 121, 132,
    133, 138–9, 140
chronological problems 3, 4, 34–41, 108,
    114–15, 121–3
Cicero 43, 45, 61, 64, 68
Cyclops 11, 76, 113, 119
Cycnus 124, 125

death of the author, as source of
    inconsistency 2, 5, 56, 133, 138

emendation, textual, as solution to
    inconsistency 4, 5, 27, 36, 56, 58, 60,
    69–74, 75, 77, 92, 125
Empedocles 60, 68
Empson, William 23
Ennius 40

felix 47, 50
fiction, modern 14, 36, 44
films, continuity errors in 38
future reflexive allusion 30
  future reflexive contrary-to-fact
    48

163

gate of false dreams 95
gigantomachy 4, 78, 98–101, 102, 141
Goldberg, Rube 67
Golden Age 75, 83, 100–1, 102, 115, 129, 141
golden bough 77, 91

Heath, Malcolm 10, 22–3, 41
Helen 13, 14, 15, 17, 18, 48, 77, 86–7
Hellenistic poets, *see* Alexandrian or Hellenistic poets
Hephaestus, thrown from Olympus 15
Hercules 91, 122
Herodotus, commenting on Homeric variant 15, 85
Hesiod 14, 15, 28
Homer 2, 6, 8–15, 16, 21, 24, 29, 50, 59, 62, 76, 93, 107, 112, 113, 119, 133, 136
Horace 22, 127
Hyacinth 125

Ino 115
Italians in the *Aeneid* 11, 76, 77, 80, 96–101, 123

Joyce, James, on Shakespeare 2, 3
Jupiter (Zeus) 4, 10, 28, 42, 44, 64, 77, 79–82, 84, 89, 98–101, 102–3, 109–12, 116–18, 128–30, 141

Lucan 1, 3, 4, 5, 6, 42, 56, 64, 78, 131–42
Lucretius 1, 3, 4, 5, 11, 41, 55–76, 78, 83, 84, 94, 108, 111, 114–15, 118, 123, 126, 132, 133, 134, 136–7, 138–9, 140, 141
Lycaon 109–12, 116–18, 128
lying 2, 5, 10, 17, 49, 53, 82, 83, 86, 89, 109, 116, 117, 118

Medea 31, 38–40, 48, 111, 118, 124
Meleager 111, 118–19, 124

misdirection 10, 64
Monty Python 56

Neoplatonism 23
Nepos, Cornelius 40
Nero 4, 5, 64, 132–5, 136, 138, 139

Odysseus 11, 12, 14, 17, 81, 86, 92, 95
Ovid 1, 3, 4, 5, 6, 10, 39, 48, 55, 56, 64, 78, 102, 103, 104–30, 132, 133, 139, 140, 141

Palinurus 77, 95, 141
Parker, Herschel 36
Patin, M. 4, 65
Penelope 12
Petronius 6, 43, 46, 131, 133, 138, 140
Phaethon 108, 114–15, 121
Philodemus 42
Pindar 14, 15, 28
Plato 2, 6, 8, 11, 18–20, 23, 90
Polignac, Melchior Cardinal de 59, 64
Priam, death of 86
prophecy 1, 14, 17, 37, 78–82, 102, 127, 141
  death and the optimistic prophecy 52, 89
pseudo-scientific 126–8
Pythagoras 123

reading, cheating in 52, 61, 67, 75, 133, 139
  first-time vs. second (or linear) 56, 60, 61, 75

Sappho 29, 87
Scodel, Ruth 5, 9, 13, 16, 17, 125
Shakespeare 2, 20–2
speaker, as source of inconsistency (or solution from character speaking) 10–11, 42, 43, 45, 86, 103, 109–12, 116–18
Stesichorus 15

thematization of inconsistency 5, 10, 17

Theocritus 24, 27, 29–30, 87, 119

Timpanaro, Sebastiano 36

Todorov, Tzvetan 9

tragedy 2, 8, 14, 15, 16–18, 87, 131, 140

Turnus 96, 99, 108

underworld 4, 12, 14, 77, 78, 80, 86, 91–5, 102, 141

Valerius Flaccus 31, 132

variants, mythological 4, 13–15, 28–32, 40, 49, 78, 82, 85–6, 95, 97, 102, 110, 115, 116, 118, 124, 129, 141

Varro of Atax 43, 46

Vergil 1, 2, 3, 4, 5, 6, 10, 12, 17, 41, 56, 64, 77–103, 107, 108, 111, 114, 119, 123, 128, 132, 133, 138, 140
  Georgics 4, 64, 76, 78, 83–5, 100, 102, 132

Zeus, see Jupiter

Zwierlein, O. 83